Nathapanth in Western Himalaya

Nathapanth in Western Himalaya

Tobdan

Kaveri Books
New Delhi-110002

First Published in 2015
ISBN 978-81-7479-171-9

Published by
Kaveri Books
4832/24, Ansari Road
New Delhi - 110 002 (India)
Tel.: 011-2328 8140, 4707 2321
E-mail: info@kaveribooks.com
kaveribooks@gmail.com
Website: www.kaveribooks.com

Laser Typesetting by : Deep Graphics, Delhi

PRINTED IN INDIA

Preface

Nathapanth remained a very powerful religious force in the past for long period pervading every walk of life across whole of India. It made immense impact on the scholars, rulers, religious leaders and others. Many rulers were its followers. One of the most valuable contributions it made was that it created an atmosphere of social and religious harmony in the country. For this it had to pay a great price.

Its geographical spread and reach had been unparalleled. It reached even the remotest corners and inaccessible areas like Bir Bhanghal and Lahul in Himachal Pradesh. It spread even beyond the borders of the country to Tibet following after the Buddhism there. But ultimately this powerful wave also fell to become a part of history. Some communities of the sect can still be seen as a distinct social group retaining some old practices. Some of their practices are still being followed with great reverence by all the sections of the society. In Himachal a good effort is being made to collect the oral literature, much of which concern the Nathas, and publish them.

During the course of my study I have received help in different ways from numerous persons like Hira Lal of Sharan, Khub Ram Khushdil and many others. As always, C. Dorje of Archaeological Survey of India had been guiding and helping me as and when I requested. I express my deep gratitude to them all. I am greatly thankful to Shri Rakesh Goel of M/s Kaveri Books for accepting the work for publication and bringing it in an excellent form.

Tobdan
Kullu

Contents

List of Plates

1 Nāthapanth: Some Contributions

Nāthapanth remained a strong religious movement for long period and occupies an important place in the religious and cultural history of India. It has made immense contribution in the areas of religious, social, literary, linguistic, cultural, etc. developments. In its heydays it spread over the whole country touching its four corners: Kāmrūp in the east, Kashmir in the north, North West Frontier Province in the west and Kerala in the south.

It had penetrated even into the remotest corners of the country. In Himachal Pradesh it reached the extremely inaccessible and remote areas like Bharmaur, Bhangāl, Lahul and Kinnaur. Even after the Independence it took long time to open up these areas and link them with the outside world through the motorable road. Bhangāl could be linked by vehicular road with the adjoining areas only sometime after about fifty years of the Independence. In other areas like Kullu, Shimla, Mandi, etc. the cult had extended to the extreme heights which are called *gohar.* It covered the whole of Himachal, whole of the hilly regions of Uttar Pradesh or the present Uttrakhand. It crossed the heights of the Himalaya and reached beyond India to Nepal and Tibet.

Worship of Śiva is the principal element of the faith of the Nāthas but its character had been generally flexible and all absorbing. At its ultimate stage it presented a mixture of elements merging from different faiths, including the Islam. It overwhelmed many small sects and dissolved them in itself indistinguishably. The principal gods of the Hindu pantheon worshipped in the Nāthapanth are Śiva, Brahmā, Viśṇu, Rāma, Hanumān, Bhairav, etc. In the Nātha Cult some of them have been propitiated in new forms. There are gods of the Panth, of its own, like Ādināth, Matsyendranāth, Mīnanāth, Gorakhnātha, Bhartharī, Gopīcand, Guggā, Vīr, Yoginīs, *Siddhas*, and other numerous religious teachers and leaders who have been deified. It may be that lately the temples dedicated to Śiva and Śakti, in their various forms, have lost their distinctiveness of belonging to any particular sect and have become common worship place for all. But there are number of temples which can still be identified as exclusively belonging to the Nāthapanth like those of Ādināth, 64 Yoginīs, Bhairava, Gorakhnātha, Nārasiṁha, Guggā, etc.

The cult attracted teachers, devotees and followers from diverse faiths and all sections of the societies. They were rulers, brāhmans, rājpūts, professionals of low and high class, and many of them came from the lowest classes of the society. The founder of the Panth Guru Gorakh, according to one version of the story of his life, belonged to the profession of cowherd.

It gave refuge and consolation to many hopeless and desparate seekers. It broke the domination of certain orthodox sections and created opportunities for the numerous aspirants for rising up from the bottoms of the social and religious ladders. They worked for the social integration and religious harmony. Many of the ideals were, however, inherited from the high traditions of the *siddhas*.

Bhakti Movement: Bhakti Movement, the movement of love and devotion, and also a literary movement was greatly influenced by the thoughts, teachings and ideals of the Panth and the lives of its leaders. Gorakhnātha remained one of the principal subjects of inspiration of many literary giants of the movement. Great saints, literary persons, religious leaders and social reformers like Kabīr, Nānak and others adopted Gorakhnātha as their model and made him a subject of their works. In a literary work as a dialogue between Kabīr and Gorakhnātha, it depicted as if the two were personally known to each other. This description at one time had even created a notion that the two great saints were contemporary. References to Gorakhnātha in the writings of Kabīr, Dādulāl, Nānak, etc. is frequent. They have been ardent social critics and reformers. In the hymns of Nānak conversations with the Nātha *siddhas* like Bhartharī, Gorakh, Macchendra, etc. occur at several places, says Mohan Singh. Kabīr was a great saint poet of this period. He belonged to a low professional class of *Julāh*, weaver. *Śabad*, word, a form of literary composition in Hindi poetry current in the medieval period, is said to have been enunciated effectively by Gorakh. Later poets carried the tradition forward. In the movement great amount of contributions came from the writers belonging to the depressed classes.

Hindi literature: There are good number of works in Sanskrit and other archaic Hindi languages written by the Nātha scholars on the philosophy, etc. of the Panth. But special credit has to be given to the Panth for the promotion and development of the vernacular languages and literature. It contributed in the development of the languages and literature of Hindi, Bengali, Marathi, Punjabi, etc. which are presently great regional languages having vast store of literature. Mohan Singh writes that, 'The credit for writing in the vernacular for Panjabi should go to Gorakhnātha and to Nivrtinātha, the Marathi saint, for Marathi'.

Hindi language and literature inherits the works of the early *siddha* writers who wrote in Apabhranśa. In a collection of works of these *siddhas* named 'Baudh Gān o Dohā' about fifty percent of the writers belong to the group of the 84 *siddhas*, which also include Nātha-*siddhas*. The number of such writers must have been much more. In this way they have enriched the Hindi literature. Dvivedi observes that the treatment of the subjects concerning the Nātha *siddhas*, like the explanation of the path of *sādhanā*, religious beliefs of the *yogis*, their philosophical and moral views, etc. are to be found more and better explained in their literature in Hindi rather than in Sanskrit.

The poets belonging to the Sufī following, a companion of the Nāthapanth, also contributed greatly in the movement of the Bhakti and in enriching the Hindi literature. Muhammad Jāyasī's Padmāvat, an epical work, is an invaluable contribution to Hindi literature. Besides, there had been a series of Sufī poets who have contributed to Hindi literature.

Vernacular languages and folk Literature: Contribution of Nāthapanth in the promotion and development of the vernacular languages and folk literature is specially of great value. They have contributed even in the development of certain scripts. The impact has penetrated even to the remotest areas. Himachal owes to Nāthapanth in a number of ways. Nātha literature is found in Himachal in good amount in many languages viz. Bilāspurī, Mandīyālī, Kāngrī, Bharmaurī, Kullui, Sirmaurī, Mahāsuī and some other smaller languages. The songs encompass a variety of subjects. They throw light on the thoughts of the Panth, euologise the cult leaders like Bhartharī, Guggā, Gopichand, etc. The epics of Bharthari and Gugga were extremely popular among the people. There were specialised bards, singers, musicians and dramatists. The songs like Ainchlī and Blāj besides being epical compositions are of great religious and cultural importance which were celebrated at least once in a year. Many of these songs were also dramatized and were great source of entertainment and enjoyment for the people. They were played generally in the form of *swāngs*, i.e. comics. *Bāṁt+hd+ā* and *Karyālā* are very popular dramatic entertaining performances. Playing dramas was an essential part of the fairs which went on throughout the night. The fairs in the olden days lasted for a number of days.

In the winters when the nights were long and outside it was freezing cold, people gathered in small groups in different houses in the village and sat round big fires, talking and joking, alongside working on wool uninterruptedly. Such occasions were enlivened frequently by the presence of the professional bards and storytellers, who sang and related stories, occasionally accompanied by music. They entertained and generated energy in the audience.

The verses contain interesting stories of the cult heroes *viz.* Bharthari, Gopicand, Gugga, etc. and messages for their followers. Besides there were other interesting stories like the stories of Nal-Damyantī, Hīr Rānjhā, Rājā Rasālu, Pūran Bhagat, etc. A great Rājā called Sātavāhan or Salwān lived at Siyālkot. He had two queens named Acran and Lonan. With the former he had a son called Pūran Bhagat. He always kept on meditating on Gorakhnātha, whom he considered a magical man. Guru Gorakhnātha bored his ears and made him his disciple. The son of Lonan was named Rasālu. He too was a Nātha and a well known figure. The story of Rānjhā of Takht Hazārā and Hīr of Jhang Siyāl is another famous epic song. Rānjhā was disciple of Gorakhnātha. He visits Gorakh Tilā upon which sits Gorakh. The way was difficult and the road was steep. Asta and Masta (followers of Gorakh) were sitting there on the way. He bowed and offered them some money and went past them. Rānjhā wanted to become disciple of Gorakh. He stole his conch escaping the eyes of the nine Nāthas. Hīr too was disciple of Gorakh. Adati Raja married his grand daughter Hīr to Rānjhā and the two went to Mecca.

Annual mountain pilgrimages: The Nāthas followed the annual ritual and cultural affair of going to the mountain tops and lakes strengthening the old traditions. In Chamba, there is the tradition of annual visit to Manimahesh lake situated at a great height in Bharmaur. The scene of Rūpkund in Uttrakhand also may be connected with similar tradition. The old traditions of annual fair of ritual trips going around the villages called Nāthe-rī-Pherī (Rounds of the Nāthas) and the eight day visits during

Guggā Naumī singing Guggā-ri-bār, Hymns of Guggā, have not yet died out completely. Groups of Nātha followers go in traditional dress singing and playing the musical instruments round the villages. Then the festival is celebrated.

Sāñcā Vidyā, Sorcery: The difficult terrains in the highlands of Himachal had undisturbed and quiet environment favourable for the development, preservation and continuance of certain traditions and practices in small pockets in seclusion. In the high reaches of the areas of Shimla, Solan and Sirmaur there were concentration of magical practitioners, mostly Brahmans. Their descendants are in possession of some manuscripts called Sāncā and many of them show authorship of the Nātha scholars. The highly secret *tantrik* practice was known as Sāñcā Vidyā. These manuscripts are known to exist in four scripts viz. Pābucī, Candvāṇī, Bhīūñcāṇī and Paṇdvāṇī which are supposed to have developed from Bhaṭṭākṣrī, of the class of Tāñkrī. The script is akin to Tāñkrī, the common script of Himachal in the medieval period. The diversity developed perhaps because of the tendency of the practitioners to keep their knowledge secret from one another.

These books contain *mantra*, *tantra* and *yantra* on many subjects like controlling the opponents, hypnotizing, killing, reviving, blessing, showing magical powers purporting to cure all kinds of problems, even the smallest problems like a cow does not give milk, or the child does not take milk etc., for which they have *mantra* and they have *mantra* for every cause. For the treatment of a problem of more serious nature like possession by an evil spirit, the priest applies *mantra* (formula), *tantra* (a magical diagram) and *yantra* (articles like mustard seed, piece of thread, a piece of the skin of serpent, etc. which are to be injected with *mantra*).

They trace the origin of the knowledge similar to other branches of knowledge from Śiva. The practioners of Pābucī, a similar art like Sāñcā, in district Sirmaur, claim that the chief of the *Yantras* is Śañkar Bhagwān. Guru Gorakhnātha spread this knowledge. The following legends tell the source of the strength of the practitioners and exhibit how powerful and impressive is their power. It is said that once Matsyendranāth organized a *Bhandārā*, feast, for which he roamed from place to place and collected alms. He also received valuable jewels. When he reached back at his place, his pupil Gorakhnātha asked him, if all of his alms were snatched away, what would he have done? The Guru simply replied that there would have been no *Bhandārā*. Gorakhnātha snatched the alms from his Guru and threw it into the well. The Guru felt sad and was prepared to finish himself jumping into the well. Gorakhnātha said, "Why do you want to die? I can gather this material within a moment." Then Gorakhnātha urinated on a rock and the rock turned into gold, with the power of his *mantra*.

In another legend, it is told that once Mother Śakti intended to test the strength of Gorakhnātha. She became a fly and as Gorakhnātha opened his mouth she entered into his mouth and then moved into his stomach. Guru Gorakhnātha shut the paths of the breath and imprisoned the fly within his body. The *devī* requested him to let her free, since she came to know the extent of power of the Guru. She also offered him the power to control Bhūt, Gandharva, Piśāca and promised, 'I will always live on your mouth'. Then the Guru let her free.

Yet another story reveals that once the *devī* lifted a part of mountain and threw it on the Guru. The Guru charmed two seeds of *mash dāl* (black pulse) and stopped the rock in the sky. Judging his power, she compared him with Mahādeva, (Jasrotiya,1998: 90-101). In this way the *mantras* are empowered by Guru Gorakhnātha, who is mightier than any other power.

The Nāthas have thus made great contributions in the development of culture in its numerous aspects.

2

Nāthapanth: The Panth

Ādināth: Nāthapanth traces its origin from Ādināth, the Śiva. In the incarnation of Ādināth, Śiva explained the *mahāyoga jñāna*. This has been expressed by the Mahāyogi Gorakhnāth. In his well known writing '*Gorakspaddati*' it is stated that *Yogśāstra* has been pronounced by Ādināth. A temple dedicated to Ādināth is located in Khajuraho in Madhya Pradesh.

Matsyendranāth: Matsyendranāth gained the knowledge from Śiva. When Śiva was delivering the doctrine on *Yoga*, the Nātha yogajñān, to Bhagwati Pārvati, Yogindra Matsyendranāth overheard the pronouncements, and further Mahāyogi Gorakhnātha obtained discourse from Matsyendranāth. Matsyendranāth thus was the direct descendant of Ādināth Śiva and therefore the first teacher of the Nātha Sampradāya and the *Siddha* of the Kaulācār. It is also said that he was born in Kāmrūp and had meditated there.

Matsyendranāth also received the instructions on Kauljñāna, the secret knowledge, the Kulāgama, the Canon of the Kaula school from Śiva. Micheal Magee relates a legend from the Kauljñānnirn+aya and says that the legend of Matseydranāth, as is told in the work, is the oldest available source of information on Matsyenderanāth and his school.

Magee relates that Bhairava, Śiva himself, while speaking of his different incarnations as *Siddha* identifies himself with Matsyendranāth and says, 'I am that fisherman the best of heroes'. Further on he tells his consort that it was he who revealed the secret knowledge to her at Kāmarupa. It was the knowledge of the Kulāgama – the Canon of the Kaulas of which he was the repository at Candradvīpa. Then he relates that while he was staying at Candradvīpa with his consort, Kārttikeya came to him as a pupil. Being under the influence of nescience the latter stole the Śāstra, which contained the mystic knowledge and threw it into the sea. Bhairava, incarnate as Matsyendranātha, went to the sea, caught the fish which had devoured Śāstra, cut its belly open and recovered the sacred canon. The thief being enraged at it dug an underground passage, stole it again and threw it into the ocean. It was eaten up by a fish of immense size. This caused the rise of Bhairava's anger who prepared a net with his spiritual powers, *śaktijāla*, caught the fish and began to drag it to the shores. But the fish would not come as it held as much strength as Bhairava did. Besides, it was possessed with spiritual power and was not to be easily conquered even by the gods. Then Bhairava abandoned his Brahmanhood and assumed the character of fisherman to enable himself to fight with the fish better. The fish was then dragged by the net of spiritual powers and the Kulāgama was recovered from its belly cut open. 'Though I am a Brahman I have become a fisherman'. This Brahman is called Matsyaghna as he killed the fish and he is a fisherman, because he acted as a fisherman. Thus Matsyendranāth, the incarnation of Śiva, received the mystic knowledge of Kulāgama and he delivered it to others at Kāmrup (Micheal Magee, Introduction: 9-11, in Bagchi, 1986). Thus Kaulmārg was founded by Matsyendranāth. He is also said to be the first teacher of *Haṭhayoga* after Ādināth. Scholars maintain that Nāthapanth developed from the already existing sects like *Siddha* Kaul Mat, etc.

Atkinson tells that in Nepal the legend of origin of the Nāthapanth is mixture of the Hindu and Buddhist doctrines. Gorakhnātha is regarded as the special protector of the Gorkhalis. 'Avalokiteśvara Padmapāni, according to a local legend, descended by command of Ādi Buddha as Matsyendranātha. Matsyendranātha is Lokeśvara in Nepal'.

Sylvain Levi writes that, 'Matsyendra Nāth in Nepal is mentioned by the tradition as belonging to historical times. Narendradeva reigned about the middle of the seventh century. He had abdicated his throne in favour of his son, Varadeva and had consecrated himself to a religious life. At that period Goraksa Nāth came to Nepal in the hope of meeting and worshipping Matsyendra Nātha who still frequented his most preferred residence mount Kamāni to the south of the valley' (Levy,1979-1980: 17-18).

Mīnanāth and Matsyendranāth: It is found that the same stories as are related about Macchendranāth or Matsyendranāth are also wholly attributed to Mīnapa or Mīnanāth. There is also a debate as to whether Macchendranāth and Mīnanāth are two different entities or are the same. They were both ordained by Śiva, Ādināth, as is given in different stories. In the account of 84-*siddhas* no story about Macchendranātha is found but instead it is that of Mīnapa.

Tibetan historian Taranath, in his work *bka'-babs-bdun* shows the two teachers as different entities. He writes: 'The pupil of Mīnapa were *Ha-li-pa* (ploughman), *Ma-li-pa* (gardener) and *Tai-bo-li-pa* (?) (*so-rtsi-mkhan*, counter of teeth). Macchendra's pupils are Caurañgī and Goraksnāth. The first is son of a king.' Further we also learn from Taranath himself that Mīnapa was the teacher of Goraks. Taranath at one place also shows Mīnapa and Macchendra as one entity.

Taranath writes that the section of the 'twelve yogis' tells that Mīnapa meditated upon the god Maheśvara and accomplished the *siddhi*. Goraks sought discourses from Mīnapa and meditated on it and accomplished the self-born knowledge of the Mahāmudrā. SD Gupta considers Mīnanāth and Matsyendranāth as the same person. PC Bagchi also holds from the sources from Bengal that Mīnanātha, Macchendra and Matsyendra all three are the same.

Matsyendranāth's functions are important and abounds slightly wider spheres. The important work named Kaulajñānanirnaya, which expounds the thought of the Kaul cult, is attributed to Matsyendranāth. In Nepal only Matsyendranāth is known. There Matsyendranāth and Gorakhnātha are worshipped as deities. The two were exhibited on the coins and currency notes also.

The scriptures of the Doctrine also maintain the same mystery and we are not able to say confidently one way or the other. Michael Magee mentions two manuscripts of the work called *Akulavīrtantram* which he distinguishes as Akula A and Akula B, found in Nepal. A was found in the Darbar Library while the B belonged to the Collection of Keshav Shamsher Jung Bahadur Rana. Manuscript B has been dated in the colophon corresponding to 1610 CE, but on other grounds Magee places it to 13th century CE. The most striking fact about the manuscripts is that although the two works have the same title and dwell on the same subject, the work *Akula* A is authored by Mīnanāth and Akula B by Matsyenderanāth. Moreover in the work Kaulajñānanirnaya some chapters are authored by Mīnapāda and some others by Matsyendranāth, or under his variant names. In this regard Magee writes that Mīnanāth and Matsyendranāth are synonyms. 'Besides, if the names of Mīnanātha or Mīnapada had occurred in the colophons of the last chapters of the Kaulajñānanirṇaya we would have been justified in taking him to be a successor of Matsyendra. But the chapters at the end of which his name occurs are in the middle. It may therefore be presumed that when the present work was composed the two names were still considered to be synonymous being applied to the same person. Besides Akula A has in its colophon the name of Mīnanātha whereas Akula B has

Mcchendrapada in its place. The two texts being only different versions of the same text we are justified in thinking that when these texts were compiled the two names were still applied to the same person'(Michael Magee, Introduction: 8, in Bagchi,1986).

Mīnapa: Following is the story of Mīnapa from the Account of 84-siddhas. In Kāmrūp in eastern India there lived a fisherman who earned his livelihood by fishing. One day he tied a piece of flesh on the tip of the cotton thread and threw it into the water. A big fish was caught and then the fisherman tried to drag it. But the fish was so powerful that it dragged the fisherman back who fell into the water. A big fish swallowed him but the fisherman survived due to the strength of the merits accumulated in his former life.

Meanwhile Umā requested Maheśvara for granting her instructions on *yoga*. Maheśvara said, my instructions are extremely secret. Nobody should come to know it whatever may be the cause. Therefore get a house constructed under the water. The needful was done and Maheśvara began his discourse. At that moment the fish, who was carrying the fisherman in his stomach and was passing through the house, stopped under it. During the discourse Umā fell asleep. When Maheśvara was asking in the course of instructions, 'Do you understand me?' He heard, saying 'Yes, I understand.'

As the discourse was over, Umā got up from sleep. Then she requested Maheśvara to continue his discourse. Maheśvara replied that he had already finished his discourse. Maheśvara then through his superior vision learnt that there is a man in the stomach of a fish under the house who heard his discourse. Maheśvara made the fisherman living in the stomach of the fish his pupil and bound him by the vow of secrecy. The fisherman meditated for twelve years in the stomach of the fish. Then another fisherman from the Śrītapa Hill caught that fish and brought out of the water. The fisherman looking at the inflated stomach of the fish, thought there must be some valuable thing like gold, etc. When he pierced the stomach he found a man alive. He asked, 'Who are you?' 'I am also a fisherman. During the period of a king named so and so this fish carried me away.' Hearing this everybody was surprised and he became famous called as Mīnapa (Fish-man). Thereafter he worked hundred years for the welfare of the beings.

The story shows that Mīnapa belonged to Kāmrūp and he is the Guru who first received the sermons on *yoga* from Ādināth, Maheśvara, Śiva.

Gorakhnātha: In the lineage of the Nātha Teachers Guru Gorakhnātha was the successor of Matsyendranātth, Macchendranāth or Mīnanāth. However there are scholars who hold that Guru Goraks or Gorakhnātha was the propounder of the Gorakhpanth or Nāthpanth or Kānphata sect. A story tracing origin of the Panth from him is given below.

Most of the traditions make Gorakhnātha the incarnation of Śiva, who is the divine source of all *yoga*. It is believed that it was Gorkhnāth who popularized, if not introduced, the principles and practice of *yoga* throughout the length and breadth of India. In fact Matsyendranāth or Mīnanāth was the spiritual head from whom the Panth traces its origin and receives inspiration. The worldly act of propounding the Doctrine was done first by Guru Gorakhnātha.

There are certain legends telling how Gorakhnātha was born and how he acquired this name. Once a devotee of Śiva desired an off-spring, so the god, at Parbati's intercession, gave him some ashes from his *dhūnī* or fire and told him that his wife should eat them. The lady, however, was incredulous and threw it away. The ashes fell on a heap of cowdung. Eventually the devotee found a child where the ashes had been thrown. The man took the child before Śiva who said it would grow up as a great ascetic. He named it Gorakhnātha and instructed him to find a Guru. Gorakhnātha set forth to seek a teacher. Reaching the sea, he offered there a large loaf on a pipal leaf. This was swallowed by Rakho, the fish, who twelve years later restored a child whom Śiva named Macchendranāth, who became Gorakhnāth's Guru. Another version makes Macchendranāth the issue of Gorakhnātha himself. In either version Gorakhnāth's position appears superior.

Śiva then told Gorakhnātha that he must, through an ascetic, have children, and advised him to make disciples. Śiva also gave him *dūbh* grass, saying it should be his clothing, and a stick cut from an *ak* tree, saying it should be tied to his garments, and a *nād,* to be sounded thrice daily, in the morning, in the evening and once in front of the Guru. He also asked Pārvati to bore Gorakhnāth's ears and place earthen ear-rings in them. This she did. Gorakhnātha then made twelve disciples; Sant Nāth, Rām Nāth, Śārang Nāth or Bhārang Nāth, Dharam Nāth, Bairāg Nāth, Daryā Nāth, Nāik Nāth, Nāg Nāth, Gangai Nāth, Dhajjā Nāth and Jālandhar Nāth.

The above story reveals the origin of the name Gorakh from the fact that the child was found on a heap of cowdung. In another instance it is said that Niranjan Nirankār, the formless Creator, created Gorakhnātha from the sweat of his breast, whence he is also called Ghor Nāth (Ghor, filth).

Life of Guru Gorakhnātha: The life story of the Guru as is found among those of the 84-*siddhas* given below explains the etymology of the term Goraks more appropriately.

In the eastern portion of India in the family of a king named Devapāla a son was born. As the boy attained twelve years of age his mother fell ill and was nearing death. Then the mother pronounced her last words to her son. She said the pain and happiness of the living beings originate from their sin and good deeds respectively. 'Therefore don't commit the act of sin even if your life is at stake'. So saying, she passed away. Then the subjects pleaded to the king, to bring a bride for the prince. The king acted accordingly. A few days thereafter the prince was going to the jungle for change of his mood. The princess sent messengers with the orders to request the prince to come back. But the prince did not agree. The queen was filled with anger. She ordered her attendants to bring the prince back or otherwise to kill him. They advised that it would not be good to kill the prince. He is the dearest of the king. The queen played a trick. She tore off her clothes and scratched her body with her own nails. She covered her body with blood and lay lying on her bed.

When the king came and saw the princess in disheveled position he asked her for the cause of her unhappiness. The princess said: 'your son disfigured my body and I have become like this'.

The king said if the prince behaves in this manner, he should be killed. He appointed two executioners and ordered them to kill the prince. The executioners came to the prince but thought that it would not be right to kill the prince. They then told the prince, 'Lord, we are not able to kill you. Instead we will kill our own sons.' The prince told them not to do like this, but to follow the orders of the king. 'My mother in her last will had advised me not to do sin for the sake of body and life. You do as you have been ordered by my father.'

Then the executioners took the prince to the jungle and placed him under a tree, chopped off his limbs and then came back to their home. At that place there came a great *yogi* named Acinta. He gave initiation to the prince and gave discourse to him. Then the *yogi* went about a *kos* afar where there were seen a group of cowherds. He told them about the sick person and requested them to help him. A boy left the cows under the protection of the friends and went to the place with the mark shown to him by the *yogi*. He remained with the sick man and built a hut of leaves for him around the tree. He served him food and removed his filths with his own hands.

Then one day the sick prince showed his body to the boy and said, 'Look, I have my legs and arms grown afresh', and asked him, 'Should I give discourse to you?' The cowherd said, 'I have no desire for discourse. I have an Acārya, he told me to serve you. I did as he told me to do.' So the cowherd came back and began tending his cows again.

The *yogi* Acinta came to the cowherds and the boy related him the whole story. The teacher was very happy. Acinta gave him initiation and discourse. At that time the teacher told, 'you will be able to liberate ten thousand animate beings,' and then he went to some other place. The cowherd meditated and accomplished the *siddhi* of Mahāmudrā. At that time he also received initiation from Mahādeva and he acted accordingly. As he did the act of tending cows he became famous in all the directions as Goraks.

In the above story lives of three important characters come to play. The main actor of the story, the prince, son of Raja Devapāla becomes Guru Caurañgipa and the cowherd, *ba-lang-srung* (who tends cattle), who tends the limbless and helpless prince becomes Goraks. Both of them are initiated and given discourse on the Doctrine by Guru Acinta.

Some important modern works on the basis of this story have shown Goraks as the son of Devapāla which fact as we have observed here may require modification.

It is also to be noted that in Tibetan translation in the work 'Account of 84-siddhas' the name Caurañgipa is translated as *rkun-mo-chan* which may be translated as 'Thievish'. If we follow this translation the word can be translated as: caur = thief, then it leaves the other half of the word 'añga', meaning 'limb', unexplained. Therefore the word Caurañg may have to be read as (cau=four; añga=limb) and translated as 'Four Limbs'. This is more appropriate in the context of the story also. In the story of Goraks as above we observe that the term Goraks means the one who tended cattle. Caurañgi had his four limbs cut, by the order of his father, the king, and had later on regained due to his own meditative efforts.

Birthplace of Gorakhnātha: Gorakhnātha, in many stories current in Himachal Pradesh, it is told, belonged to Jālandhar. Jālandhar through Tibetan sources can be identified with ancient Kangra, in Himachal. Briggs has gathered similar view who says that the Nepalese hold that Gorakhnātha came to Kathmandu from the Panjab. Other traditions from Oudh, Nasik and Gorakhpur in U.P. also seem to have some bearing about his connection with the Panjab. Therefore, on the basis of these traditions and the presence of a monastery at Gorakh Tīlā in Panjab, Briggs says, it would seem best to hold that Gorakhnātha was a native of the Panjab.

In the story above we have seen that Goraks was a native of Bengal which information carries greater weight.

The Period of Gorakhnātha: Atkinson notes that, 'Gorakhnātha, according to the Nepal annals, visited the valley in order to see the great Macchindra in the reign of Raja Bar-deva in the year 521 CE. Bar-deva is reckoned as the seventh in descent from the Lichchhvi Ansu-Varma, who was Raja of Nepal shortly before Zuanzang visited the valley in 637 CE, so that the Nepalese Macchindra may be assigned to the middle of the eighth century' (Atkison, II-II:505). Taranatha also gives a reference to Goraks to the same date in his famous work *History of Buddhism in India*. But generally the scholars consider this date and also some more evidences pointing to the same period as little too early.

Briggs has investigated the issue in great detail. He discusses several streams of the sources and has arrived at the conclusion that Gorakhnath lived not later than 1200 CE, more probably early in the eleventh century (Briggs, 1938: 249-250). Goraks, according to the story in the Account of the 84-siddhas, as we have seen above, was contemporary to the son of king Devapala (c. 810-850 CE) from which it may be derived that he belonged to the second half of the ninth century CE, which is more likely and acceptable date.

According to the Vaṁśāvalī of the rulers of Chamba, Sahila Verman (920-960) was the first who founded the capital at Campā, the present Chamba. He was accompanied from Bharmaur, the former capital of the State, by *siddha* Carpatnāth, the famous *siddha yogi*. In all matters connected with the settlement of the new capital the Raja was guided by the advice of the *yogi* Carpatnāth; and in recognition of this a shrine was afterwards erected for him near the Laksmīnārayana temple at Chamba, where worship is done morning and evening. This shrine is ascribed to Sahila Varman (Hutchison & Vogel, 1933-I: 283). Thus the date of Carpatnāth works out to circa first half of the tenth century CE. We observe that at places Carpatnāth and Gorakhnātha are shown as contemporary.

The period of Nāthapantha: Beginning of the Nāthapanth naturally has to be reckoned from the time of Gorakhnath. Scholars discuss the topic from various angles. Some sources place the period of some of the important *gurus* of the sect at around 6th-7th century CE. Most of the scholars consider that it began in around ninth-tenth century CE. Acharya and Gautam presume that, 'Middle of the 9th century A.D. is considered the beginning of the *Nātha-sampradāya*. Its closure is in the 12th century A.D. However, the representatives of the *Nātha-sampradāya* like Kapālika, Aughar, Kānphata and Yogācārī upāsak and the others like *yogi*, Dādu-panthī and Kabīr-panthī, exist even today throughout the country,' (Acharya and Gautam 1978: 17-18).

Manjul says that the *Siddha guru* of Northern India Guru Gorakhnātha came in the 10th century and all the Navnāth were influenced in one way or the other from him. Therefore sometimes they are called nātha-*siddha*. Dvivedi writes, the great guru of India, guru Gorakhnātha was born in the 10th century of *Vikram samvat* i.e. ninth-tenth century CE. The *yoga-mārga* of Gorakhnātha was the most powerful religious movement before the Bhakti Movement. His birthplace is not known. Some indications are that he was born on the bank of Godavari in the South, or in Punjab, or in Bengal, etc. There are many books in the name of Goraksnāth. Even today his followers can be found in every corner of India. There is no language in India which does not contain the story of Gorakhnātha (Dvivedi, 1996: 95).

Briggs holds that the Kānphatas are said to have remained with the *Siddhas* of Bengal. They composed poems, known as the Caryāpadas, between 950 and 1200 CE. With the help of traditions and literary evidence, it may be said that Gorakhnātha or the sect of Kānphatas flourished about the end of the eleventh and the beginning of the twelfth century CE and anyway not later than 1200 CE. SD Gupta writes that many of the traditions taken together will strengthen the belief that Matsyendra, the first Nātha Guru, flourished at the latest in the tenth century CE. Thus we observe that the consensus on the origin of the *Panth* is on near about the tenth century CE. Among the plethora of data we cannot arrive at a conclusive point of time but we have a broad idea about the period of beginning of the *Panth* on which majority of the scholars show consensus.

Jālandharīpa: Jālandharīpa is stated to be founder of a Panth, separate from the Nātha. Perhaps he was contemporary with Goraksnāth and sometimes he is shown anterior to Goraksnāth.

Dvivedi shows him as a Kapālika. His descendants are Kanipā and Gopīcand. He is known to have been active in the east in Bengal and Bihar.

In Nepal in a tradition Ādināth is shown having two branches of Matsyendernāth and Jālandharnāth. Further Matsyendranāth had four branches: Goraksnāth, Carpatānāth, Revānāth and Mīnanāth. Jālandharnāth had two branches: Karnipa and Gopīcand. Similarly other scholars hold the same opinion about Jālandharnāth. This must have been a powerful branch in the beginning of the movement.

Jālandhar is ordinarily called Jālandharipa. Jālandhar was a *siddha* and we find his story mentioned among the eighty-four *siddhas*, which goes as follows. Jālandhar, jāl-dhar, hunter, belonged to the place named Nāgar-thong-bra (?Nāg-kot-ra or Nāgar-kot, i.e. Kangra). He belonged to a brahman family. Fed up with the household life he made his residence at the cemetery. One day as he was sitting on a branch of a tree he heard a voice from the sky. A dākinī said, 'Oh, son of noble lineage, consider in your mind the thought of the welfare of the worldly beings'. He became pleased and prayed again and again. Then the Jñān-dākinī (Dakinī of Wisdom) appeared in reality and gave discourse on Heyvajra and other subjects including on the *dhūtī* and *avadhūtī*. On accomplishing the meditation and attaining the *siddhi* he gave benefit to a number of beings.

We also find some information as a part of another story from the same source. In the life story of King Indrabhūti, there is contained some information about Jālandharipa. The country of Urgyan (Uddiyāna) consisted of five lakh villages. Indrabhūti ruled over half of the kingdom named Sambhola. Over the other half named Lañkāpurī ruled king Jālandhar. Indrabhūti's daughter Laksmiṁkarā was married to the son of Jālandhar. Some sources show Laksmiṁkarā as sister of Indrabhūti. Laksmiṁkarā was a *siddha* among the eighty-four. A work named *Advayayasiddhi* is attributed to her and is supposed to belong to middle of ninth century CE.

It is observed that the two traditions assign Jālandharipa two different places of his origin. According to the first he belonged to the east and according to the other he belonged to the north-west of India.

Indrabhūti is also related to Padmasambhava, according to his biography, the great Buddhist Vajrayāna Master of the eighth century CE, who also belonged to Uddiyāna.

Development of the Sect: There are some instances explaining how the *Panth* exerted itself to expand and assumed the extended dimensions.

In the Gorakhvānī at one place it reads, 'Oh Avadhūta! Get the essence of the word (Śabad), get the word. The body is attained by the word. Only for attaining this word ninety-nine crore Rajas became 'Celā' (followers), however, there is no limit among the subjects who became adepts to the faith.' This paragraph gives a glimpse of the manner of propagation of their faith and the extent of their reach. They directly approached the rulers and gained their favour. By convincing the Rajas and converting them into their faith they could influence the masses easily.

Certain religious sects existing before the emergence of Nāthpanth like Buddhism, Siddhasampradāya, Śaiva, Kaul, Śākta, Pāśupata, Kāpālika, etc. all were attracted and merged fully or partially with the Nāthpantha and gave it a great fillip. It shares much of the Buddhist traditions and thoughts.

Atkinson writes that the Pāsupata, one time popular sect of Kumaon got merged up with the Kānphatas, so much so that there is a total disappearance now of the former sect in the region of Kumaon. Dvivedi writes that the Nāth-paramparā developed from the Siddha Kaul Mat. Nāthpanth thus started on the fully developed structure of the *Siddha* and Kaul sampradāya, and others.

Nomenclature: The *Panth* is known by various names as Nātha, Yogī, Nāthapanth, Gorkhapanth, Kānphata, Darśanī sadhus, etc. They are called Kānphata, because they wear a ring piercing their ear. On the name of this ring they are also known as *Darśanī sadhu*.

In the Punjab and in the Punjab Hills and elsewhere they were called simply Nātha, which is a general term meaning 'master'. In Western India they were generally known as Dharamnāthī after a famous disciple of Gorakhnātha of that name. In other parts of India the names like Kānphata and Gorakhnāthī were commonly used.

Īśra the Creator: There are some instances in which the term *īśra* i.e. *īśvara* (Śiva, God) is used distinctly indicating that this also once formed one of the cult term of the *Panth*.

Taranatha informs that Śākyaśrī of Kashmir (1127-1225) in about 1203 CE went to Tibet and ordained many monks there and then came back to Kashmir. About this time the Turuskas had invaded Magadha and many *pandits* and scholars had fled to different directions and a few to Nepal and Tibet. Taranatha remarks: "At that time, most of the yogi followers of Goraksa became the followers of Īśvara. They used to say, 'We are not opposed even to the Turuskas.' Only a few of them belonging to the Nateśvarī-varga remained insiders", that is Buddhists (D. Chattopadhyaya; 1970: 319-320).

In the important song of Aincalī sung by the *gaddis* in Chamba it refers as *Iśru* i.e. *īśvara* for their Lord, Mahādeva, Śiva. The story says in the first Brahmā was born. Then the *pandits* were invited and they were consulted to foretell whether the child will grow as *īśar*, creator of man? They tell that the child is a hero. He has very good qualities. But the power of kingship is not in his fate. Then Viśnu was born. Then the third child 'Bhole Mahādeva', i.e. the Śiva was born. It was foretold that the child was hero, he possessed the perfect qualities. He will be ruler and *īśar*, the creator of man. In the story told in Lahul also, as we will see later, the creator of the man is named *īśru* i.e. *īśra*.

The Order in Practice

The Initiation: One of the essential features and distinctive marks of the Nātha *yogis* is that they have split ears. Therefore they are known as *kānphata*. This is done at the time of their initiation into the faith. At this time they wear ear-rings which are of different sizes at different places.

The term *yogi* is applicable to the practitioners of *yoga*. There are certain classes of them. The followers of the ascetic class of the Nāthapanth or Gorakhpanth are generally called *yogi* or *jogi*, more properly as *kānphata yogi*. The *kānaphata* were also known as *Darśan*. There is another class of *yogis* of the same cult who did not pierce their ears and did not wear rings. They were called *Aughars*.

It is said that those who have undergone the first stage of initiation are usually termed as *Aughars*. Some *aughars* keep their hair long and unkempt. They serve their *guru*, obtain teachings from them, and perform certain duties about the establishment where they live. Aughars pretend to some magical powers, and some approximate them with the Aghori. Others say that they are followers of Kanipā, pupil of Jālandhar. At some places Aughars (Oghaḷs) are an inferior class. Aughars do not wear ear rings.

According to Briggs the regular *yogi* who slits the ears of a novice inserts the knife and then asks him whether he is willing to renounce the world or not. If the novice says that he is not willing, he withdraws the knife. If the novice says that he is willing to follow the precepts of the sect and become an ascetic, the ear-slitter moves the knife up and down, finishing the operation. Piece of a twig of nīm-wood, soaked in oil are inserted in the wounds for three days, when ear rings called *kuṇḍal* or *mudrā* are inserted.

By slitting the ears the Aughar becomes a *yogi*, and may add to his name the word '*Nātha*', lord. Often he takes a new name to which he adds the word '*Nātha*'. When the wounds have healed, the yogi resumes his sacred thread, smears his body with ashes, and appears before his guru. Ear-rings of clay are now put on, the mantra '*Om sauhaṁ*' being used. In some parts of India the rings are of lacquered earthenware. After a period varying from fifteen to twenty, or forty days, or a year, rings of some other substance may be substituted for those of clay.

In the final stage of their ceremony of initiation a specially chosen *guru* or, teacher, splits the central hollows of both ears with a two edged knife (or razor). The slits are plugged with sticks of nīm-wood, and after the wounds are healed, large rings (*mudrā*) are inserted. These are symbols of the yogi's faith. The yogi, wearing the *mudrā* or *kundal*, becomes immortal.

The ceremony of initiation is completed with the worship of the nine Nāthas, the eighty-four *Siddhas* and Bālsundrī. After initiation a novice may elect to become a *yogi*, move to celibacy. In this case he would be known as Nāga, Nihang, or Kānphata. On the other hand, quite contrary to supposed regulations, he may become a householder or grhastha. That he need not remain in the monastery is allowed by the Hathayogapradīpikā, writes Briggs.

There are various views concerning the origin of the practice of wearing the rings. As stated above, the initiation of the custom is attributed to Gorakhnātha. However, Śiva is the great ascetic and he wears huge ear-rings. Some trace the practice to Macchendranāth, the *guru* of Gorakhnātha. But the origin of the practice of splitting the ears is traced to others as well. Some say that Matsyendranāth himself started the tradition. He saw *kundal* in the ears of Śiva and he performed difficult penance for getting it. Another story is that in order to keep itself above from the other sects, on the request of Gopicand, Jālandarnāth started this tradition. Some sources say that Gorakhnātha started this tradition piercing the ears of Bhartharī. The *guru* tied the earthen *kundal* to the ears of Bhartharī. Some *yogis* still wear the rings of earth. But it being subject to easily breakable, therefore rings of metal, horns of deer are worn.

On the name of ring they are known as *Darśanī sadhu*. This *mudrā* is made of different metals and also of ivory. More rich *sadhus* wear golden rings. Rhinoceros' horn is a favourite substance for ear-rings. It is not easily broken. Rhinoceros is a sacred animal.

Rings are of two types, flat and cylindrical. The former is called *darśanī*; the latter *kundal*. *Darśan* is a term of extreme respect. Dvivedi says *Darśan* is respected more because it is believed that the person wearing this ring has the audience of the Brahmā. The word *kundal* simply means round. *Kundal* is also called *Pavitrī*.

The rings worn in Western India were said to have been about seven inches in circumference and weighed two and quarter ounces or more. Weight is dependent upon the substance out of which the rings were made. In Kacch, where some of the *yogis* wear *mudrās* of gold, the strain of their weight was carried by a string, which is passed over the head. In Himachal the householders who are initiated were seen wearing rings of a small size of the diameter of about three or four cms.

Wearing of ear-rings is of great importance. If, by accident one is broken, a model in cloth, or so, must be substituted before the yogi may partake of food, or perform his religious duties. Or, he must bathe and procure another before he eats with his fellows or engages in conversation. A *yogi* must protect himself from having his rings torn out. In the old days he, whose ears had been mutilated, did not survive; he either died outright or was burried alive. It is claimed that the practice was surviving in Kumaon till the twenties of the twentieth century. Even now a *yogi* with mutilated ears cannot face the world. He must flee from his brethren; he must never face the old. He is ex-communicated; no tomb is erected over his body, when he dies, others will not associate with him; and he is not allowed to share in religious ceremonies and he loses his *pujāri* rights, writes Briggs.

In Kulu the ear-ring, named as *mudrā* or *mundrā* is the chief sign of a Nātha household follower. It is made from the skin of Rhino obtained from the discarded ḍhāl, battle-shield. It is quite light in weight and black in colour. This is the only kind of *mundrā* known to be worn throughout Kullu. This ring is worn only by men who are householders and have been initiated into the sect. Women don't wear ear rings.

The men wear ring first when they are initiated by the *guru*. For the first three months during the period of his apprenticeship he wears earthen or wooden rings. Then when three months are completed he wears the regular rings. Again at the time of death this ring is taken away and an earthen ring is placed which is buried with the body.

Dress and artifacts: It is said that the *yogis* of the Nāthapanth may come from any caste; they live as ascetics, either singly or in the *math,* shrine. They officiate as the priests in some places. They dress in various style, but in travelling usually wear a cap of patchwork and garments dyed with red ochre. Some wear simply a *dhoti* or cloth round the loins. They had some features common all over the country but also exhibited variety in many respects from area to area. Following are some of the important items of dress and the artifacts the Nātha *yogis* carried with them.

Kapāl: Kapāl, also known as *khappar* or *kheppar*, signifies begging bowl, a skull used as begging bowl. Later on the term was used for begging bowl made of all kinds of material, like wood, metal, etc. They also used begging bowls of the bitter gourd and also broken pieces of earthen pitcher.

Tūmbā : *Tūmbā* means the dried shell of bitter gourd. It is broad based and light. It was used as the base of the *ektārā* or *kindrī*, guitar, which was also sometimes double based, placed on the both sides of the guitar. It was also used as begging bowl and as bottle for carrying water.

Jholā or Jholī: *Jholā* is a bag hanging from the shoulder used by the household followers for collection of the flour or grains received in alms during the long rounds.

Phāvlī: *Phāvlī* means spade. It is a wooden article in which both the blade and the handle are made of wood. Its handle is small in size of about one or one and half feet long. When a man sits on the ground crosslegged, for taking rest, he places the article before him with the blade upwards upon which he places his palms turned downwards. Then he places his chin over the palms giving rest to his head.

Nāda or śringī: *Nāda* is made of horn such as of deer or rhino. It was blown on special occasions. Because it was made of *śrñga*, horn, it was also called *śriñgī*. The article was kept in its natural shape.

Gudrī*:* *Gudrī* is a dress of the *yogi* which was extensively patched and sewn and threaded with hand. Earlier it could have been a long cloak. Lately the householders also used patched and intensively threaded coats. The Nātha householders in the hills, who had been initiated, sometimes could be seen wearing coats which were patched or even if it was made of a new cloth it was threaded all over it very systematically. Lūhipa, first among the 84 mahāsiddhas had been wearing such a clothing and some others also. Sylvan Levy quotes that a disciple of Hieun Tsiang describes the followers of Pāśupata like, 'the ascetics who cover themselves with ashes, they cover the whole body with ashes and now shave and now allow their hairs to grow. They wear soled and worn clothings, which only differ from the others in that they are not red. These sectarians worship the god Maheśvara.'

Kanthā, khintharī: The blanket or the quilt the Nātha *yogis* or the householders used was also wholly patched and threaded which was called, *kanthā, khinth, khinthī or khintharī*. This was built by laying patch over patch. It may be wholly built by joining and overlaying patches. The term is extant in the folk usage for a ragged or old and patched quilt, at places as *khind* and at others as *khandolu*.

Rosary: Briggs tells that although Kānphata *yogis* wear no distinctive rosaries, they do use some that are of significance and of interest. One of these consisting of *rudrāksa* berries is that commonly worn by Śaivites. It is hung around the neck and consists of thirty-two, of sixty-four, of eighty-four, of one hundred and eight or even more berries. A smaller one having eighteen or twenty-eight berries, is worn on the wrist or elbow called *sumarnī*. This was worn both by the householder and celibate. Eighty-four beads make up the proper Śaivite rosary. Both Aughars and *Yogis* of the sect wear a *janeo*.

Important Practices: Nāthapanthīs have inherited certain unique practices in tradition from their predecessor the *siddhasampradāya* and some of them had origin even before them. Some of these practices, as observed, are: using ragged clothes, adopting the periodicity of twelve years in the meditations, etc., serving the thick cakes called roat at sacred occasions, keeping oneself continuously busy, etc. Some of them are symbols of renunciation. The Nātha *yogis* appear to have brought about some modifications in these articles or practices and also have made certain innovative additions.

Keeping oneself busy: One practical definition of *siddha* is: 'the one who roams lonely is a siddha'. If two move together, they are *sadhus*. *Yogis* cannot be said to be different from *siddhas*. Wilson writes that a *yogi* should keep on moving on the paths, or one should keep on sewing the *kanthā*, patching clothe, or should remain in meditation and remain engaged in teaching. Nāthas followed several methods for this purpose. In this manner by remaining alone or remaining in the company of the *siddhas*, one's mind is not distracted. Counting the beads and reciting name of the God and mantras by the practitioners and the followers of a religion is a general practice followed by many.

Dhāndharī: Dhāndharī or Gorakhdhandhā was an interesting invention, perhaps, of the Nāthapanthīs, as may be assumed from its name. Dvivedi tells that *dhāndhrī* is a type of wheel. The Gorakhpanthī *sadhus* construct a wheel from the small pieces of wood with a hole in the centre. They put *cowarī,* shell, or thread in the shape of rosary. Then pronouncing *mantra* they try to extract it out. Without practice and knowledge, nobody can take out the *cowari* or thread. This is called *dhāndhrī* or Gorakhdhandā. Wilson writes that the Gorakhnāthīs believe that by taking out thread out of the Gorakhdhandā by reciting *mantra*, the god is pleased with the mercy of Gorakhnātha and the person caught in the web of the world is freed from this web. In Kullu Gorakhdhandhā is an instrument like and equal to the size of fire-tong used in the hearths in the households. It is made of iron and has about a dozen holes and small rings put through them. The adept can keep himself busy by playing on it, locking and unlocking the rings which is a task of a well experienced player.

Worship of idols: Liñga was universal object of worship of the Nātha followers. Images of important deities whose statues have been found raised and are worshipped are: Śiva in various manifestations and members of his family, *Devī* having many manifestations, Bhairava, Gorakhnātha, Nārsimha, Guggā, Nāgas, etc. With regard to iconography the statues of the Panth, as may be observed from a few of them seen in the hills, are simple and folkish exhibiting minimum of attributes but assuming a distinctive style. The figures exhibit simple body posture, standing erect or sitting in a particular manner, with minimum amount of garments and ornaments and holding a few distinctive artifacts in their hands.

Women: It is said that women who wear *mudrā* are numerous. They are chiefly widows who have become *yogis*. The widowed women and the wives of the household *yogis* also wear *kundal*. However, not all women whose husbands are *yogis*, have their ear split.

Occupation: The Nātha householders were following numerous economic activities, some of the professions are peculiar to the community. These days in the rural areas they are mostly agriculturists like other zamindars and have entered into various other professions. However, some villagers still continue following some of their old traditions and celebrate traditional festivals for which they go round the villages, singing, playing musical instruments and dancing, thus continuing their old traditions. In the olden days this was combined with the economic objective.

Atkinson tells that in Uttrakhand the Kānphata *yogis* conduct the worship in all the Bhairava temples that are not ministered by *Khaśiyās*. Their principal seat is at Dāmódhar on the edge of the Ran of Kacch about twenty miles north-west of Bhuj in the Bombay-Presidency. They wear brickdust coloured garments and are remarkable for the large ear rings of rhinoceros horn, agate or gold worn by them and from which they are named. They are very numerous in these hills and possess several large establishments. They follow the *tāntrik* ritual, which is distinguished by its licentiousness for both the *liñga* and the *yonī* are worshipped by them.

The Gorakhnāthis made charms for themselves, and some sold them to others. They pronounce spells and practice palmistry and juggling, tell fortunes and interpret charms, they sell a woollen amulet to prohibit children from the evil eye, and they pretend to cure disease, muttering texts over the sick, practising medicine and exorcism and mending drugs.

There are *yogis* who are engaged in extensive commercial enterprises, others like those in Benares are rich, still others are enrolled in the armies of Hindu kings. Others are engaged in trades; and some sell small wares and silk thread. In Almora they are to be found as tailors and sellers of milk. In many parts of India *yogis* are found as weavers, and are rated as inferior *sudras*, illegitimate and semi-legitimate descendants of *Yogis*. Some sell apron strings and lace. Others are engaged in agriculture, their women helping them in sowing and weeding.

In Garhwal there are still large number of followers of *Nātha sampradāya* whose profession is chiefly recitation of Gorakhvānī. The instruments of music used are *ektārā*, *khanjrī* or *daphlī*. Besides the Gorakhvāni, the Nāthpanthi *jogis* also possess the knowledge of Jhadkhanḍi arrangement of Ḍholsāgar, which is based on *tantra* and *mantra*.

Death Rites: Briggs gives an elaborate description of the process of the death rite performed by Nātha followers. Gorakhnāthis bury their dead but rarely employ the services of Brahmans, the rites being performed by the fellow-*yogis*. A legend is sometimes given which accounts for the practice. There was once a dispute between Hindus and Musalmans as to who were masters of the earth. To disapprove the claims of the latter, Gorakhnātha sat on the ground, placing his food and belongings beside him, and called upon the earth to yield to him, if he had a share in her. The earth opened and he sank below the surface of the ground. Similar stories explaining the same theme but in different form are told at other places also. The practice of burial is not confined to Kānphatas, being followed by some other ascetic orders. The dying *yogi*, especially if he be an adept in *yoga*, is made to sit cross-legged, as in meditation.

After death the body is prepared for burial. It is washed by *yogis*, rubbed with ashes of cow-dung, or with ashes from the *dhūnī*, sometimes with sugar also, and pressed in new garments of everyday life. Or the body may be covered with an ochre coloured shroud. A new sacred thread, with the *nād,* ring and *rudrāksa* berry, and a rosary are hung around the neck. Some say that the ear rings are removed and replaced by earthen ones. A *tīkā* of sandalwood or of red lead is drawn on the forehead. Five things are put into the mouth - gold, silver, a pearl, a charred wick from a lamp (*cirāg*), used in the worship of a *devī* and incense. The body is then placed in a position of meditation (a sitting posture) on a seat and is supported by one crutch or by three. Under the body sugar, and sometimes earth, but not salt are placed. Flowers also may be put on the seat. A potsherd is placed on the head, but for this a silk cap or a turban may be substituted.

The grave is a pit, dug deep, three and half hands (*hāth*) and circular. In the south wall a niche is cut for the reception of the body which is set facing north. Under the seat one rupee and four annas or five and one-fourth rupees and sugar are deposited. The platform is made of wool, grass, etc. At the right end in front of the body is placed a guard full of water; and at the left a *rot* (a thick loaf of unleavened bread), a saucer of rice and milk, and another of water. A loin cloth and a staff (*kanak*) are laid in front of the body. The begging bowl is filled with milk and is placed in the wallet which is hung from the right shoulder. Sugar and gold are put into the grave. It is then filled in with earth, and a mound is raised over it. Later, a masonry platform, or a tomb may be erected over the grave, in which case it will be surmounted with the *yoni-liñga*. The *pādukā* (caran) of the deceased may be put on the *samādhi*.

If the deceased had been a rich *Yogi*, or if he had been the disciple of a guru, who owned land, his body would be placed in a chair shaped like a *doli*, it would be adorned with flowers, and he would be carried to the grave in a procession led by musicians. The grave is called *samādh* or *samādhi*. In some places, especially in Benares and in Almora, *yogis* were formerly burried in their own houses. For ten or twelve days after the death offerings are made to the deceased. Bel leaves and flowers are placed on the grave and upon it a lamp is kept burning.

The Pantha on the Decline: K.P. Nautiyal, giving history of the Panth in Uttrakhand, notes that the Kānphatas dominated Kumaon from the very beginning of its inception. They are found during the present time at various shrines of Bhairava or Bhairoṁ. At Srinagar in Garhwal, Gorakhnātha is worshipped as an incarnation of Śiva. Below Srinagar there is a small cavern where there is a gilded image of Gorakhnātha. Besides, they have temples in Naini Tal, Almora and Dwarahat. In Almora there is another private establishment. The temple contains small images of gods and goddesses including an image of Gorakhnātha with large ear rings greatly exaggerated. At Dwarahat in village Kama there is a temple ascribed to Nāganāth. A *pīr* looks after the temple. They have their dominance in the entire Garhwal and Tehri. At Dewalgarh and several other places near Pauri Garhwal, such as at Daduwa Devi and nearby it, there are temples of Kānphatas. They are now householders, have landed property and several other paraphernalia. But their customs are still the same and they follow the rules laid down by the sect.

At one time the Nāthapanthīs enjoyed a very high social status. They had free communication with the members of the highest class in the society, with the rulers and the high official circles. The Panth continues to be practiced even today. There are ascetics and household settlements. But it had been on the declining trend since long.

In Kullu, it is told, the Nātha gurus once were so close to the Raja that the Raja would not eat himself unless he had offered meal to his guru. Then a conflict between the Nātha and Vaishnava leaders occurred during the seventeenth century in which the Nātha leader was vanquished, a point of beginning of its downfall. But as Kullu is situated in the interiors of the country, the incident must have happened some time after the trend had set in the plains. The practice of the Panth still continues. All their creations continue to enjoy the same respect as ever. Many social customs and cultural traditions initiated and introduced by them continue to be practiced to a great extent unnoticed. Temples, festivals, deities, literatures, written and oral- all are respected and followed without any distinction. But some of them have transformed to new practices and faiths. The class of the followers has however lost the ancient high social status.

Naunāth: In the Nāthapanth there are some widely recognized organizations viz. Naunāth, Bāvanjā Vir, Causath Yoginī, etc. Naunāth or Navnāth, nine Nāthas, is an ancient and elite institution of the sect, but not much is known about it. The only confidently known fact about the organization is that it consisted of nine members and they were elite members of the Panth. It is not definite as to who were the nine original members of the group and what were the functions of the organization. Dvivedi says that Naunath founded the Panth. In the ceremonies on the occasion of the initiation into the order of Kānphata *yogis* there is the custom of worshipping the nine Nāthas and the eighty four *Siddhas*. They are worshipped on many other occasions also.

There are number of lists of the Naunāth but they don't agree with each other except a few. Das Gupta says that there are two lists which are most reliable. In the *Śodasa-nityatantra* quoted in the *Goraksa-siddhānta-saṁgraha*, mention is made of the nine Nāthas who are said to have preached the Tantras in the different ages. In the *Tantra-mahāranva* (quoted in the same text) eight Nātha are said to be residing in the eight directions and one in the centre. These Nāthas are Goraks-nāth in the east (residing in the forest of Jagan nāth?), Jālandhara in the northern region (Uttarā-patha, in a forest near Jvālā-mukhī?), Nāgarjuna (in a forest near Godavari in the south?), Dattātreya in the west (to the west of the river Sarasvati?), Devadatta in the south-west, Jada Bharata in the north west, Ādināth in the land of Kuruksetra in the mid-land and Matsyendranātha in the south-east in a land near the sea-coast. The Ninth is not named.

Some scholars say that the nine Nāthas are *avatars* of Nārāyans. Some scholars enumerate some common names of the lists as Ādināth, Matsyendranāth, Jālandharnāth and Goraksnāth. But this statement also does not appear to be absolutely true.

In the *Goraksa-siddhānta-saṁgraha* edited by Dr. Gopināth Kavirāj, the names of the nine Nāthas, is given as follows: Ādināth as Guru, then Matsyendra, Udaynāth, Dandanāth, Santosnāth, Kurmanāth, Bhavanarji and Gorakhnātha, the son of God.

In Garhwal the following nine names are given in the list of the Navnātha: Nagarjun, Jadbharat, Harischandra, Satyanātha, Bhimanātha, Goraksnāth, Carpat and Malayarjuna which is based on the work entitled '*Goraks Sidhanta Sangrah*'. It is said that Ādināth and Gorakhnātha are not included among the Naunātha. Dvivedi writes that in the beginning there were the Navnātha who initiated the sect. But about their names it is not definite. There are number of lists.

Ganesh Singh Bedi, a renowned Hindi and Panjabi poet, of the period of the second half of the nineteenth century, who remained for sometimes with the Rajas of Bilaspur in Himachal Pradesh, and wrote a Vaṁśavālī, geneaology, of the rulers of

Bilaspur in 1882, gives names of the nine Nāthas, as follows, as quoted by BR Sharma (1986:145). He writes:

> सब ही सिद्ध कहावत नाथा। इनमै है नवनाथ विसाला।
> सुनो तिनों के नाम रसाला। प्राणनाथ ओ गोपी चन्दा।
> सुरति नाथ जानो सुखकन्दा। गोरखनाथ मछिन्द्र बखानो।
> मंगल चरपट चम्बा जानो। घुगूनाथ लखो सुख धामा।
> जानो नवनाथन के नामा।

It says that all the *siddhas* are recognized as Nāthas. BR Sharma extracts names of nine chief Nāthas as: Prānanāth, Gopīcand, Suratināth, Sukhkanda, Gorakhnātha, Machindranāth, Mañgal, Carpat and Ghugūnāth. Here interestingly the poet inserts the word Chamba. Therefore BR Sharma explains that Mangalnāth and Carpatnāth belong to Chamba, but expresses doubt about the name of Sukhkanda. There was a sect of the Panth named Mangalnāthpanthin whose founder may be identified with the present Mangal. Here we may follow Briggs. He quoting the above list from a different source gives the name of Cambānath in place of Sukhkandā. He further says that they are not related to the divisions of the order but have much wider relevance. The nine great or deified and immortal teachers of the sect now live far back in the holy Himalayas and Gorakhnātha is called the chief of them (Briggs, 1938: 136). Following Briggs, SD Gupta states that these Nāthas are believed to be immortal demigods and preachers of the sect for all ages, and it is also believed that they are still living in the Himalayan region, sometimes they are regarded as the guardian spirits of the Himalayan peaks. Then quoting a legend he tells that Nine Nārāyanas incarnated themselves as Nine Nāthas.

3 The Tradition of *Siddhas* and Nāthas

Siddhasampradāya preceded the Nāthapanth. Many Nātha gurus are placed among the 84-siddhas of the Buddhist tradition, although it is difficult to distinguish between a *siddha* and a Nātha *siddha*. Nātha *yogis* are also generally designated as *siddhas*. *Siddhas* were revered by the followers of different sects and faiths.

Dhuta and Dhutāñgas: The basic form of asceticism followed by the practitioners of almost all the religious systems originating in the country existed since ancient times in the time of Brahmandharma. Rules for the mendicant *yogis* had been coded. Discussing the influence of Brahminism on the Buddhism, Acārya Narendradeva relates that in Indian culture there have been running two mutually confronting waves of Brahman and *Śraman* since the ancient times. *Śraman* were shelterless and practised celibacy. The ascetics under the Brahmandharma followed certain codes which were enshrined in the treatise called *Vaikhānassūtra* and the practitioners following such rules were known as Vaikhānas. This custom was adopted in Buddhism from the time of the Buddha.There were bhiksus who practised the Vaikhānas codes. These rules are known as *dhutāñga*, which were for example like: *vrkśamūl-niketan* (living at the root of tree), *aranya-nivās* (living in the forest), *śamśāna-vās* (living in the cemetery), etc. By bearing hardship a bhiksu purifies himself. Those who had undergone such hardships were known as '*dhut*'.

Acārya Narendradeva further writes that the first Council was held after the *parinirvān* of the Buddha in the rainy season for the collection of the *dharma-vinaya* in which about five hundred

Arhatas had gathered. Conspicuously Acārya Mahākaśyapa, the leader of the Dhutvādīs, headed the first Council. Its reference is also found in the *Abhidhammgrantha* and *Visuddhīmago*. In the *Milindpanho* thirteen *dhutāñga* are applauded.

Some scholars say that when Buddhism travelled from the east to west, it adopted this change. Brahmans were more influential in the west, as compared to in the east. According to these scholars, in the earliest times Buddhism was very simple. This change came after the conversion of the Brahmins in the west and a *bhiksu* practicing the *dhutāñga* was seen as more respectable one (Narendradeva, 2000: 2, 12).

I-tsing, a Chinese Scholar, who visited India between CE 671 and 695 finds the rules of *dhūtāñga* in practice among the Buddhist monks. Speaking about some of the codes intended for the ascetics, I-tsing notes: 'The four Refuges, the four Actions, and the thirteen dhūtāñga were ordained for men of superior faculties.' 'It is only reasonable that we should support our life practicing the twelve dhūtāñga.' It further states at some other place, 'it is right to perform the devotional exercise six times day and night, carrying out the dhūtāñga' (I-tsing 1896: 56, 166).

Takakusu, the translator, explains that the thirteen dhūtāñga are certain ascetic practices, the observance of which is meritorious for a Buddhist priest. He gives the list of the thirteen dhūtāñga, as follows (I-tsing, 1896: 56 note-3):

The above codes are basic to be followed by a monk. The same basic principles as were laid down for the Buddhist monks as had been handed down from the ancient times were later on continued to be followed by the *siddhas* and *nāthas* and ascetics of different religious sects. We observe some of the above rules being followed in the Nāthapanth. The term *dhūt* re-emerges later on but the meaning and character then becomes much transformed and had lost the status carried by the ancient term.

Pali	Sanskrit	Literal Translation from the Chinese
1 *Pamsukūlikañgam*	*Pāmsukūlika*	Having the garments made of rags from the dust-heap (pamsu).
2. *Tekīvarikañgam*	*Traikivarika*	Becoming a man who wears only (three) garments.
3. *Pindapātikañgam*	*Paindapātika*	Begging constantly.
4. *Sapadānakārikañgam*	*Deest*	Begging from door to door.
5. *Ekāsanikañgam*	*Ekāsanika*	Eating at one sitting.
6. *Pattapindikañgam*	--	Begging with a bowl.
7. *Khalupakkhābhattikañgam*	*Khalupaskādbhaktika*	Not receiving food Twice (or afterwards).
8. *Āraññakañgam*	*Āranyaka*	Living in an Aranya (forest).
9. *Rukkhamūlikañgam*	*Vrikshamūlika*	Sitting under a tree.
10. *Abbhokāsikañgam*	*Ābhyavakāsika*	Residing in an unsheltered place.
11. *Sosānikañgam*	*Smāsānika*	Visiting a cemetery.
12. *Yathāsanthatikañgam*	*Yathāsamstarika*	Taking any seat that may be provided.
13. Nesaggikañgam	Naishadiyika	Being in a sitting posture (even while sleeping).

The Primer of alphabets and the Siddhas: The *siddhas* made a great contribution in the field of learning and the spread of knowledge, bringing it within the reach of the common man. It appears that they had prepared complete course material, the primer, literature for the elementary course of learning the language and the lexicons. There are some titles of works known and associated with the term *siddha* which can be identified as remnants connected with the *siddha* tradition.

Siddhamātrkā is an important term related to the subject. Lexicons describe the term *siddhamātrkā* as a kind of script or a name of a particular set of alphabets or the like. According to one source *Siddhamātrkā* is considered equivalent to the present term *bārākharlī:* twelve columns i.e. the consonants arranged in the columns joined with twelve vowel signs.

Suniti Kumar Chatterji writes that Siddhamātrkā is a North Indian script of the seventh century CE. He writes, 'In North India, through various stages like Kushān Brāhmī, Guptā Brāhmī and Siddhamātrkā of the 7th century A.D., we arrive, through the Nagar style of writing at Siddhamātrkā and through the Śārdā and Kutila styles at the modern North Indian scripts' (SK Chatterji, 1966: 8). He also writes, the Asokan Brāhmi of the 3rd century B.C. , 'about the time of Christ it became modified into what is known as Kushān Brāhmī, then about 400 A.D. it became Guptā Brahmī, and then in the 7th A.D. it came to be known as the Siddhamātrkā form of writing. Ultimately, by about 1000 A.D. it became a kind of Proto-Nagari and a Proto-Kutila scrpit' (SK Chatterji, 1966: 11).

VS Agrawala also, tracing origin of the term, writes that Brāhmī script underwent evolution after the time of Asoka. 'During the sixth and seventh centuries, there was a further evolution, due specially to the cursive form of the Guptā script which was given the name of siddhamātrkā and which became the universal script for writing religious texts right from India to Central Asia and to Japan. The earliest manuscript in the Siddham lipi is in the Horiuzi temple in Japan written on palm-leaf in the cursive hand of the sixth century A.D. The term Kutila script was also applied to this nail-headed variety, but the same is not now approved and it appears that Siddham lipi was its correct name since the alphabet written in that script was begun with the words *Om Namah Siddham'* (Agrawala, 1966: 13-14). We observe that the association of the term *Siddha* with the writing system and literature has an implication very wide and spanning much longer period in the history.

The Tibetan script has origin from a north Indian script or scripts in about the same time, around mid seventh century CE. During the first half of the seventh century Thun-mi Sambhoṭa, a wise minister of Srong-btsan sgam-po was sent with some associates to Kashmir to study the writing system extent there and the language. There he studied under Pandita Devavidyā Siṁha and learned the writing system and the Sanskrit grammar. They formed thirty consonants in conformity with the requirement of the Tibetan language from out of the fifty alphabets then existing in Kashmir. Gu-ge mKhan-chhen Ngag-dbang Grags-pa in his mNga'ris rGyal-rabs names the Kashmiri script as Nagar. rGyal-rabs gsal-ba'i me-long names two scripts: Nagar and Garata. The work gives some more information on the subject. It may be noted that nearly fifty percent of the letters of Tibetan script resemble with those of Kashmiri Śārdā found on comparison with the inscriptions of Chamba State in Himachal Pradesh.

I-tsing records existence of a primer, a book named *Si-t'an-Chang,* which J. Takakusu translates as *Siddha*-Composition and considers equivalent to *Siddha*-vastu, a book for the beginners. "This is also called Siddhirastu, signifying 'Be the success' (Complete be good luck) for so named it is the first section of this small (book of) learning. There are forty-nine letters (of the alphabet) which are combined with one another and arranged in eighteen sections,' (I-tsing, 1896:169-171). William Moniers translates *Siddha*-vastu as a Buddhist spelling book. Siddhavastu according to Hieun Tsiang, another Chinese scholar who completed his travel in India in 644 CE, slightly earlier than I-tsing, contained twelve chapters and the young boys in order to educate and encourage them were first taught to study this book of twelve chapters. Evidently the literature was developed by the *siddhas* and was current among them. Quoting a paragraph from the record of I-tsing Takakusu gives full list of the sixteen vowels and 35 consonants (I-tsing, 1896: lx-lxii). In the main text I-tsing gives total number of alphabets as 49. Hieun Tsiang gives this number as 47. Takakusu from the same source of I-tsing, but outside the travelogue which is a separate document of the scholar, gives two more names of ancient books on the same subject as *Siddha*-letters and *Siddha-koṣa*, perhaps lessons on composition and a lexicon. These were the literature, which we know, were in use among the beginners of the Buddhist monks.

Alberuni, a great scholar from Central Asia of eleventh century CE, records that the most generally known alphabet in India is called *siddhamātrkā* which is by some considered as originating from Kashmir for the people of Kashmir use it. But, he says, it is also used in Varanasi. The same writing is used in Madhyadesh, the country around Kanauj, which is also called Aryavarta. The alphabet used in Malwa was named Nagra (Sachau, 2002: 160). By this period the Gupta script had evolved to new forms and Nagari had taken birth yet the term *siddhamātrkā* was still in use. The term Nagari for the script probably existed in the middle of the seventh century CE. During the time of visit of Alberuni 1030 CE the script current in Kashmir was *Śardā*.

From the above descriptions it appears that the *Siddhas* had prepared several works of the basic material for learning the language. Therefore even the chart of alphabet came to be named after them. As regards script, there were more than one script in existence during the Gupta period. We cannot say much about *siddhamātrkā*.

The *siddhas* had also introduced some procedures in the system of learning. In Himachal Pradesh while learning the alphabets of *Tāñkrī* script, an offshoot of the Kashmiri *Śardā*, there is a tradition of writing at the beginning of alphabets a formula like: *U Mā I, II siddham*. This reads as *Aum ekāñka dvī-cheka siddham*, which is translated as *Om*, figure of one, two bars, *siddham*. *Om* stands for *Om* as usual. *Ekāñka* is the numeral of One, as it is written in *Tāñkrī*, and the two bars represent stop in a sentence and function as full stop. Lastly the word *siddham* stands for accomplishment, or a kind of prayer that, as a work of study has been initiated, this may be fulfilled. In Tibetan writings we very often come across the phrase, *Om swasti siddham*, a method of salutation, written at the beginning of certain texts.

Literal meaning of the word *siddha* is given as to prove with logic. In the religious aspect it conveys the meaning of attainment or accomplishment. Amar Singh, the ancient author, places *siddha* among the ten classes of gods. Alberuni explains the term *siddha* in the following manner, "After the Deva comes the class of the Pitaras, the deceased ancestors, and after them the Bhūta, human beings who have attached themselves to the spiritual beings (Deva), and stand in the middle between them and mankind. He who holds this degree, but without being free from the body, is called either Rishi or *Siddha* or Muni, and these differ among themselves according to their qualities. *Siddha* is he who has attained by his action the faculty to do in the world whatever he likes, but who does not aspire further, and does not exert himself on the path leading to liberation. He may ascend to the degree of a Rishi. If a Brahmin attains this degree, he is called Brahmarshi; if the Kshatriya attains it, he is called Rajrishi" (Sachau, 2002: 77). Here the *siddha* exhibits the characteristics of a Bodhisattva.

The Tradition of the 84 Siddhas: Acharya Abhyakar Gupta, an Indian *Pandita*, belonging to twelfth-thirteenth century CE, was, according to Rahul Sanskrityayan, a resident of Campāran, who wrote a book giving the account of the 84-siddhas which was translated into Tibetan by dGelong sMon-Grub Shes-rab. Rahul Sankrityayan and Bhattacharya have fixed the period of the 84-*siddhas* expanding between 633 and 1200 CE.

This important work possesses a large amount of information about the *siddhas*. It covers many aspects about the subject like the social background, profession and many other things. Some of the *siddhas* came from the families of elite class like the rulers and Brahman families but mostly they belonged to other small social and professional classes. The pupils from the former class were able to get the teachers themselves, they could call a teacher as they felt need of. Others, even if one had desire to be initiated into the order, feeling remorse, would say, who will teach me? But they got teacher unexpectedly. Ascetics coming begging would ask them if they needed teaching for the benefit of their next life. On saying yes, which is always so, the teacher generously bestows him with the sacred instructions.

The names of the *siddhas* do not appear to be their original names, names received in their family. These are nicknames acquired on attaining the *siddhī*, showing that they have severed their past connection. The new name is based on many grounds like a typical individual background, trait, etc. like nobleman, weaver, lazy, etc.

Some salient features observed in the accounts of the *siddhas* may be enumerated below:

1. The list contains names of eighty-four *siddhas* and among them four are lady *siddhas*, who are called *yoginīs*. Perhaps it is for this reason that sometimes the work is called *rgrub-thob rgyad-bchu*, eighty *siddhas* instead of eighty-four.

2. The *siddhas* are of mixed educational background. Some are highly learned scholars. *Śāntīpa* was versed in the five branches of learning Some are illiterate and they had been doing manual work whole life long.
3. They came from many professions, covering the whole gamut of the social classes.
4. Generally, their fixed place of meditation is the cemetery with a few exceptions.
5. The *yogis* have prescribed dress, artifacts for carrying and manner of behaviour.
6. The philosophical ideal of many of the *siddhas* is realistic, short and simple.
7. They generally meditated for twelve years (more than 90%), in rare cases they accomplished in three, six and nine years, and in one case in six months.
8. They belonged to various kingdoms from all over India, all the four directions, but they mostly belonged to Magadha and Eastern India. Lū-hi-pa, the first in the list, however, came from *Sıñgala* (*Siṁhala*).
9. Most of the teachers show practicing the Law, but a few of them pray the gods both from Buddhism and Brahmanism. Sarahapa practiced Brahmanism in the day and Buddhism in the night. One of the teachers, Mīnapa, is wholly Brahmanic.
10. The deities meditated upon are Mahāmudrā, Vajravarāhī, Avalokiteśvara, Maheśvara, Umā and Vajrahās.
11. They on attaining the *siddhi* teach and give discourse to others.

Social background: Majority of the *siddhas* came from the lower section of the society. They represent the various social classes and variety of professions of the time. Thirteen *siddhas* come from the royal families and fifteen from the brahman class. Nineteen are of low caste who come from the lowest rung of the society and fourteen are from the middle class. The rest are professionals, viz.: hunter (2), fisherman, musician, weaver, leather worker, swordsman, *kāyath* (accountant), beer seller, washerman, woodcutter, wood seller, meal seller, ironsmith, cultivator (2), trader, oil expeller, potter, sweeper, shoe maker, sheep rearer, tailor, belonging to priestly class, wild tribe, basket maker, baker, king's priest, minister, beggar, shepherd, cowherd, made grass rope, collected precious stones from the sea and sold, agricultural labourer, and carried a basket and collected whatever he could find. One of them was of haughty nature. Some others possessed unusual character like: one was lier or cheat; one always shouting; voracious and ate everything; madman; most of the time sleeping; gambler; and the one who has been expelled from his family.

The narration of life of Guru Tantrīpa is a typical example of the style in which the life of a *siddha* is given in the account. Tantrīpa was a weaver and was economically well off, having worked hard and earned wealth from his profession. He had a number of sons, who were married and had sons. His wife had expired while he had reached the age of eighty-nine years. He had become physically weak and was blind. The daughters-in-law in the family felt his presence awkward, specially before the guests. So they got prepared a cottage of grass for him in the corner of their garden where they served him food from time to time.

By chance once Guru Jālandharīpa passed through the place. Jālandharīpa advised Tantrīpa: 'All accumulated wealth is short-lived. All those born in this world are bound to suffering. All religions are self-less. The state of Nirvana is peaceful and happy. Therefore don't you need instructions for preparing the food for the path after the death?' The Teacher gave him teachings and initiated him into the faith. The old man meditated for twelve years and accomplished *siddhi*.

Geographical background of the Siddhas: Below are given names of the regions and places, and the number of *siddhas* belonging to the place as have been specified in their Accounts.

a. North-West India: Urgyan (Uddiyāna) = 2

c. Eastern India: Eastern India (Not specified) = 5

Magadha = 5; Bhangala (Bengal) =4; Sālīputra= 7; Kāncī = 2; Visnunagar = 3; Devīkota = 2; Nālandā, Nalendra = 3;

Others: Sendhonagar = 3; Manidhara = 2; Campaka = 2; Siṁhala, Tre-ūr, Rā-jñī, Kāmrūpa, Kauśambī, Pātliputra, śrāvasti, *Mantra* Vikrama, Māgh-hur, Gha-hur (Gaur?), Sompurī, Balhipura, Gandhapura, Rājpura, Kañkarama, Kabilasakuna, Kaharī, Vikramapura, Bhanīrūpa, Dhanjur, Rāmeśvara, Nagar thoñ-da (Nagarkota, Kangra?), Bodhinagar, Autantpuri (Uddandapurī), Mangalpura, Dirunagar, Cambarnan (Campāran), Sarvatīr, Ae-patra, Jomanśrī, Abhacī, Bhirling, Dhokar, Grahara, Abhīra.

Some of these *siddhas* receive teachers from among themselves. The following teachers come from among the 84 *siddhas* and the numbers against them represent the number of pupils initiated by them from among the 84.

Kānhapa = 5; Lavapa = 3; Acinta = 2; Jālandharipa = 2; Lūhīpa = 2; Nāgārjuna = 2; Tillipa = 1; Naropa = 1; śantipa = 1; Maitripa = 1; Kukkuripa = 1; Sarahapa = 1.

These teachers are not from among the list of the *siddhas*. They are Maheśvar, Mahādeva, Ratnākar-śānti, Buddha-pa and Pandita Bhatna. They taught one pupil each. Besides, six pupils were initiated by *ḍākinīs*. The rest who number around two thirds of 84, are not named, they are merely stated to be well versed *yogis*.

Dress and Artifacts: The *yogis* and yoginīs ordinarily had a prescribed dress, artifacts to be carried and codes to be followed. Many of them carried a *kapāl* (skull bowl) as begging bowl, wore *gudrī* and carried *kanthā,* worn out and overlaid with patches and stitchings. How nauseating were these things to an initiate, can be gauged from an example from the life of Guru Kañkana, who was a king, that he exhibited for such things.

The ruling king of Visnunagar was initiated as a *yogi*. The Teacher advised his pupil, "O, king! There is no essence in the kingship. Everybody who is born in this world is subject to misery. Birth, sickness, ageing and death are like water-mill, rotating continuously."

The disciple asked the teacher, "Without discarding the objective of obtaining the desired knowledge, if there is any other way of practicing the Doctrine, I will do. Else, I cannot live on the wholly stitched dress and the food from alms.'

The *yogi* replied, "The stitched clothe and alms both are essential. You will have to adapt to this way of living."

The king said again, "I feel like vomiting with patched clothes. I will vomit by eating the victuals received in alms and eating in the vassal of Kapāl. I cannot live in this way. There is no end to the sufferings. The happiness of the heaven is also doubtful."

The *yogi* termed this kind of attitude of the Raja as haughtiness. He advised the king to practice the Doctrine and thus was initiated. *Siddha* Kanthali belonged to a poor family and wore *kanthā*, ragged and patched clothes, therefore, he was named Kanthali, wearing ragged clothes. Lū-hi-pa, the first among the 84 *mahāsiddhas*, also wore ragged clothes. Dhukhandhī spent most of his time in picking rags and sewing them into clothes.

It was essential that there should be a Guru who would initiate the pupil and give him teachings. The Teachers are selfless and generous. They are ready to teach anybody who wishes to receive teachings. Even they ask themselves whether somebody needed instructions. In return they don't ask for anything. Sometimes the *yogis* were called by the would-be pupil, who were resourceful, to become their teacher. Some teachers came themselves before the pupil and offered them teachings and initiated them. The pupils from the lower classes and poor are initiated by the wandering *yogis* who come to them for alms and in the conversation they get closer to each other. The *yogi* then gives instructions and teachings and the pupil following the instructions of the Guru sits in meditation, usually in a cemetery, and after a certain period accomplishes *siddhi*. These are some of the essential steps in the practice of the *yogis*. After accomplishment of the *siddhi* they became *yogi*. They similarly teach others and liberate them.

The Doctrine: Philosophical idea of an individual *siddha* has been explained metaphorically in very simple way sometimes taking example of the life story of the *siddha* himself. One of the *siddhas* before entering into the Law belonged to a destitute family. On attaining the accomplishment his life of poverty was explained as 'voidness'. We take another example.

Camarīpa was a shoemaker. His art has been explained as: Recognising the hide as the cognition of suffering, it was sewn with the needle of the teachings of the Guru and the thread of eight Doctrines, into the shoes of the self-born essence.

Guru Dhobīpa: In a town named Saliputra there lived a son with his father. They earned their living by washing clothes. Once there came a well versed *yogi* and begged for food from them. They fed the *yogi* and then the son asked from him, 'Do you have any clothe for washing? I will wash them." The *yogi* held a piece of charcoal in his hand and showing it to the boy, asked. 'If it is washed, can its dirt be removed? Can it be cleansed?' The washer boy replied, 'If the black coal is washed it will remain black.' The Teacher then told, 'Even if you wash a thing from outside, you cannot wash the three inner impurities which you need not wash constantly. It is enough if you wash only once. I have discourse for this. Don't you need it?' The boy said, 'I want'. The boy was blessed with *mantra*, *mudrā* and contemplation. The boy meditated on *saṁvar* and on these three kinds of thoughts for twelve years. When he accomplished the *siddhi*, *mudrā* cleansed his body, *mantra* cleansed his voice and contemplation cleansed his mind.

Below are given the names of the *siddhas* from the Account of 84 Siddhas in Hindi and Tibetan. Generally we find that Hindi names and their Tibetan translations agree. But at places it would appear that in the course of long history Hindi names have become corrupted and unrecognizable in the Tibetan transliteration. Tibetan translation is literal translation of the original Hindi names, therefore they are also helpful in many cases in recognizing the original Hindi term. English translations given here are those of the Tibetan translations. The new proposed readings of certain Hindi names have been given at the end of the sentence, after the English translation. In some cases the names can be derived clearly from the life story of the Teacher. But this method is also not helpful always. The list runs thus:

1. Lū-hi-pa (*nya-'i-rgyu-lto gsol-ba*, one who lived on the food of fish intestine.).
2. Līlāpa (*sgeg-pa'i-zhabs*, sportive).
3. Virūpa (*ngan-pa'i-zhabs*, violent).
4. Dombhīpa (*g-yang-mo*, Living with a *Ḍom* girl).
5. Śabarīpa (*ri-khrod*, living in the forests).
6. Sarahapa (*mda'-bsnun*, playing with arrow).
7. Kañkrīpa or Kañkālīpa (*keng-rus*, skeleton)

8. Mīnapa (*nya-pa'i-zhabs*, fisherman).
9. Goraksa (*ba-glang-srung*, tending the cattle).
10. Caurañgīpa (*rkun-mo-chan*, a thief; four limbs).
11. Vīnapa (*pi-wang-brdung*, who plays on vīna or guitar).
12. Śāntīpa (*zhi.ba'i-zhabs*, peaceful).
13. Tantrīpa or Tantīpa (*thags-mkhan*, weaver).
14. Camārīpa (*lham-mkhan*, shoemaker).
15. Khañgapa, Khadagpa (*ral-gri pa'i-zhabs*, sword holder).
16. Nāgārjuna (*klu-sgrub*, who meditated on serpent).
17. Kanhapa (*Nag-po-zhabs*, Black).
18. Karanīpa, Karanaripa, Aryadeva (*Ka-na-rī* or *zhang-'zin*, blind by one eye, kānā).
19. Thaganpa (or Thakanpa) (*brzun-smras-pa*, lier/cheat, Thag).
20. Naropa (*mi-mchhog*, a noble man, Narottam).
21. Śyālīpa (*spyang-kyi'i-zhabs*, leading a jackal).
22. Tillī pa (*til-rdungs*, who pounds *til* seed).
23. Catapa or Catrapa (*slong-mkhan-zhabs*, begs carrying a book).
24. Bhadrapa (*bzang-po'i-zhabs*, noble man).
25. Dhukhandhī (*gnyis chig-tu byed-pa*, to join two to make one).
26. Ajokī (*le-lo-chan*, idle man, Ayogī).
27. Kalpa (*smyon-pa'i-zhabs*, mad).
28. Dhobīpa (*khrus-mkhan*, washerman).
29. Kañkana, Kañganī (*gdu-bu-pa, rlung-rtag-pa*, wearing bracelet).
30. Kambhala (*lva-ba-pa*, wearing blanket).

31. Dingapa, Dengīpa, (*'bras-brdung*, rice pounder).
32. Bhandhepa (*nor-lha'm nor-'zin-pa*, god of wealth or carrying wealth).
33. Tantīpa (*chho-lo-ba*, gambler).
34. Kukkurīpa (*khyi-mo-chan*, leading a female dog).
35. Kucīpa, Kusulīpa (*ltag-wa-chan, kub-ste-skur-bo-chan*, hunch backed).
36. Dhama-pa, (*thos-pa'i shes-rab bya-ba*, learned man).
37. Mahila-pa (*nga-rgyal-chan, chhen-po*, haughty, great).
38. Acinta (*bsam-du-med-pa, dran-pa-med*, without worry).
39. Babhahī, Badheha (*chhu-las- 'o-ma len-pa*; who separates milk from water). 40. Nalinpa (*padma'i rtsa-ba*, Lotus Root).
41. Bhusuku (*zhi-pa-lha,'du-shes-gsum-pa*, god of speech, knower of three times).
42. Indrabhuti (*dbang-po'i 'byor-pa'i zhabs*).
43. Mekopa (*'jigs-su lta-ba*, fearful).
44. Kodālīpa, Kudālīpa (*tog-tse-pa*, spade holder).
45. Kamparīpa or Kamaparīpa (*mgar-ba*, ironsmith. Kampā = pincers.).
46. Jālandharīpa (*dra-ba 'dsin*, hunter).
47. Rāhulpa (*sgra-gchan-'zin*, Rahul, son of the Buddha.).
48. Dharmapa (*chhos-pa*, holder of the Doctrine).
49. Dhokrīpa (*snod-khur-bya-ba, rdsa-snod*, holding a vessel, earthen vessel).
50. Medhinī, Medanī (*zhing-las-chan*, agriculturist).
51. Pañkaj (*'dam-skyes*, born from mud, lotus).
52. Ghantapa (*dril-bu'i zhabs*, holder of bell).

53. Jogīpa (*rnal-'byor-pa*, *yogi*, diligent).
54. Cālukpa (*gnyid chhe-ba*, who sleeps long).
55. Godhura (*bya-rngon*, hunter).
56. Lucīka-pa (*kog-'dug-langs mkhan*, cheat, Luccā).
57. Naguna, Nigunapa (*yon-tan med-pa*, without knowledge).
58. Jaya Nandhī, Jyananta, (*rgyal-ba kun-dg'*, Jaya Ānanda).
59. Pacarīpa (*khur-ba 'tshong-ba*, sweet-meat seller).
60. Campaka (*tsampa-ka*, flower campaka).
61. Bhiksana (*bsod-syoms-pa*, beggar)
62. Dhilīpa, Bhalīpa (*mar-nag-'tshong-pa*, seller of oil)
63. Kumbharīpa (*rza-mkhan*, potter)
64. Carbarīpa (*spyod-gos*, wearing dress of ascetic, Cīvardhārī).
65. Mani Bhadrā (*nor-bu bzang-mo*, noble jewel),Yogini.
66. Mekhalī (*ske-rags-chan*, having waist band), Yogini.
67. Kanakhalā (*dsegs-ma i g-yul*, play of water drops), Yogini
68. Kīlapa or Kilī-Kilīpa (*ku-cho-chan*, shouting man, kilkārī).
69. Kantalī (Kanthalī, *hrul-chan*, ragged).
70. Dhañgulī or Dhagulī (*rtsva-thags-mkhan*, made grass rope and sold)
71. Udhilī-pa (*'phur-ba*, Flying Guru).
72. Kapālī-pa (*thod-pa-chan*, holder of skull bowl).
73. Kirbala-pa (*sna-tshogs sngags-pa*, numerous *mantras*).
74. Sakarapa, Sagarpa (*Sa-ro-ruh ste mtso-skyes*, born from lake, lotus).
75. Sarvabhaksa (*thams-chad-za-ba*, eater of things indiscriminately).

76. Nāgbodhi (*klu'i byang-chhub*, Serpent Bodhisattva).
77. Dārikapa (*chhung-ma-chan*, a married man).
78. Sutlī-pa, *Pu-tra-li-pa* (*sku-bsnyen-pa'i zhabs*, holding a picture).
79. Upahānpa (*lham-mkhan*, cobbler).
80. Kokili-pa (*khu-byug*, Cuckoo).
81. Anañga-pa (*lus-med*, not having body, Kāmdeva).
82. Laksmīñkarā (*dpal mdzad-ma'i zhabs*, who acts nicely), Yogini.
83. Samudra-pa (*rgya-mtsho'i zhabs*, ocean).
84. Byālī-pa (*stag-chan-nam sbrul-chan*, holder of tiger or serpent).

From the above eighty-four teachers four were *yoginīs*, women *siddhas*, as follows: 65. Mani Bhadrā 66. Mekhalī 67. Kanakhalā 82. Laksmīñkarā.

Nātha-Siddhas: Among the above 84 *siddhas* Dvivedi recognizes 34 as *Nātha-Siddhas*. These are those at serial numbers: 3. Virūpa, 5. Shabarīpa, 8. Mīnapa, 9. Goraksa, 10. Caurañgīpa, 12. śāntīpa, 13. Tantrīpa or Tantīpa, 16. Nāgārjuna, 17. Kanhapa, 19. Thaganpa, 21. śyālīpa, 24. Bhadrapa, 28. Dhobīpa, 30. Kambhala, 31. Ḍingapa, Ḍengīpa, 32. Bhandhepa, 36. Dhama-pa, 38. Acinta, 44. Kodālīpa, Kudalīpa, 45. Kamparīpa, 46. Jālandharīpa, 50. Medhinī, Medanī, 59. Pacarīpa, 60. Campaka, 61. Bhiksana, 63. Kumbharīpa, 64. Carbarīpa, 65. Mani Bhadrā, 66. Mekhalī, 67. Kanakhalā, 70. Dhañgulī or Dhagulī, 72. Kapālī-pa, 76. Nāgbodhi, and 77. Dārikapa.

Dvivedi has also given a separate list of *Nātha-Siddhas* from the work named Varnaratnākar and they are 75 in number.

4

Nāthapanth: Expansion towards Tibet

Nāthapanth had been so exuberant a cult that it not only reached the extreme corners of the country but also crossing the borders reached in Nepal and Tibet. Nepal was connected with the faith since its inception. Regarding Tibet, it is known that Indian *panditas* had been visiting Tibet for the spread of the knowledge of Buddhism since long past and Tibetan teachers were visiting India for study and to carry back loads of books with them. Since the decline in the growth of the Buddhist knowledge in India, the place was taken over to a small extent by the other developing faiths like the Śaivite, Nāthapanth, etc. The tradition, however, remained live by the pilgrimages undertaken by a number of devotees regularly to the important holy places in India. Some indications are available that Nāthapanth exerted for expansion towards Tibet.

Taranath informs that about the beginning of the thirteenth century the Turuskas had invaded Magadha and many *panditas* and scholars had fled to different directions. It is told that at that time a few of them went to Nepal and also to Tibet. On the event Taranath remarks: "Most of the *yogi* followers of Goraksa became the followers of Isòvara. They used to say, 'We are not opposed even to the Turuskas.' Only a few of them belonging to the Natesvarī-varga remained insiders", that is Buddhists (Chattopadhyaya, 1990: 320). From Taranath's statement it is evident that during this period Nāthapanth was thriving vigorously. It was one of the moments when Nāthapanth expanded towards Tibet. Among those who had fled to Nepal and Tibet some of them must have been Nāthapanthīs.

During the time of Taranath (1575-1634) a Buddhist *sadhu* named Buddhagupta from India visited Tibet. Tucci translated a resume of his travelogue from Tibetan into English. He writes that it is quite certain that Taranath's meeting with Buddhagupta exercised a great influence upon the formation of Taranath's mind. Many of the information embodied in one of his works named *bka' babs bdun* must be directly derived from the teachings of Buddhagupta who is there considered as belonging to the Goraksasampradāya (Tucci, 1931: 686).

Taranath also says that he received discourses and also much information from Śantigupta, who had received similar knowledge from his teacher Buddhagupta, and Buddhagupta in turn from his guru Tīrathnātha, Brahmanātha and Kṛṣṇanāth. Taranath had gathered information for his works from many other *siddhas* and sources. His work '*History of Buddhism in India*' is well known. As far as the Nāthapanth is concerned, the works of Taranath on the stories of some *Mahāsiddhas* like Mīnapa, Goraks, Carpatnāth, etc., are rare and to some extent different from those found in other sources. Taranath himself writes that in his works his sources include other than those found in the scriptures.

Buddhagupta was born in Indralinga near Rameśvara in South India, in the family of a rich merchant, whose name was Krsna. Name of his teacher was Tīrathnāth. Buddhagupta was a Buddhist but he was trained in Nātha *yoga* practices. Probably he was more a Nātha. He was initiated into the doctrines of the *Siddha* Goraksanāth's teachings by his three teachers. Tucci writes, at the time of Buddhagupta, it seems that the school of Goraksa was greatly flourishing in India, though it was divided into a series of sub-sects. There were number of branches of the sect which are named as follows: Nāthapanthin; Bakṣapanthin; Gopālapanthin; Pāgalapanthin; Āyī-panthin; Colipanthin; Hoḍupanthin; Dhvajapanthin; Verāgīpanthin; Mañgalanāthapanthin; Pathopanthin; Sattanāthapanthin;

Naṭeśvarīyogins. About this last sect Tucci writes that, 'There was also another rather dissident sect more strictly Buddhist called Naṭeśvarīyogin to which Tīrthanāth, Brahmanāth and Krsnanāth, the gurus of Buddhagupta belonged, and which must also be connected with Taranath' (Tucci, 1931: 686-687). This Naṭeśvarī sect was also followed at Gorakh ṭilā. Buddhagupta, like many of the Indian *sadhus*, was a great traveller. He visited many places in India and outside India in far away countries in order to find traces of Buddhism and Buddhist remains. Buddhagupta visited Tibet and many places in the Himalaya and then went down to Māru (Rajsathan). Then he went to Nāgartata (= Nāgarkota, Kangra), Multan, Kabul, Khorasan, Gosa, Uddiyān, etc. He also travelled to Africa.

It appears that Nātha teachers were visiting Tibet since earlier than Buddhagupta had visited, we have seen an incident above, and there were other similar visitors contemporary to Buddhagupta. Semdong Rinpoche (S. Rinpoche: Foreword, xiii, in Chattopadhayaya, 1990) informs that Taranath was named as such by an Indian *yogi* named Jvālānāth. This is said to have happened in a dream. We presume, there must have been a cause to arouse the particular dream. Jvālānāth lives today more like an important historical person.

It is important to note that Taranath gives information on Bharthari and the story matches wholly with the story existing in Himachal and elsewhere in northern India in oral folk tradition. He writes that in the country of Mālwā the dynastic line of the kings continued after the death of Viṣṇurāj. After him Bhartharī became king. A sister of the king was married to Vimalacandra, apparently in Bengal. King Govicandra, i.e. Gopicand, was born of the union (Chattopadhyaya, 1990: 249). His source might have been oral through some visitor from the northern India, confirming the proposition that there were other Nātha *yogis* visiting Tibet besides Buddhgupta and his companions.

It is almost during the same period that one of the Tibetan Teachers sTagtshang-raspa (1574-1651) was on a pilgrimage to Uddiyāna in the Swat valley, now in Pakistan. There he was initiated into the Nāthapanth, given a new name as Śyāmnāth and was also given instructions on a certain work. We observe that in a few of his early sketches the Guru is represented in the garb of an Indian saint wearing a loose cotton sheet, a typical round hilly cap and large ear-rings of the Nāthas. However, his statues in the monasteries are in the usual lamaistic style. After his return from the travel he once visited Tibet but he spent rest of his life in Ladak. In Mandi in Himachal, he worked for sometime for preparation of a work on some mystic formulas, under the Raja of the State and at that time he was named Taranath. All these were great events but its impact was shortlived.

Uḍḍiyāna: Uḍḍiyāna or Oḍḍiyāna, in Sanskrit and Urgyan or Orgyan, in Tibetan, was an important place and a place of pilgrimage in the tradition of Tantrik Buddhism since early times. In the Tibetan tradition Urgyan is associated with Padmasambhava, the great Vajrayāna Acārya. The king of Tibet decided in order to impel the rebellions of Buddhism to invite the famed Acārya Padmasambhava from Nalanda. The knowledge of Urgyan in Tibet might have begun just before their association with the Guru as we find that his name is always associated with the place as Urgyan Guru Padmajungne, Guru Padmambhava of Urgyan. The interest for pilgrimage to Urgyan in the Tibetan *siddhas*, it is observed, started from the first half of the thirteenth century.

Uḍḍiyāna, the Pīṭha: Uḍḍiyāna was, in fact, a famous Pītha in the tradition of Indian Buddhism. DC Sircar writes that mention of Uḍḍiyāna is found made in the Hevajratantra during the time of Gopāla, in the middle of the eighth century CE, recording an earlier tradition, as a *Pītha* among the four viz.: Jālandhara, Odiyāna or Uddiyāna, Pūranagirī and Kāmarūpa (Sircar, 1973:

12). More detail on the subject is available in the Tibetan Buddhism.

Pīṭha, sacred place, is an important subject under the tantrik system. DC Sircar has given above names of four principal *Pīṭhas* under the Buddhist tantrik system. The same four places, under the same name, with equal status, are recognized as *Pīṭhas* under the Śaiva system. DC Sircar lays down that early tradition in both Buddhist and Hindu system regarding *Pīṭha* is that of *Catuṣpīth,* Four Pīṭhas. Sircar (*ibid*) quotes a list of four *Pīthas* from Kālikā Purāṇ which after a little transformation all agree with the above four names.

Hemendra Nath Chakravarty, in his chapter on Introduction to his translation of Tantrasār of the famous Acārya of Kashmir Śaivism and author of several authoritative works, Abhinavgupta of the 11th-12th century, gives list of 33 *Pīṭhas*. The principal *Pīṭhas* are three namely: Kāmarūpa, Pūrnagiri and Uḍḍiyāna. All the three names agree with the list above but it unusually drops the fourth name Jalandhar, although it has been given a minor place in the list. Jalandhar has been known as a *Pīṭha* in the history very widely.

Abhinavgupta defines *Pīṭha* as a place of meditation. He tells that mountain-tops, river banks and kaliñga (sea shore?) called *pīṭhas* are good for meditation, although they are useful only externally. It also tells that just as there are a good number of holy spots outside, similarly they have locations inside the human body, similar to as is followed in Buddhism.

Chakravarty gives, in all, list of 33 *Pīṭhas*. The *pīthas* have been classified in six divisions: *Pīṭha*, *Upapiṭha*, *Sandohaka*, *Kṣetra* and *Upkṣetra* and *Upsandohaka*.

1. Pīṭhas are three namely: Given above.
2. Upapīṭha: Devīkoṭṭa; Ujjayinī; Kulagiri.

3. Sandohaka: Pundravardhana, Vārendra, Ekāmra. Against the three Upapiṭhas and three Sandohakas names of the parts of the bodies have also been given.
4. Kṣetra: They are the petals of the heart lotus. Prayāga, Varaṇā, Aṭṭahāsa, Jayantikā, Vārāṇasī, Kalinga, Kulūtā, Lāhulā.
5. Upkṣetra: The eight tips of the lotus. Vīrajā, Eruḍikā, Hālā, Elāpū, Kṣirikā, Rājapurī, Māyāpurī, Marudeśa.
6. Upasandohaka: The eight meeting points of petals. Jālandhara, Naipāla, Kaśmīra, Gargikā, Hara, Mlecchadigdvāṛtti, Kurukṣetra, Kheṭaka, (Hemendra Nath Chakravarty, Introduction in Abhinava Guptaācārya, 1935).

It may be noted here that Lāhulā is found at number eight in the important category of *kṣetra*. This identification of the name Lāhulā with Lahul is corroborated from the presence of the name alongside Kuluta which stands for Kullu. We also see a Lāhulā Vir described in a *mantra* from outside Lahul in Himachal. These facts indicate that Lāhul was recognized as an important place as a Tāntrik Pīṭh. In this tradition Lahul is known as Gar-zha Khaḍoling, Lahul the country of Ḍākinīs. Near the renowned monastery of Gandhala or Gandhola is situated the meditation place of guru Ghanṭapād, one of *mahāsiddhas* among the eighty four Indian *siddhas*. It is called Drilbu Ri, the mountain of Ghanṭ apa, in folk tradition.

Pīṭha in Tibetan System: In the Tibetan system of Tantrik practice Vajrakāyā, the body of the Vajra deity, is divided into twenty four parts, and each of these are identified with twenty-four *Pīṭhas*, places or regions of India. At each of these 24 places there resides a guardian deity called Vīr. The vajrabody is first divided into three main spheres: I. Sphere of the Spirit: II. Verbal Sphere, and III. Sphere of the Body. Then in each sphere eight places are allotted in the following manner:

I. Sphere of the Spirit: Pullīra Malaya (head), Jalandhara (top of the head), Oṭṭiyāna (right ear), Arbuda (nape of the neck), Godavari (left ear), Rāmeśvara (space between the eyebrows), Devīkoṭa (two eyes), Malavar (two shoulders).

II. Verbal Sphere: Kāmarūpa (two armpits), Oṭre or Oṭeviśa (breasts), Tiśakune (navel), Kośala (tip of the nose), Kaliñga (mouth), Lampaka (neck), Kāñcī (alternately Campā) (heart), Himalaya (pupils of the eyes).

III. Sphere of the Body: Pretapurī (sexual organs), Gṛhadevatā (anus), Saurāṣtra (thighs), Suvaraṇadvīpa (calves of legs), Nāgara (sixteen fingers and toes), Sindhu (upper part of the foot), Maru (four thumbs and big toes), Kulūta (Knees). Tucci gives name of each of the twenty-four presiding deity, Vīr alongwith some other details.

Regarding the identification of the places Tucci remarks that, 'While in the school properly Indian, this "adamantine body' is identified with twenty four places mentioned above, corresponding, except for few exceptions, to countries easily identifiable in the Indian territory in a large sense, in a second time, and possibly when the fortune of Buddhism started declining, the zone of the geographical Vajrakāya has been limited to the Himalayan region. This transposition which has often done violence in the geographical traditions of India, is already an accomplished fact in the tantric schools of Tibet. For instance, Urgyanpa and Stag tshañ ras pa do their pilgrimages from Tibet to the valley of the Swat taking care to visit the twenty four places of the Vajrakāya already presided, according to the theories of the Śaṁvaratantra, by the twenty four vīras. Now all these places are through Zanskar, Kashmir, Kullu, the district of Hazara and Swat' (Tucci 1935, III-2:42-43).

Tucci further writes that, "This adamantine body" is reconstructed, so to say during the liturgical process, in the body of the person who meditates.'

The same list taken from a different copy of *bDe-mchhog-rgyud*, Śaṁvaratantra from Lahul supplied by Nawang Norbu Kukuji, reads as: 1. Gar-zha'i Pu-li-ra-ma-ya, 2. Jālandhra, 3. Great Tīrtha Ma-ru, 4. Au-ḍi-yāna, 5. Arputa, 6. Godāvarī, 7. Rāmeṣvra, 8. *Devī* ko-ṭa, 9. Mālvā, 10. Kāmarūpa, 11. Au-dre, 12. Triśkune, 13. Kośala, 14. Kaliñka, 15. Lambaka, 16. Kāncī, 17. Himalaya, 18. Pretapurī, 19. Gṛhadeva, 20. Saurāsṭ, 21. Suvrṇadīpa, 22. Nagar, 23. Sindhu, 24. Maru and Kuluta.

On comparison of the two lists we observe that the names of the places in both the lists are almost the same and they maintain the number restricted at twenty four. There is one exception. In the Norbu's list Maru of Tucci at III-7 has been shifted to serial number 3 and with due regard to its importance it is mentioned as the 'Great Tīrtha Ma-ru'. Then a new Ma-ru has been inserted and clubbed with Kuluta at serial number 24.

The copyist of the work Śaṁvaratantra was aware that Lahul is known as a *tantrik Pītha*. He perhaps he desired that this fact should be reflected in the grand list. In the first step in this direction, he locates the *Pītha Puliramaya* in Garzha i.e. Lahul. This is a rare example. This name has not been found used in this manner.

In the second step Maru and Kuluta have been clubbed and have been shown as one centre. No doubt in the ancient tradition Kuluta stands for Kullu. But presently the Tibetan *siddha* travelers and the lamas in Lahul identify Kuluta with Gus (Guī) i.e. Gushal village on the confluence of Chandra and Bhaga in Lahul. sTagtshang raspa while going through Lahul mentions the place as Gus Mandal, Kuluta, corresponding to knee. Similarly Maru is identified with Margul, Udaipur, near Triloknath in Lahul. Further two entries of Tucci Pullīra Malaya and Malabar have been given here as Puliramaya and Malva.

Pilgrimage to Uddiyāna or Urgyan: Pilgrimage to Urgyan was not an easy task to perform. From the records of individual traveller available it is learnt that four lamas attempted for the pilgrimage out of which two succeeded in completing the journey. rGod-tshang-pa and Nawang Tshering of Zanskar returned from Kangra without completing their journey. Urgyanpa and sTagtshang Raspa were able to complete their journey. Those who succeeded in the journey came to be known as Urgyanpa, i.e. he who has performed pilgrimage to Urgyan. The tradition is followed in the Dugpa Kagyud sect. Tucci has studied the works of the three pilgrims (Tucci, 1940) leaving that of Nawang Tshering of Zanskar, Ladak (1657-1730).

Siddha rGod-tshang-pa (1189-1258) was the first Tibetan Lama to attempt pilgrimage to Urgyan. But he did not go beyond the modern Kangra in Himachal Predesh, which Tibetan writers also identify with Jālandhar. This teacher calls the place as Nāg-ko-te and at another as Nāg-ko-tre but both forms are read as Nāg-ko-te which is a near perfect transcription of the term Nāgkotra of Sanskrit. He translates the name as *klu'- mkhar,* castle of serpents. *mKhar* here stands for a standing rock or the face of the earthen cliff. The rock situated at the junction of the two rivers rises straight up on the face of which there might be numerous hollows inhabited by snakes. At the top of this is situated the renowned ancient fort of Kangra. This is one of the earliest source quoting the name of the place in this form. All the later Tibetan sources name it Nagarkot, following the local tradition, which can be translated as the city of fort.

Two Tibetan *siddha* lamas Urgyanpa (Dharma-Singge rNam-rgyal (1223-1303) and sTagtshang Raspa (1574-1651) successfully completed the pilgrimage to Urgyan. They have left detailed account of their journeys.

Urgyanpa visited Urgyan in the second half of the thirteenth century CE. During his time the socio-political conditions existing there were not so difficult although the areas were being taken over by the Turks, as he writes. However, by the time of visit of sTagtshang Raspa the conditions had become very difficult. The Teacher escaped attempts on his life several times. His indomitable determination and courage only could keep him surviving and continuing his journey, even under the extremely harsh conditions. He covered a substantial part of the journey, in the last, alone. In the extreme conditions of tension in the mind, the Teacher writes, he tried to get himself relieved of the tension by remembering and praying for his teacher, and composing songs and poems. Below is given a brief account of the journey of guru sTagtshang Raspa to Urgyan.

Travel to Urgyan, the Land of Ḍakinīs

sTagtshang Raspa visited Urgyan, Uddiyana, twice in 1613 and 1615. In the first attempt as he came from Tibet went straight through Kinnaur, 'reached Su-ge-thang (Suket), and then Kañkra-kot (Kangra)'. He says, Tibetans call it Nagar-kot. 'In the east of it there is a temple in the style of a *caitya.* There, one night in the dream, I visualized bcom-ldan-'das-ma, Bhagwati. I prayed her to foretell, 'I want to go to Ti-la and Kashmir. Is there any obstacle, if I go?' 'There is no hurdle,' was the reply.'

'Going west for one day from Kangra, we reached Nu-ru-phu (Nurpur), Śrinagar, Pa-thā-nan, (Pathankot?), No-sar, (Nauśahar?), etc. We reached Ba-la-nāga Ti-lā (Bālanāth Tilā). There reside a class of *yogis*. Siddh Bhā-nath (Bālnath?), the incarnate of Jinta-pīr, was a young person. There is also a *siddha* named sTag-le Nāth. On a rock on the southern side of the hill there is seen clearly the self-born image of Urgyan

(Padmasambhava). Jā-pīr and Jint-pīr had treaded over the land, signs of which are still visible. From there came back to Kashmir.'

The Teacher then through Jammu came to Zanskar. He stayed there enjoying the hospitality of a renowned local *siddha* Devā Gya-mtsho. He was invited by the king of Ladak but the Teacher was not willing to accept his offer this time. After about six months, he came to Lahul where he stayed for full one year. Then a lama named Zhi-ba Namgyal, who also knew some conversational Hindi, agreed to accompany the Teacher and the two started their journey again from Lahul. The Teacher this time was very firm and intended to ensure that the journey did not fail due to their personal weaknesses. At the initial point the Teacher bound his companion by entering into an agreement of no-responsibility and no-liability towards the other fellow for any reason whatsoever during the journey. Both were free to leave the journey and the companion in the middle of the journey at any stage without taking care of the conditions of the other fellow. This was based on the experience the Teacher had gained during his first visit. At that time some of his fellow pilgrims had fallen ill and one or two had even died, for which reason he had to leave the journey incomplete. If he had not executed this agreement perhaps he would not have been able to complete his journey this time also. The Teacher had with him as guidebook the *Namthar*, travelogue, of his predecessor, *siddha* Urgyanpa.

The Second journey: From Lahul through Pangi they reached the head of the valley of Tsam-bhe dam-pa (Chamba). 'From there in seven days we reached Nu-ru-phu (Nurpur), Śrinagar, Pa-ṭha-nan, No-sa-ra (Nauśahar), Ka-ṭhu-har, Bā-tu-rar, Pa-ṭhan-mo-sur, Sa-kī-rī, Sa-lau, Bhe-tsh-rbhur, Sa-la kau-ṭu, Sau-ṭ Kau-ṭ and Gho-tso-rāg. Nearby it flows the river coming from Kashmir down towards the south. In the travelogue of *Siddha* Urgyanpa it is given that on the other side of the river there is the town named Wa-ra-mi-la. We tried to locate the place going towards the south for seven days but failed. Zhiba Namgyal did not believe in the facts recorded in the *Namthar*.

'Then going north-west for five days we reached a place named Hi-la. The place named Ho-ra given in the Namthar was unknown to the people. They also did not know the hill named Bang-ho-tòi from where salt was extracted. Salt is extracted even at present. Then we walked for three days through the wasteland and reached Mu-ra-ga and La-phī-ra. From there crossed a river. In three days reached Tso-śara. There are rocks of salt.

'In its south there are the large cities of Dha-gan and Za-mo-la which are both still Buddhists and there are many *sangha,* clusters of monks. From there salt comes to this side to Nagarkot, Lahore and A-bhe-ra, it was told. To the other side it is exported to Aś-kam in Gho-tha.

'From Tso-śar we went to Dho-dho-śt+ and Va-va-la. From there in two days reached Ma-lo-ṭṭa. It is told that there is the Vihār of king Hu-la. It has been destroyed and a settlement has come up over its ruins. Going north-west there is the city known as Ru-kā-la, but nobody could tell about it. Zhi-ba Namgyal said we will visit Ba-la Nāg Ti-la (Bālnāth ṭilā) and go back. I said, somehow we will be able to search it out. No purpose will be solved by going back.

'We moved towards west-north. There we met a trader from Lahore. He asked, 'where are you going?' We told, 'we are going to Rukāla'. We asked from him the way. He told, there are many robbers. "Don't go, they may kill you. We will not show you the path".

'We went together upto some distance. Then there appeared some five or six persons who were working in the salt mines. They asked us, "where are you going?" and asked whether we were insiders or outsiders. He said, "you greedy" and one of them hit me on my head with the hammer used for extracting salt. He held me by my breast and tried to hit with a dagger.

'We returned. But we missed the path and went towards the right side. There in a deep ravine, there were many people who had gathered to collect salt. On asking them about the path they were able to tell the road to Rukāla. We tried to go there. Then an old man said, you come here near to me. He gave us meal and we took it. During this time he said, "I am a Brahman". He accompanied us. We walked for nine days together and then reached near a lake. "It is sacred", he told.

'Again walking for three days through the waste land we arrived at Rukāla. From there we went to Po-ra, No-śa-ra, Ma-tang-ga-na, Mi-ṭha-pa-ni. There we met a Brahman. He forbade us from going to Kapur and said, "Go back to Ghor-kh-ṭi-la (Gorakh ṭīlā)". He pushed me back by holding my chest. Zhiba Namgyal said, "We shall go back, it is not right to move like a butterfly jumping into the fire".

'I said, yes, you can go back. I will keep on going, even if I have to die. From there I and Zhiba Namgyal departed.

'From there I went to Mā-dh, A-tsi-ma, Pa-kśi-li, Dho-dho-ri, Kā-tu-har, Bha-thu-rvar, Pa-ṭṭòh pañ-ge, Ka-po-la, Kandha-har and Ha-so-nagar. After crossing a river I came to Pa-ru-ka, Nas-bhal, Si-khir. There by the mid day I met with about sixteen robbers. I asked, "are you coming from Kapur?" They replied, "Yes, we are from Urgyan (Kapur)". One of them hit me with a sword twice on my head. Another one also hit me. I fell on the ground. They tore off my clothes. One person sat over me. The robbers talked among themselves and exchanged money. I thought they had sold me. Two brothers who had bought me, were leading me. Then on the way we met other six robbers. They snatched me from them. Then I reached Na-mol va-jra. I made a prayer.

'There an old man hit me with a stick twice. I fell on the ground. I thought this is because of my former actions and in my thoughts I offered a prayer for my teacher.'

'Then I reached at Si-thar. A villager held me and did not allow me to go further. "You will be killed". There I met a Buddhist Brahman.'

'The Brahman said, "You cannot go further from here. Come with me to Bhyāsahur." There at Bhyāsahur there live a large assembly of *yogis*. The teacher there was named Pīr Buddhanāth. I was also initiated as a *yogi*. On this everybody became pleased. In the Indian system for becoming a *yogi* one has to get his ears pierced, wear *munda* (ear-rings) and then he receives a new name. I was named Śvā-mo-nāth i.e. Śyāmnāth. All the people of Bhyāsahur greeted me saying Śvāmonāth. They made me sit in a corner near the door in the room of Guru Jñānanāth. I was taught lessons of yoga on *sa-tva pho-ro bhi-bhūti*, etc. by Jati Gurgnāth.'

'At that time I realized: 'My thoughts are like the commands of my teacher. As regards *siddhi*, I accomplished the Bodhisattva. O knowledgeable, Nawang Zangpo (Teacher of sTagtshang Raspa), look at me with compassionate eyes. I have reached in India but culture and language are not understandable. I am forgetting the distinction between the east and west, and south and north: they all appear alike. I, Śvāmonāth, a thought of repentance arose in me. I had a companion he went back. Even though I had no liking, I had to accompany others. Even though having power in me, I lost control over myself to the others. Even though I did not like, I had to contest with the others. I, Śvāmonāth, a thought of repentance arose in me. I was in hurry, but the people created obstructions. Even though not liking, I have to stay in a foreign land. "O, 'Ḍakinīs of Wisdom' of Urgyan, may I be able to see you soon!"

'On the first day of the first month (perhaps of the Tibetan calendar, February-March) there was a big celebration. Many *yogis* and sanyāsis gathered there. I met one *yogi* who had come from Urgyan and was going on pilgrimage to Mahā-tshin-dar Ti-lā. The *yogi* knew that I was caught by the robbers, they had sold me, and had kept me in confinement.

'The *yogi* said to me: "If you want to go on pilgrimage to Urgyan, I will accompany you and we will go together".

'He was going to Hasonagar. He told me to wait. He would reach back by ten days. "Then we will go together". I waited there for ten days. The *yogi* did not return. I told the *yogis* there, "I am going to Kapur". The *yogis* of Bhyāsahur, and Pīr Buddhanāth caught me. "If you don't want to stay here, go to Dha-gan, go to Hindustan or go to Lahore. You cannot go to Kapur, at all. The area is extremely dangerous".

'I thought, my constantly saying that "I am going", might be irking them. So thinking, I said. "I wish to go to Hindustan. Please show me the way". On this everybody became happy. Everybody said, "Go to Hindustan" and showed the way. From there I went to Hasonagar. There I met the former *yogi* named Balanāth.

'There were traders, we joined them and went with them. We crossed a small river. Then came to Pa-ruba, Nya-pa-la, A-pu-ka, Killi-hila, Si-kir, Mo-mo-la ba-dsra, Si-nora, Pe-la-har, Mu-thilli, Mu-śi-li, Mu-thikśi. Maha-tilli, Sa-tā-hul-dhya, Ka-la-bhya-tsi, Sangi-la-dhuba and Aā-śa-kam. Then we crossed a high pass and reached Kapur. Going on the other side of the pass, we reached Urgyan. Going further for three days from there, reached Zo-mo-kha-dir. There is a palace of a king who is named Par-tsha-ga-ya. In Urgyan, it was told, there are seven lakh villages. The ruling king of the State and the *yogi* Balanāth were known to each other. Therefore the king sent a man to show us the way. Going for five days we reached at a place in the east. The mountain range named Aya-lom Be-lom is said to be one among the eight Śriparvatas.

'From there in five days we reached at Ra-yi-śar. Upto this the customs of the people of Urgyan and other Indians are similar. In three days we reached Kha-rakṣ. The people upto this region, both men and women, wear necklaces of jewels obtained from snakes. Some wear necklaces of jewels obtained from black serpent and others of those of mixed colours of white and black. The men wear black cap of wool, having pointed tip like tufted hair, and studded with numerous jewels. Nearby it in the north-west direction, there are the remains of the burnt palace of Acārya Padmasambhava. Then we came to Kha-rakśar. Then in five days we reached Rā-yi-śār. Upto this place the manners of the people of India and Urgyan match.

'On the backside of the mountain here is situated the famous Dhanakoṣ and beyond this is Sindhu Sāgar which in common Indian language is called Samundra Sindhu. It is told that there can be reached in one day. I expressed my wish to go to visit the place. Balanāth asked, "Where will you go? Aalom Bilom is the last sacred place. The place beyond this is uninhabited. There is only sea. There is no holy place at all". He was feeling angry, so I could not insist. On its southern side there is a small hillock which is also called Mangal-pāni.

'There we saw ten women bathing and sporting. When I reached near them, they taking the form of birds, went flying towards Kāmalpīr. Balanāth, clasping with both hands, said, "Well done, good". Balanāth said, "We have visited all the holy places of Urgyan country".

'Then we turned back and in two days reached Urgyan. It is also called Dhumthala. Sahujanāth on that day was bestowing blessings of Varāhī on many people. I also received the blessings. Then reached at Rayiśār.

'Then, after crossing many towns and villages, moving through the level path reached at Puṣp-hāri in Kashmir.'

sTagtshang Raspa after completing the journey stayed in Ladak. He acted as adviser to the king Singge Namgyal. He actively participated in the religious and social affairs of the State. He is associated with the construction of the famous Hemis monastery of Ladak, although in history the holy place goes back to the time of rGod-tshangpa. During this period he also visited Tibet.

As we learn from the account of his journey, sTagtshang Raspa was initiated into the Nātha following at Bhyāsahur by the teacher named Pīr Buddhanāth and was named as Śyāmnāth. He was also given lessons on a certain subject. Bhyās-hur appears to have been another important centre of the Nātha *yogis* where there lived a number of *yogis*. The Teacher does not indicate whether he visited Balanāth Tīlā or Gorakh Tīlā in the second journey. Nāthpantha was flourishing in the region during this time and was at its peak. Gorakh ṭīlā was sacred and an important centre of the Nāthpanth and it has been described by many scholars. A brief introduction is given here.

Gorakh Tīlā: Gorakh Tīlā, an important Nātha centre, is situated somewhere near Urgyan but has been referred to by our pilgrim Teacher in his account only in passing. The place was in the knowledge of the pilgrim before starting his first journey to Urgyan as he asks from the devi at Nagarkoṭ to forecast about the success of his journey to Tīlā and Kashmir. Alexander Cunningham has treated the subject comprehensively and describes its history, geography, location, etc. "From Jhelam to Jalalpur the course of the river is from north-east to south-west, between two nearly parallel ranges of mountains, which are generally known as the Tilā and Pabhi Hills. The Tilā range, which is about thirty miles in length, occupies the west bank from the great east bend of the river below Mangala, to the bed of the Bunhar river, 12 miles to the north of Jalalpur. Tilā means simply a 'peak or hill,' and the full name is Gorakhnātha-kā-Tilā" (Alexander Cunningham, 1924: 189-190).

Briggs adds that the most famous establishment of the Kānphatas in the Punjab, and in fact in all India is at Gorakh Tilla. The hill is rugged and difficult to ascend. There is a steep, almost perpendicular cliff on one side of it. This is accounted for by the following legend. Lakṣmannāth the Jogi of Tilla, was once visited by Siddhvacārnāth (Bhartrhari), and was unable at the moment to provide food for the guest. So Bhartrhari carried off part of the hill to Kirāna Bar, threw it down, and founded a new monastery. This explains the steep ascent at ṭilla.

Describing the establishment he writes further that it is situated on the top of the hill and is enclosed by a wall. One of the principal temples in the main enclosure is dedicated to Hanumān. The elevated portion to the west within the enclosed wall contains *samādhis* in three corners and a temple of Śiva to the east of the centre of the platform. In front of this and at the north is the *caran* (foot) of Laksman. By itself, in the platform, north west of the temple is a large trident. North of the temple is a small shrine of Bhairom, and just to the east of this is an old tree under which is a niche marking the place there where Gorakhnātha used to sit (Briggs, 1938: 101-103).

Abul Fazl writes that in the middle of Sindh Sagar near Shamsabad is the cell of Bālnāth Jogi which they call Tilah Bālnāth. Devotees of Hindustan regard it with veneration and Jogis specially make pilgrimage to it. Rock salt is found in this neighbourhood. There is a mountain 20 *kos* in length from which they excavate it, and some of the workmen carry it out. Of what is obtained, three fourth is the share of those that excavate and one fourth is allotted to the carriers. Merchants purchase it from half to two dāms a man and transport it to distant countries (Ain-i-Akbari, Vol. II: 315).

The place is known by several names viz. Bālanāth, Bālanāth-ka-ṭilā, Jogion-ka-ṭilā, Gorakh Tilā, Hill of the Sun, Hill of the Elephant, etc. Bālanāth is the oldest name of the place. It is stated that the place was formerly dedicated to the sun, as Bālanāth, but is now devoted to the worship of Gorakhnātha.

Abul Fazl, as we have seen above, names the place only as Bālnāth. Cunningham writes that Gorakh ṭilā is a recent name as Mogal Beg, who surveyed the country between 1784 and 1794 CE calls the hill 'Jogion-kā-Tilā', or Tower of the Jogis, whose chief is called Bilnāth. sTagtshang Raspa also visited the place. He himself refers the place as Bālnāth. But from the mention of the place by some local people he also records the name as Gorakh ṭilā. From all these it appears that Bālanāth is the older name of the place. During the time of sTagtshang Raspa the new name was also in currency.

Cunningham also writes that according to Mogal Beg the chief of Jogion-ka-Tilā was called Bilnāth, i.e. Bālnāth. It appears that this might have been the title of the chief of the establishment. sTagtshang Raspa also refers to a similar personage named Bha'a-nāth, i.e. Bālanāth.

Cunningham says that the name of Bālnāth is most probably even older than the time of Alexander, as Plutarch relates that, when Porus was assembling his troops to oppose Alexander, the royal elephant rushed up a hill sacred to the Sun, and in human accents exclaimed, "O great king, who art descended from Gegasios, forbear all opposition to Alexander, for Gegasios himself was also of race of Jove."

Briggs records that it is believed that Bālnāth underwent his penance here, and it was from him that Bhartrhari learned the practice of austerities. The *samādh* of Bhartrharī is at Tilla, and the cave there is named after him. The monastery is now in charge of the Lakṣmaṇ or Daryā or Hethnāth panth of the sect, and they have disciples beyond the Afghan frontier. The place has also been named as Pīr.

A stone slab at this place marks the spot where Rānjhā used to sit and where he was initiated. Gorakhnātha pierced his ears. Thirty or forty *yogis* are usually in residence. A special mela is held at Tilla in March. The monastery is in possession of a deed granted by "Akbar confirming earlier grants". At Sargoda there is a branch of Tilla. He further says that at Till candidates are drawn chiefly from Khatrīs, Arorās and Brhamans (Briggs, 1938: 101-103).

During the time of Briggs the Chief of the establishment was named Laksmannāth. It is told that Bālnāth and Laksòmanònāth both are the same person and that the latter succeeded Gorakhnātha on this Tilā. As regards the name Bālnāth the explanation of the Nāthas is that Bālnāth was Bāl-yati, a celibate from childhood.

It is told that the Panth followed at the Tīlā was named Nateśarī and the other one branched off from it is named as Daryā which is situated in the plains. Nateśari is also considered as the original Hethnāth Panth of the original Gorakhnāthis. Rānjhā belonged to Nateśri. The Jafir Pīrs followed Rānjhā.

5 Nātha Mythology

A. Creation of Universe and Evolution of Man

There exist some important songs in Himachal current in the folk tradition which record the myths of the Panth about creation of the universe and the evolution of man. Among them the two most important songs are Aiñcalī, an asset of the *gaddī* community in Chamba, and Blāj or Bralāj sung in the region of Upper Shimla. Both are found in their respective languages. The two regions are separated by a large tract lying in between. The songs, however, dwell on the same subject and relate the same story with slight difference, which may be owing to the two separate composers. Their source appears to have been the same. Aiñcalī, the Chamba version is more realistic and Blāj, the Shimla version is slightly imaginative, may be that the former retains some archaic and original characteristic. The latter might have been somewhat modified in the nineteenth century when it was first put down to writing. Internally both of them are equally ancient and the Shimla version has some additional subjects, which are unique. They are the expansion of the grain, its measurement and the context of Rājā Bali. Independently both are compact and interesting. Summary of the stories may be given as: Originally there was nothing. There appeared the Guru or there was only the Guru, the Teacher, named Nārāyana. Then Mansā *devī*, the goddess, was created or was born. The Guru created the earth, the moon, the sun and the stars. He created Brahmā, Visnū and Śiva. Then Śiva took over the task of creation of man. He experimented with materials and in size. Ultimately he was successful in evolving the man of three cubits high, with all its desired qualities of a man from the soil or ash.

The subjects dealt in the epics may be given as: i. Creation of the Universe, ii. Evolution of Man, iii. Expansion of the production of grain seed and development of the scales of its measurement, and iv. A glimpse of the Natha view on the human life. The subject of expansion in the production of grain and development of the scales of measurement is found treated only in the song of Blāj. It also relates the story of Raja Bali and a reference is also made to the festival of Diwali.

The stories begin stating that in the beginning there was only voidness. The following stanza describes the condition that existed before the creation of the universe.

न थीये धरणी न थीए गासा, तां थीआ न्हेर ग्वारा न।
न थीये चन्द्र न थीये सूरज, न थीये तारा न थीये व्याहणू।
न थीए पौण न थीए पाणी।

There was neither the earth, nor was there the sky. There was no sun or moon or stars. Neither there was air nor water. There was darkness everywhere.

The following lines besides describing the conditions existing before the origin of the world, tells how the creator of the world appeared.

न थी धरती न था कासा, बरसेया धुंधकारा।
न था चन्द्र न था सूरज, न था नौ लख तारा।
न थी स्याही न था समाजन, न था लिखन हारा।
न थे सन्त न था भेदी, न था ज्ञान बचारा।
न था कटुआ न था बछुआ, न था सरजन हारा।
बिच समुन्दर परगट होआ, अलख पुरख नरवाणा।

There was no earth or the sky. Neither there was moon nor the sun, nor the nine lakhs of stars. Neither there was ink nor paper. Nor was there any writer. Neither there was any saint nor scholar. Nor was there any seeker of knowledge. Nor was there any creator. Then there appeared smoke. In the middle of the sea there arose the Pure Man, the Nārāyana.

Another similar song adds that there were neither Brahmā, nor Vishnū nor the Vedās.

न थू ब्रह्मा न थू अम्बर, न थू वेद बचारा।

From the different stories it is known that when it was void, there was only darkness. Then the Creator of the universe, the Nārāyana, appeared. He was a self created Power. According to one version he was incarnated. From another version he appeared out of the water from the ocean. From the Shimla version it is given that the guru, i.e. Nārāyana who created the earth, which was all covered with water, already existed. He was the cause of the creation of the universe.

From a fragment of source from Chamba it relates that Nārāyana was self created. He rubbed the right side of his body and out of the filth he created the earth. From the similar object from the left side he created Mansā *Devī*, a girl, a renowned deity now a days. She was to be married and thereafter it was to be decided as to who was to hold the weight of the earth. According to one story the responsibility of holding weight of the earth was given to the 'Dhaulā Bail', the 'White Bullock'. In the hills there are *devīs* and *devatās* in most of the villages. A few of them have tradition of telling on special occasions the story of his own origin and of the universe.

Aiñcalī: Aiñcalī is a song of the *Gaddī* community of Chamba. This religious song is sung at the time of some important celebrations. It describes the position of nothingness as it existed in the beginning, like in the previous stanzas. Then it explains how man came into being. While other songs explain the things in pieces, Aiñcalī covers a number of subjects in sequence.

एंचली

जलथल धरती गुरूए न्यारे, नाज गुरू अवतारे।
नहीं थी धरती नहीं था कास,
नहीं था मेरू कैलास। नहीं थीए पौण
नहीं थीए पाणी, तां थिए गुरू न्यारे।
नहीं थिये चन्दर, नहीं थीए सूरज, तां थिए गुरू न्यारे।
नहीं थिये तारा, नहीं थिये भ्याणू। तां थिए गुरू न्यारे।
बुध तां गुआई मेरे गुनाजरू ने, गुगले री धूणी धुखाई।
गुगले री धूणी धुखाई गुरूए, सै धूणी भसम कराई।
से इओ धूणी गुरूए भसम कराई, अंगे मली मली लाई।
अंगे मली मली मलूणी कराई, तिस मलूणी री मूरत बणाई।
पढ़ी तां गुणी दिता जीव दान, खड ी होई मनसा देई।
बारह बरहे दी होई मनसा देई,
तां नदी पर नहाणा जांदी।
कपड़े उतारे देई करया स्नान, गुरू दी भ श्टा लगाई।
नाज गुरू दी भ श्टा लगाई, मनसा होई पैरां भारी।
मनसा जो लगी प्रसूता।
पहली आसा दसवां महीने
जनमया ब्रहमट कयाला
सद्दे बहु पंडत रास गणाई
'ऐ बेटा कै इसरा होला
जनमे रा सूरा करमे रा पूरा
राज इस खटोरा नाही'
दूजी आसा दसवां महीने
जनमया बिसनू दुठाई

सद्दे बहु पंडत रास गणाई
'ऐ बेटा कै इसरा होला
जनमे रा सूरा करमे रा पूरा
राज इस खटोरा नाही'।
तीजी आसा दसवां महीने
जनमया भोला महादेव
सद्दे बहु पंडत रास गणाई
'ऐ बेटा कै इसरा होला
जनमे रा सूरा करमे रा पूरा
राज इस खाणा जरुर'। (B R Sharma: 1986, 19-20).

The Teacher was incarnated. There was neither the earth, nor the sky, nor the Sumerū and Kailāsh mountains. There existed neither air nor water. There was only the Teacher. Neither there was the moon nor the sun. Neither there were stars nor was there the morning. The Teacher created the Universe. He created the earth, all covered with water. He was then lost in thought and made the smoke of guggul incense. After the guggul was burnt there was created ash. The Teacher smeared the ash to his body and with this dirt he created a figure of man. After studying and thinking, he infused life in it. Then there was standing Mansā *devī*. The stories in the Shimla region tell that Mansā *devī* was born out of the mind of Nārāyana, the self-created Teacher.

Mansā *devī*, when she was of twelve years of age, went to take bath in the river. She took off her clothes and began taking bath. The Teacher's mind became lusty. Mansā *devī* became pregnant. Mansā *devī* was now prepared for delivery. She gave birth to the first child in the tenth month. Brahmā was born. Many panditas were invited and they measured the movements of stars and planets. They told that this son will become Īśra (Lord). By birth he is a hero and by actions he is complete. But he is not likely to become the ruler. Next was born Vishnū. His fate was also forecast as similar. Then the third son was born, 'Bholā Mahādeva', the Śiva. It was declared that he will become the ruler. The stories in the Shimla region tell that these three gods were born out of pitchers which Nārāyana gave to Mansā Devi for keeping guard over them. Then the story runs further:

> नीले गगन बसाए, सिरथी उपाई भोले स्वामी ने, रचना रचाणा लाई।
> रात ते ध्याणी उपाए, भेड़ा त बकरी उपायी, गौआं ते महियां उपायीं।
> चीड़ू ते पखेरू उपाये, नर ते मादीन उपाये।
> बिजन मनुखे संसार न बसदा। मनख उपाणा लाए।
> लोहे रा मनख बणाया। भरे मनखा हुंगतारा।
> नहिं भरदा मनख हुंगतारा, तां नी बसदा संसार।
> चांदी रा मनख बणाया, सोने रा मनख बणाया।
> सोने रा मनख फिरी हटी जांदा, फिर कुसे रा बारा आया।
> नौ गजिए फिरी उपाये, नौ गजिए रा बारा आया।
> त्रै सौ सठ दिहाड़ी उम्मर उपायी, नहीं पांदे घरबार।
> थोड़े जीणे रे तिक्कर किज्जो, फिरी पाणे घर बार।
> गिठ मिठलू फिरी उपाये, गिठमिठलू रा बारा आया।
> गिठमिठलू लड़ी लड़ी बौहंदे, तां नहीं बसदा संसार।
> माटी रा फिरी मनख बणाया, भोले त्रै हथा उपाया।
> मासे री फिरी जीभ लुआई, भरे मनख हुंगतारा।
> तां भरया मनखे हुंगतारा, तां बसदा फिरी संसार।

(B R Sharma, 1986: 22-23).

Then the Bholā Lord started the process of creation of the Universe. The blue sky was created and so the world. Night and morning were created. Sheep and goats were created. Cows and buffaloes were created. Birds were created. But without the human beings the world cannot be settled. Then he started creating the human being. Firstly a man of iron was created. It does not have voice so the world cannot be inhabited. Then the human being of silver and gold was created. He too did not have voice. Then the human being of nine yards long, having the life of three hundred and sixty days of age, was created. He did not get house to live. For so short a period of life there is no reason why a house should be built. Then dwarfs were created. They quarreled among themselves, therefore the world could not be inhabited.

Then the Bholā Mahādeva created the man of earth which was three cubits high. He placed a tongue of flesh in it. This man now started answering the calls. Bholā the Lord cautions man: The streams are cold and hot. You will come naked and will go hungry. What will accompany you, when you go from this world? You will take with you two and half yards of cloth and two pieces of wood. Sin and virtue, truth and false, these will go with you. Oh, White Bullock! you will hold the weight of the world. When the world is now settled, Śiva is settled on the Kāli Dhār, the Black Ridge.

This story tells how the self created Teacher created the universe out of nothingness. He first created Mansā *Devī*, then the creator of the man who then created the man and then the world became inhabited with many species of beings and the human beings.

BR Sharma says that in Bilaspur area there is a custom of singing songs by the Nātha adepts. Before starting singing some important songs like Guggā Jāharpīr, a piece of song called *gavāh* is sung in the beginning. It is told in the story that in the beginning there was darkness on the earth. Then the sound of Huṁkār arose by itself from which was born Śiva. Śiva created the sun and the moon. With the drops of his perspiration he created the stardom. From Huṁkār developed Oṁkār. This story thus runs covering the period upto the advent of guru Gorakhnātha and tells the relationship between Guggā and his mother Bāchhal.

In Kinnaur in the song describing the story of Mādev-Yukuntras, a similar story is told. The point of action in this story starts with the birth of the creator of the universe, Mādev (Mahādeva), Śiva. The local deity Yukantras, the Lord of the Snow, is defeated and his daughter is married to Mādev.

In Lahul this story of creation of the man is related in the following song.

छारे रा माणु

ए थाले–थाले जला कुम्भा आसे।
तेथा ऊपरे गुगलू थामा आसे।
तेथा ऊपरू महादेवा री जटा आसे।
जाटे ऊपरू सोने पादमा धरती।
ई ारू महादेव क्या दोरे कीती।
बारह वर्शे बण खण्डे जापी।
सोने खईरी मनुशा गड़ाई।
दूर छड्डी ता हाका पाई
सोने री मनुशा हुणुकारा नाई।
रूपे खईरे मनुशा गड़ाई
दूरा छडडी हाका पाई।
रूपे री माणुशे जा हुणुकारा नाई।।
त्राम्बे खईरे मनुशे गड़ाई।
त्राम्बे री माणुशे जो हुणुकारा नाई।
इशरे महादेव क्याए दोरे कीती।
बारह वर्षे वण खण्डे जापी।
लोहे खईरे मनुशे गड़ाई।
लोहे री माणुशे जो हुणुकारा नाई।
इशरे महादेव क्याए दोरे कीती।
बारह वर्षे वण खण्डे जापी।
गो ाटु डाबी धूणी जगाई।

धूणी जागी ता छारा न बणी।
छारा मुसी करी मनुशा गडाई।
छारे री मनुशा आमान बणी।
छारे री मनुशा दूर नदी पार छड्डी हाका न पाई
छारे री मनुशे हुणुकारा आसे।

The Man of Ash: O below there, there is the mass of water. Over it there is the pillar of the smoke of guggul. Over it is the bunch of hair of Mahādeva. Over the mat of the hair there is the soil of gold. Īśru Mahādeva made great effort. He meditated for twelve years in the jungles. He melted gold and created man. He placed it afar and called from distance. He found that the man of gold has no voice. Then he melted silver and created a man. It was kept afar and call was given. It too has no voice. Then copper was melted and man was made. The man of copper has no voice. Then he made a man of iron. He too possesses no voice. Īśru god made great effort to create a man. Then he again meditated in the jungles for twelve years. Then he collected cow-dung and created smoke. Then ash was created. The ash was kneeded with water and a figure of man was made. Then the man of ash was placed afar across the river. A call was given from distance from this side and the man of ash could respond to the call. Then the human being was created and the world became populated. This is an example of expansion of the culture from Chamba towards Lahul.

A Natha View on Human Life

We have seen above at the end of the song of Ainchalī a glimpse of the Nātha view on the human life where it tells about its worthlessness. The same view is expressed in the following stanza. This stanza is part of the song of Bhartharī found in the beginning.

काची बणी काया कोठडो।
काची बणी या सन्सार।

दो आ दिने राजा जिउणा।
छाडी देणो सन्सार।
समझा शुणो राजा भरथरी।

This human body is impermanent. This world too is temporary. O, King! This life is short, only of two days. Then you will have to leave the world. O! King Bhartharī, listen, you must understand this.

In another story on the advice of his mother as above, Bhartharī, asks her, 'how to make this body permanent on this earth?' The answer is that one should become a *yogi*. So the son becomes a *yogi*.

The following is a song of *gaddīs* on the life of Raja Gopīcand which explains the same point of philosophy.

चन्दन चौकी गो रुपी झरियां राजा गोपी चन्द नहाए
ता अम्बर भोला भो अघना चान्दी वरगा ठण्डी बून्द कटौण अए
ता छज्जे बो बैठी माता नैन वन्ती नैन भरी भरी रोये
ता फिरी उपरहूं हेरे राजा गोपी चन्द ता माता नैन बन्ती रोये
ता कुनी दिती माता तिजो गाली कुनी बोले मन्दा बोल
ता नहीं बो दित्ती बेटा मिन्जो गाली न बोले मन्दे बोल
ता कुनी बो हेरू माता मन्दी अखरा तिसेरी हखरी कड्डन
ता ना बो हेरू मिन्जो बेटा मन्दी हखरी न कोई गलियान्दे
ता जैसी कायन बेटा तेरी तैसी बावल तेरे री
ता जल बोल माटी हो गेई हुइ भसमां री ढेरी
ता सिख देन माता मेरी पाइये धियाना उमर कायन
ता जोग धियाना राजे भरथरी पाये उमर कायन
ता जोग बो धियाना माता मुन पानी उमर कायन
ता जोग धियाया राजे गोपी चन्दे पाये उमर कायन

Raja Gopīcand was sitting on a seat of sandal wood, with silver ewers, for taking bath. Then he felt drops of water falling upon him.

He thought, 'The heaven is clear like silver, whence do the cold drops come?' Sitting in the balcony his mother, Nainwantī, was weeping bitterly. Then again Raja Gopīcand looked up. His mother Nainwantī was weeping. He asked – Who gave, mother to you abuse? Who spoke evil words? She replied – Neither was given, son, to me abuse, nor were spoken evil words. He – Then who looked mother, with evil eyes? His eyes I will tear out. She – No one looked at me, son, with evil eyes, no one gave me abuse. As your body is, so was your father's. He was burnt and became clay. He turned into a heap of ashes. He – Then give me advice, mother, how to make my body immortal? I would become an ascetic, mother. I would make my body immortal. So Raja Gopīcand became an ascetic. He made his body immortal, (District Gazetteer, Kangra District, 1924-25, Appendix I, xv-xvi). The essence is that by becoming an ascetic one can become immortal.

The song of the Blāj

Blāj is a song sung in the Shimla region especially in the fair known by the same name as Blāj held in Balag village. The story ends with the suppression of Bali Raja by Vishnū, a reference from the scriptures. The name Blāj, from the several similar terms indicates that it is connected with the story of Raja Balī. It is sung on many occasions. The song covers some unusual and important subjects. The song was first collected by Pandit Tikā Rām Joshi and published in the Journal of the Asiatic Society of Bengal in 1909/1911 which has been reprinted by the Himachal Academy. Recently some other versions also have come up but they are incomplete.

The story of the song runs thus. Nārāyana, the God, a self-created power, created the earth. The whole earth was covered with water. Then suddenly sprang Mansā *devī* from the God's mind and the God kept her as the guard of the earth. The God gave her seven earthen pots instructing her to keep them in a store and break open in the tenth month. As she kept on breaking the pitchers, Brahmā, Vishnū and Śiva were born. The *devī* sought from each of them to marry her. Each one of them promised that they will get her married but with a man. Then they started creating man of different materials and of different sizes. Lastly Kāmdeva was created who gave answer to the call. He was called Huṁkār, his son was Nirankār and his son was Harī Chand. There was prosperity, justice and peace during the reign of raja Harī Chand. His son was Balī Chand. He built a palace and performed a yajña.

In the ceremony all the deities of the four directions were invited. But Balī Chand avoided to invite Vishòṇū. Viṣṇū assuming the form of a dwarf, arrives at the door of Balī Chand, and seats himself at the gate. He neither takes food nor takes drinks. Balī Chand says, 'O Brahman, please accomplish my sacrifice. I will give you whatever you may ask for'. The dwarf bound him by an oath. The guest brahman performed the rite by feeding the sacred flames with the fuel of iron, and lighted lamp with water. Thus accomplishing the sacrifice, he asked for the gift. Balī Chand said: 'O Brahman, ask what do you want? Whatsoever you ask for is acceptable to me'. The dwarf said I have accomplished your sacrifice. Bestow on me two and half paces of land. Balī Chand said: 'You are misled, and do not know how to ask. Gold, silver, horse and robes are gifts for a Brahman. I would have given you the fertile land in Balag, wherein grows a *khārś* of grain'.

In one step, the dwarf covered half the earth and in another the whole world. But there being no room left for the remaining half step, the dwarf put his step on the shoulder of Raja Balī Chand and cast him down into the seventh world of the lower region. Raja Balī besought Visnū, saying: 'Let not allow to disappear my name'.

Balī Chand exclaimed: 'O Diwālī, when will you come?' She replied, 'In Kātik, October'.

'With what greedy desire?' 'Of maidens and children.'

'O Diwālī, when will you come with the desire of walnuts and roasted grains? And with the desire of beautiful women and handsome youths?' So much is the song of Blāj.

John Dowson writes giving reference from the classical literature that Raja Balī was a good and virtuous daitya king. 'He was son of Virochana, son of Prahlāda, son of Hiranya- Kasipu. His wife was Vindhyāvali. Through his devotion and penance he defeated Indra, humbled the gods, and extended his authority over the three worlds. The gods appealed to Vishnu for protection and he became manifest in his Dwarf Avtāra for the purpose of restraining Bali. This dwarf craved from Bali the boon of three steps of ground, and having obtained it, he stepped over heaven and earth in two strides, but then out of respect to Bali's kindness and his grandfather Prahlāda's virtues, he stopped short, and left to him Pātāla, the infernal regions. Bali is also called Mahābali, and his capital was Mahā-bali-pura' (John Dowson 1993: 42)

Raja Bali's name has not disappeared. His name still survives in many parts of India. He is honoured greatly. The deity 'Raja Bali', who must be the same, is worshipped in Lahul in an important festival of Khogal, the new year festival annually, in some parts of the valley.

B. Expansion of Grain Seed and Development of its Measuring Units

There are songs giving description of the origin and yearly increase in the production of grain seed and alongwith it the invention of measuring units, a new unit added each year with the successive growth in the production of grain. These songs are sacred and form parts of prayers of the village deities and some are sung at the time of fairs. The following is a part of the song of Blāj, sung in the Blāj fair, treating the current subject.

The following portion of the song gives description of the evolution of mustard seed. The production increases year after year and simultaneously the new units of measurement of grain are invented.

पहला नांओं नारायणो रा, जुणिए धरती पुआनी,
जलाथली होई पिरथिवी, देवी मनसा राखी जगाड़ी।
माणु ना होले कवें रीखी, एकेई नारायण राजा होला,
सिद्ध गुरू री झोडी ता, ढाई दाणा शेरो रा झाड़ा।।
ढाई दाणा शेरो रा, महारे शवाड़िए बीजऔ,

बीजी बाजी रो शेरा जमादे लागे।
जामी रो शेरा गोड़ने लाए,
गोड़ी रो शेरा पाकदे लागे
पाकी लूणी रो शेरा, कुनुयें लाए।

गाही मांडी रो क्या होआ पवाजा?
ढाई दाणा बीजो दा छुरू होवा पवाजा।
छुरू भरी शेरो रा महारे बीजे शवाड़े,
बीजी रो शेरा जामदे लागे
जामी रो शेरा गोड़ने लाए,

गोड़यो रो शेरा पाकदे लागे
पाकी लूणी रो शेरा कुनुयें लाए।
गाही मांडी रो शेरा क्या होआ पवाजा,

छुरू भरी बीजौ रा, पाथा होआ पवाजा।
पाथा भरी शेरा रा महारे बीजौ शवाड़े,

बीजी रो शेरा जामदे लागे
जामी रो शेरा गोडणे लाए
गोडी रो शेरा पाकदे लागे
पाकीं लूणी रो शेरा कुनुयें लाए
गाही मांडी रो शेरा क्या होआ पवाजा,

पाथा भरी शेरा रा जूण होव पवाजा।
जूण भरी शेरा रा महारे बीजौ शवाड़े,
बीजी रो शेरा जामदे लागे
जामी रो शेरा गोडणे लाए
गोडी रो शेरा पाकदे लागे

पाकी लूणी रो शेरा कुनुए लाए
गाही मांडी रो शेरा क्या होआ पवाजा
जूण भरी बीजौ रा, खार होवा पवाजा।
खार भरी शेरा री महारे बीजो बलगे शेरी
बीजी रो शेरा जामदे लागे

जामी रो शेरो गोडणे लाए
गोडी रो शेरो पाकदे लागे
पाकी लूणी रो शेरा कुनुए लाए
गाही मांडी रो शेरा क्या होआ पवाजा,
खार भरी बीजौ रा होआ खार पूरा नूरा।
खार रो शेर रो भाईयो महारे मुन्दर बाणो।
सिद्ध गुरूवे मुन्दर बाणा।

Translation: This is part of the song is sung in the praise of *devatā* Blāj. It says, first take the name of Nārāyana, the God, who created this earth. This earth was covered with water. Mansā Devi was given the responsibility of looking after this earth. There was no man or *devatā* here. There was only the ruler Nārāyana. Then two and half grains of mustard seed fell down from the bag of *Siddha* Guru (Nārāyana). This we sowed in our *shwādī,* a small plot near the home. It started germinating. Then we weeded. The seeds then started ripening.

We harvested the crop and heaped up at one place. After thrashing it, with two and half grains of seed the yield was equal to one *churū*. Then we sowed one *churū* of seed and produced one *pāthā*. Then we sowed a *pāthā* seed and obtained one *jūn*. From one *jūn* we got one *khār*. One *khār* of seed we should sow in the large field of Balag. With one *khār* we got one *khārś*.

O! brothers with one *khārś* of mustard we must ask for protection. The *siddha*-guru offered protection. By the evening time, there appeared, Lūdar, Śiva who said, 'The earth and the sky are hereby protected, the sun and moon are hereby protected, the region of constellation is hereby protected, Nāga Vāsukī is hereby protected and the seven seas are hereby protected. The courtyard (of the Raja) and the four quarters are hereby protected. The saints and sages are hereby protected. The gate of the Koṭī State is hereby protected. Rānā Raghubīr Chand is hereby protected. The Heir Apparent and brothers (of the Rānā) are hereby protected. The palace and its boundaries are protected. The village deities Kḷaiṇū, Shrāḷi (Juṇgā), Sip, Dhāñdi and Korgaṇ are hereby protected. Gods and goddesses are hereby protected. The courtyard of Cāklū is hereby protected. Lastly this Blāj Fair is hereby protected.'

This production is sufficient for the whole population of the residents. Thus the abundance of production of the grain has brought about support and assurance for sustenance of all the beings and establishments here and there is prosperity all around.

The name Rānā Raghubīr Chand is a current insertion in the song or might have been a replacement. This song entitled 'Song of the Blāj Fair' was recorded by Pundit Tikā Rām Joshi who was *rājguru,* official priest, of the states of Keonthal and Kotī, near Shimla. Koṭī was a very small State. At the time when this song was recorded its parts like Kaithu etc. were then included in the Shimla town. At that time Rānā Raghubīr Chand, a historical person, was ruler of the Koṭī State. He was born in 1865 and succeeded his father Rānā Bishan Chand in 1891.

Song of Balāj from Sunnī: Below is given a piece of another similar song from Sunnī area of Shimla which also is a part of a prayer. It is short and compact. This song also covers one or two steps missing in the above song. This prayer is offered in the morning and evening. While praying in the morning the worshiper says, 'open the fist', in the evening he says, 'close up the fist'.

छुरू शेटो शेवाड़िए बोआ, मुद्रो बाज़ी।
छुरू बोई र मुठू ओआ।
मुठू बोई र ठाकरी भोई।
ठाकरी बोईर पाथा ओआ।
पाथे बोई र मणा ओआ।
मणा बोई र जूणा ओआ।
जूणा बोई र खार ओई।
खार बोई र खारच ओआ।
हलो जूंगड़े मुंदरो बाजी।
चूल्हे चौके मुंदरो बाजी।

Translation: I sowed one *churū* of seed in the *shwād,* it became our protector. From one *churū* we got one *muṭhū*. From one *mutòhū* we got one *tòhākrī,* from one *tòhākrī* we got one *pāthā.* From one *pāthā* we got one *maṇā*. From one *manòā* we got one *jūn.* From one *jūn* we got one *khār.* From one *khār* we got one *khārc.* It became protector of the kitchen.

Measurement of Grains

The above measures can be put as under:

1 Churū = Grains which can be held on the fingers on the front part of the palm. It is about one and half tolā. (One tolā is approximately equal to 11.66 grams.).

1 Muṭhū = One fistful.

1 Ṭhākrī = One handful, both palms open.

1 seer (kaccā) = six chatāk.

1 *pāthā* or *pathā* = 5 Seer (kaccā) = 30 chatāk

1 Maund = 8 *pāthā* = 40 seer pakkā

1 Jūn = 2 maund

1 lākh = 16 pathā

1 bhār = 20 pathā

1 *khār* = 20 bhār

1 *khār*c (*khār*śu) = 20 *khār*

1 battī = 2 seers

1 seer pakkā = 16 chatāk = 80 tolā.

The whole array of the above data is a mixture of weights and measures. Pathā is a wooden bowl for measuring grains in volumes and was used most commonly throughout Himachal. Its weight varies according to the kind of the grain measured. It is given as: 'The specific gravity of māś, sariārā and husked rice is about the same, and a pathā of either of these weighs four sers, four sarsahis or 4 1/3 kaccā sers (nearly 2 pakkā sers or 4 lbs.)'.

The problem is that in practice this measurement is not found as of one standard. The size of a vassal of *pathā*, the most common measuring wooden pot, may vary from area to area and one class of society to another viz. the trader and the farmer, and even in extreme cases there may be the vassal of two sizes in the same house, one for one kind of use and the other for a different kind of use: one for giving and the other for taking. There is a saying at certain places that people should carry their own *pāthā*, and also that there is one kind of *pāthā* for giving a thing and another one for receiving. In Lahul the *pāthā* is called *bre* which is slightly smaller than *pāthā* used in Kullu. *Bre* is a Tibetan term and the term is found in the ancient Tibetan documents from Central Asia.

Genesis of grain in Lahul: In Lahul there is a story that when Gepang, the deity of Lahul, came to Lahul with several devatas and devis across the Baralacha pass, they were carrying loads of grain but in the way at a place on the other side of Baralacha, called Naphen Nuphen (*lha-phug klu-phug* = Cave of the gods and nāgas) demons obstructed their way and directed them to throw away their loads. It is told that there are some heaps of earth still seen there. Gepang cleverly hid two seeds of grain, one was white and one black, in the hollow of his bamboo stick, and was able to bring them with him. With these originated the grain crops in Lahul: huskless barley from the white seed and buckwheat from the black seed. These two kinds of grains had been the staple food items of the Lahulis till the time of economic boom in the recent time.

6

Nāthapanth in Himachal Pradesh

A. An Overview

Nāthpanth at one time had spread over almost whole of the present Himachal. Further to certain degree the customs were followed by the whole population. But the household class of the Nātha was the exclusive follower of all the customs and formalities of the Panth. Presently they are seen settled in pockets in different parts of the State. They were ordinarily householders and agriculturists by profession. In Himachal the Panth has quite a long history. The earliest evidence available about the Panth is from Chamba where it reached crossing the plains and the low hills. Chamba has a distinction of possessing rich and unbroken chain of historical evidences about the history of the State covering a period of more than a millennium. In the time of Raja Sāhil Varman (920-960) area of the State was expanded greatly. The capital was brought from the interiors of Bharmaur to the broader part of the valley and was founded at Campā, the present Chamba. Carpatnāth, a great *siddha*, was Guru of Sāhilvarman and was intimately associated in the decision making processes of the State.

Besides Chamba, remnants of the strong centres of activities of the Panth are found in some other parts of Himachal also. Kashyap writes, in Sujanpur the temple of Kanikā Bābā Bālaknāth, and in Kangra the Tilā (Mound) of Bālaknāth remained centres of the Nāthas. In Sirmour and Keonthal the Nātha *yogis* had relationship with the ruling families. Kullu remained under the influence of Nāthas and *Siddhas* for long time and was centre of Nāthas like Sirmour, Bilaspur, Kangra and Chamba. Naggar in Kullu was centre of Mahāyān Buddhism which later turned to Vajrayāna and subsequently turned to *Siddha* and Nātha. Akhala Bazar was held by Nātha *yogis*. 'Tradition says that Akhala Bazar of Sultanpur was originally founded by the Nātha Vairagis.' In Mandi 'Ḍugge Nāle rā Siddha', in Hamirpur Bābā Deoṭ Siddh, in Jogindernagar the Sthān of Bābā Bālaknāth, the temple of Bālaknāth near Sujanpur and in Kangra the Bālaknāth kā Ḍholā remained centres of Nāthas. Besides there are number of temples and maḷhis, situated at many places in the State. In the festivals of Virshu, Nirshu, Karyālā, etc. folk dances are held and miracles of the Nāthas are exhibited. Songs about Rājā Bharthari, Gopi Chand, Rāni Pinglā, Rāni Virmā, etc. are sung in their praise' (Kashyap, 1986: 172-174).

BR Sharma writes that the biggest concentration of the practitioners of Nātha faith is at Jawālāmukhī where they are managing the Gorakh Dibi, the boiling water pot which is associated with Guru Gorakhnātha. At Bharmaur in Chamba the legend of visit of nine Nātha and eighty-four *Siddha* during the ancient times is recorded in the history of erstwhile Chamba State and there are various fables relating to miracles and unusual feats performed by the Nāthas or Kānphaṭa *Yogis*. Nawālā festival, a ceremony arranged to worship Śiva and Manimaheś Jātrā as well as some other fairs and festivals are arranged in Chamba region even upto the present time and are associated with the Nātha cult. Some *mantras* (chants) for curing snake bites and other poisonous effects are still exercised in the name of Natha *yogis*, especialy guru Gorakhnath in various parts of the State.

Ramlok writes that in Rampur Nātha *yogis* ranked below the *sadhus*. They carried a vessel of broken earthen pitcher and took rounds for begging in the night, singing in the praise of Gorakhnāth and Bhartharichandra every year in the month of

Māgh. They wear *pugree* and take the offerings on the day of Saturn. On the occasions of death in a household they were offered the clothes of the deceased. They are buried and the mahants, the gurus of sadhus, are also buried. These days they are agriculturists (Ramlal Pathak, 1987: 81-86).

In Sirmaur, Gautam says, the Nāthas and the *Siddhas* are very influential. Some Nātha *yogis* practice *jantra-mantra*, black magic. There are number of Nātha temples or *maṭh* in the area and those at Nahan and Thoth village are famous. It is said that the *maṭh* at Thoth was got constructed by the famous *yogi* Twārnāth. The sadhus who are its pujāris belong to the Nātha *sampradāya* and they are addressed as *guru* or Nātha. Presently the faith is prevalent mostly among the low caste section of the society. In Shillai the Kanait community also follows the faith. There are folktales prevalent among the people in which it is revealed how the *siddhas* and *Nāthas* through tricks and magic took control over the Rajas (Khushi Ram Gautam, 1992: 21).

In Himachal the faith had spread to the extreme corners of the State like Bharmaur, Bhangāl, in the interiors of Kangra, and the inaccessible valleys of Lahul and Kinnaur. In Lahul there is the temple of Naunāth having mohrās and *rath* like those of the devatās in Kullu.

The following part of a song, rather a prayer shows how the Panth had penetrated into the interiors and how deeply it had settled even in the remote Bhangāl. Here the singer praises the *gaddi* shepherd, who hails from Bhangāl, which during those times could have been under Kullu. Actually he is Nārsiṁha, a deity of the Nāthapanth, in the garb of *gaddi*.

कुलुए भंगाला ते आया मेरे मितरा ओ
डेरा बसोलिया लाया, मेरे मितरा ओ
हत्था त तेरे नरेलू बराजदा ओ
लक्का बराजदा डोरा मेरे मितरा

Nārsiṁha is now camping at Basohali. He holds a *hukkā* in his hands and on his waist he wears a long and heavy waist band. Chandrashekhar Bebas of Kullu writes that the Pādhās, Upādhyāyas, of Bhangāl are famous for their knowledge of ojhāgiri, magical acts. There are numerous similar traditions and practices existing in other districts of Kangra, Bilaspur, Mandi, Una, Shimla, etc.

Nātha literature in Himachal Prasdesh: Nātha literature of Himachal Pradesh makes an interesting study as a model of a branch of a religious sect which developed nearly into a self-sustaining distinct entity. Much of the traditional literature in Himachal is available in oral form and considerable portion of it belongs to the faith of Nāthapanth. Recently efforts have been made to collect and publish them. Some of the literature is concerned about the life of the leaders of the faith like Bharthari, Guggā, etc. Some others, even though small in quantity, deal with other important subjects. Some of the published works may be given as: *Bharthrī Lok-gāthā, Himachal Pradesh me Guggā Paramparā, Guggā Gāthā,* etc. A good amount of material has also been published in journals and some collected works. Some works also have appeared on the related subjects like *Sāncā*, a literature of *mantras* etc. in secret characters and *Karyālā*, a form of folk drama. There still remains much to be done. It is important to note that these works are found throughout the State and in several major languages of the state. These are generally in verse form. They are sung and dramas are played.

The following is a piece of verse from a prayer to Guggā Pīr current in district Hamirpur. It gives comprehensive list of the deities of the sect who were generally propitiated in Himachal and gives an outline of the kind of the faith that was followed.

झकमक झकमक आरती तेरैं गुरूआं दे डेरैं।
गुरू गोरख राणेयां मारूयें तेरैं।

पंजा पाण्डू राणेयां मारूयें तेरैं।
चौसठ जोगणीं राणेयां मारूयें तेरैं।
बूंजा वीर राणेयां मारूयें तेरैं।
चुरासी सिद्ध राणेयां मारूयें तेरैं।
काली माता राणेयां मारूयें तेरैं।
हणमत जोधा राणेयां मारूयें तेरैं।
भैरौं छडिये राणेयां मारूयें तेरैं।
चण्डी माता राणेयां मारूयें तेरैं।
नहर सिंह वीर राणेयां मारूयें तेरैं।
नौ नाथ राणेयां मारूयें तेरैं।
कलिहर नाग राणेयां मारूयें तेरैं।

We make offerings of bright lights and sing and pray you, O Guru! Guru Gorakhnātha, Five Pāndav brothers, Sixty-four Joganī, Fifty-two Vīrs, Eighty-Four *siddhas*, Kālī Mātā, Hanumān Vīr, Bhairoñ the stick holder, Candī Mātā, Nāharsiṁha Vīr, Naunāth and Kalihar Nāga, all are favourable to us (Jaswal, 2010: 49-50). The list although quite comprehensive does not include the names the heroes like Bhartharī who were very popular in the State. The phrase 'Rāṇā of Māru' repeated in every sentence stands for Guggā.

A prayer prevalent in Arki, district Solan, mentions the names of the following important deities and persons to whom prayer should be offered: Vāsukī Nāg, Dhaulā Bail, Vasudhā Mātā, Brahmā, Visnu, Sadāśiva, Mārkandā *Siddha*, the Moon and the Sun, Nine lakhs of stars, Hanumān Vīr, Bunjā Vīr (fifty two Vīr), Caurāsī *Siddha*, Gorakhnātha, Kaniyā the pupil of Gorakhnātha, Naunāth, Panja Vīr and Nine lakh pupils. This list also misses some prominent names. Here it is given at one place as Panja Vīr i.e. five Vīrs. We usually find the terms in tradition as Bāvanjā Vīr and Panc Pīr - fifty-two Vīrs and five Pīrs.

Nāthe rī Pherī: In Himachal some old customs and festivals still continue to be held at many places. In Kullu there is a tradition existing among the followers of Nāthpanth who are now settled cultivators that they go on begging round called Nātha-rī-Pherī, Round of Nāthas, annually, singing songs or prayers in the praise of Nātha gurus. These songs are related to Bhartharī and Gopīcand. In Chamba during the month of *Māgh* (January- February), the male members of this community carrying long sticks of wood covering them with a piece of red cloth, go round the villages while playing bell and *kānsi*. Similar performances are held in Kangra, Chamba, Bilaspur, etc. They sing long songs but the following piece is common which is in the form of a duet. They repeat the word Bāhatwārā at the end of every line of the song.

Joint: *Kungu ḍori bāhatvārā*

First person: *Hua biana bāhatvārā*

Second person: *Kungu dori bāhatvārā*

Joint: *Ghar Ghar ḍori bāhatvārā*

The vermillion and a band of red thread, about a foot long, *bāhatvārā*. It has become morning, *bāhatvārā*. In every house a band of cloth, *bāhatvārā*.

One of their rare and typical *mantra* is: '*aom āhe maddrā. Guru parmā siddhih*.

ओम आहे मद्दरा, गुरु परमा सिद्दिह।

Below is given sample of another *mantra*, forming the beginning of a long charm, efficacious in curing a number of kinds of evil effects:

अथ सर्व रक्षा का मन्त्र। गोरख कुंडली। 'अथ गुरु गोरख को आदेश। चन्द्रा को सूरज को आदेश। वावंजा वीर को आदेश। चौसठ जोगणी को आदेश। हनुमन्त जती को आदेश।'

Invocation to Guru Gorakh, Moon and Sun, 52 Vīr, 64 *Jogiṇī* and Hanumān the celibate.

Festivals: There are important festivals held in different districts inheriting the legacy of the rich culture of the Panth. *Guggā Naumi* is held in some districts for nine days in the month of *Bhadon*. *Kāhikā* festival is held in Kullu and Mandi. The gazetteer notes, 'In Mandi the best known god in whose name the Kaika is held is Narain of Hurang who lives in the deep valley below the Bhubhu pass. Like most of the Narains of the hills, he is a snake god. The chief actor in it is the Nār, so called from Narāin the god, but now used almost as a caste name to designate the few families in Mandi and Kulu who furnish officiants at the Kaika. Originally the Nārs were of the Kanet community and they are still higher than Kolis. He is accompanied by his wife.' The important festival of *Bhundā* is held in Kullu and Shimla districts.

The folk literature has also not neglected in highlighting some of the weaknesses of the Panth that people had observed in its practice. A great poet has summed up the scene existing in those days in his excellent composition in the following manner:

मांगी भिक्षा भरि भरि खांही,
नाथ कहावै मरि मरि जांही,
बाकर कूकर कींगुर हाथी,
बाली भोली तरुणी साथी,
दिन करि भिच्छा रात्य भोग,
चरपट कहैं विगोवे जोग।

The Nāthas feel pride in calling themselves as Nātha. They beg alms and eat to their full. They take all kinds of flesh of goat, chicken, and others. Their companions are young and innocent women. They beg in the day and enjoy in the night. Carpat is worried that *yoga* is now degenerating.

B. Chamba

History: History of Chamba in the beginning is intermingled with the history of Nāthapanth in the State. Chamba State was founded by Meru Verman (c. 680-760) at Brahmpura, Bharmaur, in the interiors of the State. He was a great builder and there are still in existence some architectural remains at Bharmaur some of which are known to date from his time. The temple dedicated to Man+imaheś (Śiva), Lakshmanā Devī, Gaṇeśa, Nārsiṁha, etc. are attributed to him. The inscription on the pedestal of the statue of the life-sized brass bull before the temple of Man+imaheś and two other inscriptions distinctly ascribe the dedication of these temples and the statues stalled in them, except that of Nārsiṁha, to Meru Verman.

This whole complex of monuments in the local tradition is known as *Caurāsī*, eighty-four. It is believed that this place was visited by the famed eighty-four *siddhas*. These *yogis* are represented by 84 lingas at this *Caurāsī* complex. 'Gorakhnātha is represented by the linga of Nau-nāth, and his two disciples Virupa and Kthād'i have also been included in these lingas representing *siddhas*. The Cambanāth, who figured in the list of nau-nātha, is also represented by a linga named Chamban (Chamvan)' (Sharma, K.P. 2001: 79). This commemorates the visit of the *Caurāsī siddhas*.

The arrival of the 84-*siddhas* is said to have occurred shortly after Sāhila Verman's (920-960) accession at Brahmapura. They were greatly pleased with the Raja's piety and hospitality, and as he had no heir they promised him ten sons. The *siddhas* were invited to remain in Brahmapura till the prediction was fulfilled and in due course ten sons were born, and also a daughter named Campāvatī. Sāhila Verman holds a very conspicuous place in the State annals, for it was he who conquered the lower Ravi Valley, and transferred the seat of government from Brahmapura to the new capital, which he founded at Campā, the present Chamba.

Sāhila Varman while coming from Bharmaur was accompanied by Carpatnāth, one of the *yogis*, and also by his queen and daughter Campāvatī. The Raja then founded the town and named it Campā after his daughter. At this time, Vogel writes, eight *caklīs* - Chamba copper coins - were minted. 'The only coin special to Chamba is the *caklī*, five of which make an *annā*, and it has been in use in all likelihood from ancient times. On it Sāhila Varman caused to be struck a pierced ear, the symbol of a *yogi*, in honour of Carpatnāth, and this has been continued down to the present day. The later Rajas added the Viṣṇu-pad, or feet of Viṣṇu, on their coins'. Of the several temples erected by Sāhila Verman, that of Lakṣmī Nārāyana or Visnu, is the principal one.

In all matters connected with the settlement of the new capital the Raja was guided by the advice of the *yogi* Carpatnāth; and in recognition of this a shrine was afterwards erected for him near the Laksòmī Nārāyaṇa temple at Chamba, where worship is done morning and evening.

Sāhila Varman retired to Brahamapura to spend the evening of his life in peace, abdicating the throne in favour of his son Yugākar. There he dwelt as a *sādhu* in the company of Carpatnāth, and other *yogis*, many of whose shrines are still pointed out on the small 'green' where all the temples stand, and which for this reason is called the 'Caurāsī'. For the same reason the Chamba State is believed to have been originally sub-divided into 84 *ilāqās*, but they are less numerous now (Hutchison & Vogel, 1933-I: 283ff).

There is an uncertainty regarding the time of visit of the group of the *siddhas* to Bharmaur whether they visited during the time of Meru Varman, as there are monuments commemorating their association with the place, or during the period of Sāhil Verman, in the tenth century CE. In this regard Goetz writes that we have to accept both the traditions. 'In all this planning Sāhilavarman was advised by eighty-four wizards led by saint

Charpatnāth. Here two different traditions seem to have been mixed up. Charpatnāth is known both to the Mahayana Buddhist and Saiva tradition as a guru respectively of the Siddhacharya, or of the Kanphata *yogi* (Gorkhanāthī) sect. Unfortunately the time of his life is more uncertain. Tucci has attributed him to the 10th century on the evidence of the Chamba chronicle. But B. Bhattacharya has pointed out that Taranatha mentions him as a contemporary of the famous Luipa and the guru Kukkuripāda whom he has dated Luipa about 669 and Kukkuripāda about 693. In other words the saint Charpatnāth would have been a contemporary of Meruvarman of Brahmor, and not of Sahilavarman, the founder of Chamba town. As a śaiva, or Buddhist, Tantrik Charpati would probably have been connected with the foundation of śaiva and especially śakti temples, such as those of Brahmor. Also the peculiar activities of the saint and of his eighty-four disciples would fit much better into the cultural context of Meruvarman's time. And finally the shrines of the eighty-four wizards are actually at Brahmor, not at Chamba. Thus it appears that the original Charpati legend referred to the foundation of Brahmor by Meruvarman. However it is not impossible that the saint was connected also with the foundation of Chamba, not of the capital of Sāhilavarman, but of an earlier settlement' (Goetz. 1955. 32-33).

The temple dedicated to Carpaṭnāth, founded by Sāhil Verman, exists at Chamba, corroborating the contemporaneousness of the two. However, regarding the group of the 84-siddhas it is well known fact that the *siddhas* belonged to different times. Their period extended to several centuries, probably going upto the thirteenth century CE.

Guru Carpatnāth, Record of Life: Carpatnāth, was a great *siddha*. He is accounted among the 84-siddhas and also among the nine great Nāthas. He was also author of certain works. D. Chattopadhyaya refers to two works attributed to Carpat in translation in Tangyur. Mohan Singh discovered certain works by Carpatnāth which showed his relationship with Gorakhnātha.

Even though Carpat is known as a great *siddha*, is known by this name in Buddhism, Śaivism, and Nāthapanth, yet the name Carpat as such does not occur in the list in the account of 84 *Siddhas*. This fact has been noted also by Vasil'ev, the translator of the work, as noted by D. Chattopadhyaya. Chattopadhyaya further writes quoting from R. Sankrityayana that Pacharī at serial number 59 in the same work has to be taken as Carpatī. And that he was resident of Campā. He was a Kahar, i.e. carrier, by caste and preceptor of Mina-pa. The second part of the statement here can be simply ignored. This important point requires elucidation. A brief sketch of life of Guru Pacharipa is given from the said work as under.

Guru Pacharīpa belonged to Campaka. He belonged to the caste of seller of cakes, etc. and was a sweetmeat seller. He sold cakes taking them from a rich household and lived on the profit earned from it. He kept the cakes cooked in oil for himself and did not sell. Once Avalokiteṣvara came before him in the garb of a sadhu. Pachrīpa had half of the cakes boiled in oil left with him which he gave to the sadhu, who then initiated him with the *mantra* of six letters. This description is not much helpful in disclosing anything about Carpat's character and in identifying the two as the same.

Carpat by Taranath: Taranath gives the story of Carpat in his work *bka'-babs bdun*. He gives the name clearly as Carpat. He writes: In one direction of Campāran there lived many families of the shepherd class. Among them one family was very rich. It owned buffaloes, ba-men (wild-ox), cattle, horses, sheep, etc. numbering around a thousand. A bride was brought for the son of the family who in the meantime conceived a son. Once there was a great feast in the town. All the members of the family went to join in the feast. The bride, daughter-in-law, and the child remained at home. Then Acārya Carpat came there begging for food. The woman gave the Acārya food. The Acārya advised the woman to give similarly the next time also, when he comes. Otherwise if the members of her family, when they return, become angry she should come to him. He lives in the jungle burning a fire. When the family members came back they found the vessels of meal in the kitchen empty. They became angry and admonished her. Then the woman taking her child with her went to the jungle near the Acārya. The Acārya sprinkled spelled water on them so that they became *vidyādhara* (knowledge holders). The Acarya became famous after that and many people came to seek discourse from him. He similarly sprinkled spelled water on them also and about three hundred of them became *vidyādhara*. Thus he accomplished a great purposeful task.

The king of Campā hearing this news came to the Acārya. The Acārya threw off the vessels of food on the ground as if he was very angry. Then the princess of the Nāga appeared from below the earth and she placed many kinds of dishes before the king. The king came to learn that this Acārya is really an accomplished *siddha*. The king got constructed two cave-temples: one for the Acārya, the woman and her son. The second for the other 300 *vidyādhara*. Now the child also became capable of bestowing *siddhis*. The boy became famous as Cambā Carpatī. Kukkutipa was disciple of Carpat.

In the account of Taranath we read that the Guru was named Carpat and the boy whom he initiated was named as Cambā Carpatī. This can be understood as Carpat of Chamba in Himachal Pradesh.

Guru Carbarīpa: This story of Carpat as given byTaranath, with slight difference, but with the same outline of the story, agrees with that of Carbarīpa at serial number 64, given in the Account of 84 Siddhas. The name Carbarīpa with the change in two letters becomes Carpatīpa.

In the work Account of 84 *Siddhas* the story of Carbarīpa goes on to say: In a village in the Magadha there lived a rich tribesman. He owned one thousand buffaloes, and many horses and sheep. Once a great feast was organized in the town. The members of this family had gone to attend the feast. Only the daughter-in-law with her son of three years old remained at home to look after the house. Then there came Guru Carbarīpa and asked for food from the lady. She gave food to the Guru. The Guru told if her husband became enraged by this she should come to him. He lived in the jungle burning fire there. If they don't become angry, she should keep on giving food to him similarly as and when he comes in future.

When her mother in-law came, she seeing the pots empty became angry. The woman then went with her child to the Guru in the jungle. The Guru changed the two to self-born stone images and then they required no food and drink. Meanwhile her husband also reached there. The Guru treated similarly with him also. Then knowing the fame of the guru there came their relatives, friends and others. They in all numbered around three hundred. They also similarly were turned into images of stone. The boy with seven others accomplished *siddhī*.

Hearing all this then there came the king of Campaka named Mahila to see the Acārya. He having great faith in the Guru, got constructed a temple for the three of the family and another one for the three hundred devotees. This became famous as a place of sādhnā and is still famous. Many *yogis* visit the place.

Here we observe that the whole story of Carbarīpa agrees with that of Carpata given by Taranath from which it can be derived that the two are actually the same. Thus guru Carbarīpa at serial number 64 in the Account of 84-siddhas should be treated as guru Carpaṭnāth.

Chamba Carpat or Carpatnāth of Chamba: There are several references indicating to the existence of Carpat who actually belonged to Chamba, sometimes indicating as a distinct person from the Carpat of the greater Tradition. As we have seen above KP Sharma states that a *linga* named Camban, among those of the 84 siddhas, at Bharmaur, belongs to Cambānāth. We have also seen that Taranath names the pupil of Carpatnāth as Chamba Carpati, although the learned scholar shows no knowledge of existence of any place named Chamba. These two statements give indication to the existence of Carpaṭ of Chamba distinct from the Mahasiddha Carpaṭnāth. Ganesh Singh Bedi, we have seen, mentioning the names of nine Nāthas depicts among them Carpat and Mangal belonging to Chamba. Even if the statement is taken according to Briggs we can assume Cambānāth to be belonging to Chamba. BR Sharma writes that Carpatnāth, one of the nine Natha *yogis*, belonged to Bharmaur village of Chamba district. This statement, however, appears to be unfounded.

From all these it may be concluded that there was a *siddha* from Chamba named Cambānāth, distinct from Mahasiddha Carpatnāth. Taranath also shows Carpat and Chamba Carpat as two distinct persons.

R. Sankrityayan gives the alternative name of Carpatnāth as Ajipālak i.e. Shepherd or the lord of Shepherds. The gaddīs have a deity named Ajepāl which can be identified with the same Ajipālak or may be a distinct personality. The deity is revered in many places in Himachal including Lahul. In Lahul Ajepāl is one of the principal deities and is revered on some important occasions. Ajayapāl or Ajaipāl is a great personality in the greater tradition who is placed along Gopicand and Bharthari. Rahul and Dvivedi say that he was a powerful king in Uttrakhand belonging to 15-16th century CE.

Traditions in Practice

Annual Pilgrimage to Ḍal Lake: In Chamba some old traditions are still practised with great fervor. Performing the pilgrimage to

Ḍal Lake or Manimahesha Lake, situated above Bharmaur at the height of about 14000 feet, for bathing there, is held annually. Above the lake there is the mountain peak named Kailāśa. The sacred annual Procession, taking place in the month of August-September, starts from Chamba. BR Sharma writes that numerous disciples of Nine Nātha *yogis* running the *Dasnāmi Akhāḷās* in the region of Chamba possess strong faith in the cult and they participate every year in the procession of leading the *chaḷī* (mace) in the name of *yogi* Carpaṭīnath in the Manimahesha Jātrā, pilgrimage to Manimahesha.

Śivabhūmī Bharmaur: Śiva is the leading god of the *gaddis*. Śiva is believed to have his abode for half the year on the Kailāśa peak at Maṇimahesha and for this reason the Brahmaur *paragana* is spoken of as Śivabhūmī or Śiva's land. On the 1st of Assuj he retires to the lower regions, called Piyālpur (Pātālpur) where he remains till the feast of Śivarātri in Phāgun, when he returns to his summer residence. The *gaddīs* who are devotees of Śiva regulate their migrations by these two dates: leaving their summer pastures in the inner mountains on the former and their winter pastures near the plains on the latter of these dates.

Importance of the god in the history of Chamba is recorded in the following manner. The old Chamba Gazetteer notes that, 'The pre-Muhammadan plates have a distinct Śaiva character. In the general formula of the grants the first place is given to Śiva. The prevalence of Śaivism is also borne out by the stone inscriptions, three of which record the founding of Śaiva temple. On fountain we usually find figures worshipping liñga'.

The story of Trīlocana Mahādeva: Newell has recorded an important story which he says to some extent acts as charter to the annual pilgrimage to Maṇimahesha. It may be that this story must have been related every year to the followers before the beginning of the expedition to the Maṇimahesha began. It was recovered from nearly a lost quarter and presently it is no more in use. This story of Trīlocana Deva explains the relationship of the lake with Śiva and underlines the importance of the annual pilgrimage to Lake Maṇimahesha.

The story goes thus: One day Lord Śiva came into a house in Sechuien village dressed as a Gaddī and called out in front of the door. An aged woman, mother of Trīlocana, came out. The shepherd requested to lend him two packs of salt. She asked, 'from where can I have so much salt?'

Then Śiva speaks to her to look in the chest. There she found two bags of salt one of white and one of black. (The white salt came from Jangthang and was used for human consumption. The black came from Gumma, in Mandi, and was used for consumption of the cattle). The old woman sent her son Trīlocana to carry the pack with the Gaddī. First stage was Sunde, then came Harsar. At Duncho Trīlocana asked Śiva, 'Oh shepherd, where is your flock?' He told that the flock had just left the place. At the back of Barcuṇḍi Śiva left Trīlocana, telling him to come slowly behind him. Meanwhile he will try to catch up with the flock and will retain them.

When Trīlocana reached the Ḍal, the lake, he saw neither the Gaddī shepherd, nor any flock of sheep. He became a little suspicious. Then he found human footprints on the ground. Trīlocana followed the lead and walked on. He took a full round of the lake. At a place on the edge of the lake he saw a square slab. There he saw splashes of water and also saw ripples on the surface of the water. Trīlocana presumed that the Gaddī might have jumped into the water at this spot. He also jumped into the lake. In the water when he came to senses he found himself in a cave. Before him was sitting a sadhu and before him *dhuni*, a fire, was burning. He understood that he was truly Śiva. He joined his hands and asked the sadhu, 'Am I before the Lord?' The sadhu answered, 'Yes I am Śiva.' Then Trīlocana took off his pack. There he was given the task of tailoring the *colās*, cloaks of gaddī, which he worked for six months. After that in the same pack in which he had brought salt, he was given the remainders of the tailoring packed in it and Śiva left him on the shore of the lake. Śiva instructed, 'Do not disclose all this to anyone in your house, for if you disclose it, you will not be able to live there.'

When he reached home, he found the tailoring remainders had turned into gold. In the family all the members asked him from where he had got it. He did not tell. But when he was compelled he had to yield to their pressure. Then Trīlocana went to the junction of river Budli and Ravi and fell down there in the water (Newell, 1965: 76-78).

In Himachal in the villages people worship many deities. They come from different sources and people propitiate them all without distinction. Newell lists the gods worshipped by the *gaddīs* in Bharmaur. These are *siddhas*, deities belonging to the Nāthapanth and others.

Gods	**Worship days**
Nāgas,	Sunday, Thursday
Siddha,	-do-
Devī,	Tuesday
Bīr,	Thursday
Bātal	Spirit of water
Joginīs	Rock spirits
Chungu	A Demon found on walnut and mulberry trees.

Kailu Bīr is the god of abortion, only worshipped by women. Kailing is Nāga worshipped on Sundays as Śiva and is associated with a sick (Newell, 1965: 81). Newell lists several articles offered in the worship to the deities.

Navālā: Navālā is another important tradition famous in Chamba. Newell names the annual pilgrimage to Maṇimahesha as Navālā.

Others describe it as a sacred rite performed in the villages. MP Bhardwaj underlining the importance of the occasion writes that, "In the Saivaite tradition of Chamba the influence of Nātha-*Siddha-Yogis* has been immense, and is extant even today. The Navālā or a typical Ratri-Jagaran, remaining unslept through out the night singing and dancing, a function in honour of Lord Śiva, widely prevalent in Chamba, is an excellent example of Nātha *Siddha* Śaivite ritual. The presiding priest in the function has essentially to be a Nātha Yogī. The mandala also corresponds to the *Siddha* ritual and tradition. In the prayer hymns sung at Navālā the florist woman is also a jogin, and both the priest and the florist are stated to have come from the south of Chamba and are unambiguous hint of Saivite influence through Natha *Siddha* tradition. The mace or the staff bearer of Lord Siva, who leads the procession from Chamba town to Maṇimaheṣ Kailāś during the annual Maṇimaheṣ Dal-Nahan (sacred bath) yatra is none other than Saivite ascetic. A Dhvaja (standard) is also carried as a symbol of Carpaṭ Nātha, underlining the linkage between Saivite practices in Chamba and the Nātha *Siddha* tradition of medieval India. I suggest that the acceptance of Carpaṭ as the most important linking point between the *Siddha* Nātha *Yogi* sectarian beliefs and practices on the one hand and the Saivite tradition of Chamba will be more cogent than insisting on the untenable proposition of eighty four *siddhas* visiting Chamba at a point of time, and the consecration of eighty four shrines at Caurāsī Brahmaur to honour their visit (MP Bhardwaj, Foreword: 17-18 in K.P. Sharma. 2001). This underlines the importance of the occasion.

The Rite of Navālā Savālā: The main part of the ceremony is known as *Navālā* and the last section of it, the departure of the deities is known as *Svālā*. The term *Navālā* has been interpreted in several ways. The most appropriate interpretation of the term appears to be *nav-mālā*, nine garlands, symbolizing the propitiation of nine deities or nine objects or symbolically could be the *Nav-*

nāth. BR Sharma, describing the rite of *Navālā* writes that the offerings of nine garlands is an important object for worship of Śiva. He tells that in the ceremony nine persons are worshipped. These are: the landlord (host), *yogi*, four singers who are called *bandey*, celā (priest), and two sevak, servants, called Katwāl and Batwāl. The rite is performed in the family at some festive occasion like worship ceremony, Śivarātrī festival, marriage, etc. It is a prayer to Śiva. It is held inside the house and in the night. *Yogi* is the essential part of the rite. Therefore it can be linked with *Siddha* and Nātha.

This ceremony is held at the beginning or the end of the celebrations of marriage, etc. It is worth mentioning that the songs of *Navālā*, viz. *Ainclīn* are sung at this moment which in the start describe the origin of the world. Many other songs in the praise of Śiva and Śakti are also sung.

The *yogi* comes in the full traditional dress with the essential items required for the ceremony, which are quite large in number, and prepares the *mandapa*, altar. He prepares 84 cups symbolizing the 84 *siddhas* in the *mandapa*, four eons at its four corners and the mount Kailāśa in the middle. Nine garlands of flowers are offered and placed on the Kailāśa mountain. On it the idol of Śiva is also placed. These eighty four cups are filled with rice, black *māś* pulse and salt. Pieces of food items are also placed with them. Then the idol of Śiva is covered with red cloth. The *celā* dances and the singers keep on singing. The prayer goes on throughout the night.

On the conclusion of *Navālā* on the third day of the ceremony *Savālā* is performed which is an essential part of the ceremony. On this day the devatās and Śiva are given departure (BR Sharma, 1986: 89).

Roopkund: Roopkund, a snowy lake, situated in Uttrakhand at a height of about 16000 ft. above the sea level was in the news prominently a few years back for the reason that there were found skeletons of human body in large numbers. The lake falls on the pilgrimage route to Nandadevi.

A Study Team under Prof. William Sax studied the phenomenon. The remains of human body were estimated to number from 300 to 700. They included men, women and children and some of them were close relations. They belonged to two races. One of them had come from the plains. The second of them was of shorter stature. Among them some were carriers. They died due to injury on the head hit by certain hard object. It is told that women here sing a song which states that a group of pilgrims came from Kannauj and they died due to hailstorm. One of the scientists, member of the team, had suggested the period of occurrence of the incident between 12th and 15th CE. Upon the scientific analysis of the materials it was known that the incident occurred in the 9th century (National Geographic Channel, September 25, 2005). We observe that customs like the pilgrimage of Ḍal Lake in Chamba existed elsewhere also. These are ancient customs, the people have been following since early times. The faith of the people changed but the customs continued to be followed uninterruptedly.

William Sax has described another traditional pilgrimage journey taking place in these areas. Ghandyal's annual ritual pilgrimage to mountain top and planting there a pole, his insignia, is one of them. Possessing by the *Vīr devatā* in the priest and some other persons in this fair obviously shows its relationship with the Nātha tradition. Nāthapanth had quite strong hold in Uttrakhand.

Tibetan inscriptions in Bharmour

Two inscriptions in Tibetan are reported to have been found in Bharmaur. One of them was found in village Goshen, on a rock below the village. There are five sentences in it and all are very common sacred formulas. The lines look still fresh and clearly legible although it appears to be considerably old. As we read from the photograph published by K.P. Sharma (2001, plate No. 17), the five sentences are: *aum maṇi padme hum, aum vajrasattva hum* (written thrice), *aum ā hum.*

This inscription reveals one unique feature. The letter 'A', the first letter of the first word in all the five sentences is subjoined uniformly below it by the small '*a*', '*a'-chhung*, thus lengthening the sound of the letter normal 'A' and giving proper pronunciation to the first word '*Aum*' of the *mantra*. This phenomenon is observable on the *mane*-stones but not frequently. This is a rare instance. It must have been an early practice which later on was dropped. The inscription is religious. On this ground this inscription can be considered of some age, could be of around 13th-14th century CE.

This was a common route of the lama pilgrims going to Urgyan (Uḍḍiyan) in the Swat valley now in Pakistan and also might have been for Jālandhar, Kangra. Through this route one could reach upto Pathankot through pleasant climatic conditions. Otherwise if one was to take up the route through Kullu, Mandi, Kangra, Nurpur and Pathankot one would have to walk through the hot climate for near about ten days. It was comparatively a difficult journey. Guru rGod-tshangpa, Urgyanpa and sTagtshang Raspa passed through this route.

Vogel (Vogel, 1911: 252-3) records another inscription which he found on the bank of Brahmi river about two kilometers from Bharmaur towards Chamba which reads as, *'khyung-po jo-nu 'phags-pas'* which is translated by A.H. Francke as 'the august younger prince of the garuda lords.' Here in the inscription if we read it as it is, it can be translated as 'by Arya Garuda Thakur.' In this manner from the word *jo-nu'* we have used the former part *jo* (=Thakur) but then the other part is left as redundant. Therefore it should be read as *gzhon-nu* (=Kumar, prince) in which form we always find the word used, instead of *jo-nu,* which is not a meaningful word nor it can be from a folk dialect. Thus the changed lettering of the inscription would have been : "*khyung-po gzhon-nu 'phagas-pas.*" Thus it can be translated as 'This inscription was written "by Arya Kumar Garuda' or 'by Arya Kumar Khyungpo". It appears that the author of the inscription is speaking about himself who might have belonged to a noble family.

C. Kullu

In the history of Kullu it is told that Vaiṣṇavism was introduced in the time of Raja Jagat Singh (1637-1672). Since then the worship of lord Viṣṇū became popular. Earlier, Devi was worshipped and the Nātha *jogis* had so strong hold over the Rajas that the Rajas would not take meal unless first they had paid respect to the Nāthas and faqirs (saints), and had offered some gift and food to them. But when Raja Jagat Singh became a follower of Vaiṣṇavism the worship of Durgā and offering respect to the Nāthas etc. declined. This fact is evident from the temples also because the ancient temples are dedicated mostly to Śaiva faith.

At this time Tārānāth was the guru and leader of the Nāthas in Kullu. It is told that Kriṣṇdās Paya-ahārī, a Vaiṣṇav saint, fought with him. In the folk tradition he is known as Phuhārī Bābā. The story is narrated comically in the folk tradition as follows: Tārānāth hurled a boulder on Kriṣṇdās. But the powerful saint stopped it by pronouncing the sound *huṁ*. Then he sent a boulder in return which crushed Tārānāth and he died spontaneously. Paya-ahārī cursed him, 'you will become untouchable'. Tārānāth cursed, 'you will not remain *Vairāgi*' i.e. he will not remain *brahamcārī*, celibate, but will become householder. It is said that thereafter the Vairāgīs became divided, some remained *vairagī* and others became householders. They also adopt pupils and they are considered more trustworthy than their own offsprings. This consideration is seen at the time of death, it is told, when in the matters of inheritance sometimes they gave preference to their celā, in preference to their real offsprings.

The same story is told in the folk tradition in another way. While the two gurus were fighting the *jaṭā* (long hairs) and *kunḍal* (ear-rings) of Tārānāth came under the feet of Kṛṣṇadās. Thus the Nāthas were vanquished. The *śail,* stone, temple at Sultanpur, which now is a temple dedicated to Lakṣmīnārāyaṇa was originally served by the Nātha. The statue of Ragunāthji was brought from Ayodhya during this time which indicates to the event of change in the religious practice in Kullu.

The actual history of Kṛṣṇadās Paya-ahārī goes like this. MR Thakur writes that Tārānāth, a Natha jogi, was the official guru of Jagat Singh. Afterwards Phuhārī Bābā, i.e. Krisṇadās Paya-ahārī who was a great *yogi* was successful in snatching the place of guru from Tārānāth. Ramchandra Shukla writes about the saint: When Kṛṣṇadās reached at Galta in Rajsthan he stayed there in the night burning fire. But the Kānphaṭas asked him to leave the place. On this Paya-ahārī also exhibited his siddhī and wrapping the fire in a piece of cloth shifted to a different place. The Kānphaṭas were surprised to see this. In Kullu he lived at Jhīḷī above Naggar (MR Thakur: 2008:122).

Kṛṣṇadās appears to have been a widely known and an influential Vaiṣṇava *yogi*.

Kshitimohan Sen writes that among the radical religious reformers of Medieval India, Ramananda (c. 1370-1440) stands foremost. He delivered teachings in Hindi instead of Sanskrit. There are some important names among the disciples of Ramananda besides the twelve principal ones. One of them is Anantanand whose *maṭh,* temple, is still in existence in Galta near Amer (Jaipur). His disciple Kṛṣṇadās was born in Kullu in the Himalayas. The ruling chief of Amer was first a follower of the *Yogi* sect but subsequently he turned a disciple of Kṛṣṇadās. Agra-das and Kilha, the two disciples of Kṛṣṇadās Paya-ahārī, were excellent poets (Kshitimohan Sen: 1935. 70 ,76.). Although Kṛṣṇadās of the time of Jagat Singh (1637-1672) and disciple of Ramanand (1370-1440) of the third generation appear to be the same, but there is a slight difficulty in reconciling the two periods reckoned through two different traditions.

Nātha householders: In Kullu, as in many other districts, there are Nātha householders who live in clusters in villages. In the year 2000 it was estimated that they had around 500 families living in whole of Kullu. They form a distinct social class and are considered slightly lower than the Rajputs. The Kanets or Rajputs can have milk and *hukkā* at the house of a Nātha. They are mostly agriculturists and own their own land. Economically they are well off. They are spread all over Kullu and some of the villages where they have more concentration are: Manikaran, Bhuntar, Annī, Nirmand, Naggar, Mohal, Katrāīn, Tegubehaḷ, Kāis, Māhilī, Shamshi, Badāh, etc. There is no social division among themselves and are endogamous. They also serve the village gods specially Vīrnāth and Mahādev. When the *devatā* dresses on special occasions the Nāthas offer flowers to them.

Among the households of this settled society there is a distinct class of the holy men. Some men of the society get initiated, get their ears pierced and wear *kuṇḍal*. In the year 2000 it was known that there were two persons living in whole of Kullu district who wore ear-rings. These are Nantū son of Belū son of Tulū, resident near Manali and Bālā son of Ḍolū near Kalāth, both in Upper Kullu.

Both of them told their age around 70 years. But Nantū admitted that he is not aware of his correct age. In my estimation he must have been near about eighty-five. Age of Bālā could be taken as realistic. He was brought *gharjawāīñ*, son in law, from a nearby village. Nantū was initiated at the age of about 20 and

Bālā at 25. Customarily, it was told, initiation was done at the age of around twenty. Thus Nantū was initiated in around 1935 and Bālā in 1955. This tradition stopped in Kullu thereafter. It was optional for the male members in a family that they could get initiated. They adopted the sacred path of their own will.

The novice first adopts a guru, anyone, who wears *kunḍal* and could pierce ears. Guru of Bālā came from Katrāīn and that of Nantū from Māhilī. When a guru is adopted, *dhām*, feasting, is done for three-four days.

At the time of piercing the ears, the *celā* wears loin cloth. He is made to sit on the ash and then his teacher pierces his ears. Bālā was initiated in the village of his guru and was kept seated on the heap of ash and his ears were pierced by five persons behind a curtain of cloth. Ash is considered pure. Nantū was initiated at the temple of Śivajī, Siyāl Mahādeva in Siyāl village, near Manali.

Generally ears are bored in the month of Posh, December-January, and *kunḍal* is worn in the month of Phālgun, March-April. At this time both the guru and *celā* dance and a large *roat* (loaf), made of rice flour mixed with *ghi* and *gur* is prepared. Then an earthen or wooden *kunḍal* is worn which he wears for three months.

Then carrying a *jholī*, the guru and the disciple roamed for three months from village to village begging and collecting alms like rice, flour, etc. At the end of the third month he comes to home, a ceremony is held in which the regular ear-ring is worn and a big feasting is done. After this the initiate returns as a householder.

Kunḍal or *mundrā* is made from a discarded *ḍhāl*, a battle shield, which is made of skin of rhino. *Mundrā* is the chief sign of the Nātha household adept in Kullu. This is the only kind of *mundrā* worn throughout Kullu. It is quite light and durable. This ring is worn only by men who have been initiated and other men don't wear it. Women also don't wear it. Those who wear white *mundrā* are considered as purer. There is none who wears this kind of ring in Kullu.

At the time of death this ring is taken out and an earthen ring is placed with which he is buried. *Mantra* is pronounced only on special occasions. viz., when the ears are being pierced, dead body is buried, etc. They don't tell the *mantras* to anybody except to their disciple.

Nāthas sing legends and songs of Bharthari. They help in the performance of traditional festival like *Shānt* and *Bhundā*. '*Alakh Niranjan*', is a popular expression which the Nātha adepts pronounce when begging.

Clan: Bālā Rām says his *gotra*, clan, is *Nīr*. He says that there are only two *gotras* of Nāthas *Nād* and *Nīr*. They equate Nīr with Nāyar.

Gorkhdhandā: Ghorkhdhandhā is an instrument like a *chimtā,* a fire tong, around 14" long and one and half inches broad, with a number of small round rings attached, all made of iron. The disciple keeps himself busy in entangling and opening the rings, which is a difficult task for any untrained person.

Burial: When a man dies the body is placed on a structure like a wooden chair especially made for the occasion, in the sitting position, and is carried to the burial place. It is called *sukhāsana* or *dhyānāsana,* posture of meditation. He is clad in ochre coloured cloth. The real *mundrā* is taken away and is replaced by an earthen *mundrā*. The body is buried. The burial place is searched near the house in a uncultivated wasteland. A pit of about 6' deep is dug and the body is placed in the same position as was brought. He is buried alongwith the *jholī* and *phāvlī* (spade). These articles were given by the guru. A woman is taken in lying position and she is not buried.

Earlier no signs of the burial were prepared. Now a days some symbolic structures are raised like cement structure in two or three steps over the pit and in the centre a small round stone is placed or it may be made of cement, which symbolizes a *liñga*. It is told that in Kullu all men of the class are buried and in Mandi only those persons are burried who wear *mundrā*.

Nātha Devatās: Nātha followers in Kullu worshipped their god named Vīrnāth or Vīr. Their number is about more than a dozen. He is also known as *Gohrī devatā*, the deity of the high hills. MR Thakur writes that Vīirunāth or Vīrnāth was a saint who came to Kullu from Mandi. Thakur tells this story from a Bhārthā, the pronouncements of *devatā*, which is a good sample of composition in verse in the folk language.

Vīrnāth is venerated at many places, at Thātch Mashānī, Magaḷ, Mandi, Sarāj, Mandrol, Fojjal, Katrāīn, Trāśi, Badagrāṁ, Sarsai-Bhosh, etc. Gohrī *Devatā* of Dhalpur is Vīrnāth, his sister is Tillo *devī* whose small temple stands beside that of *Gohrī devtā*. There is a god named *Caurāsī-siddha*, but there is no god named Naunāth. Presently these *devatās* are venerated by all the residents.

Nauḷ: In Kullu there exists a distinct social class named Nauḷ, in status equivalent to Nātha. They are professionally agriculturists and marry within their own caste. They are said to have *jajmāns*, lords, among the *zamīndārs*, like the Brahmans, and are said to perform the rites for the dead like the Brahmans. They have a special function to perform in the festivals of *Kāhikā* which is held in some large villages like Shiraḷ, Naggar, Basaunā, etc. The festival is held at places yearly and at others after two years.

Rose writes that their duties resemble those of an Achārj Brahman, and they also consecrate and purify houses. They also play a prominent part in the Kāhikā Melā where Kāhī is explained according to some as body. The following is an account of the festival: 'An expiatory festival called Kāhikā-Mela is held in many

Kullu villages generally in Bhādon or Sāwan (or at Shil village in Jeṭh) at which a Nār chosen by the deota is reverenced as Mahādeo and his wife as Sīta or Shaktī. He first visits any house whose owner is afraid that he has been bewitched and generally by the ceremony of pounding bhang (hemp) and bekar (bhekhal) together in front of a deota with prayers for his destruction (*deopane*). The man sits inside his house and the Nār outside, and a young he-goat is killed. Chidra is then performed, the man and the Nār both holding one of the goat's shoulders which the Nār cuts with a knife, uttering prayers to avert the spells. After this the Nār and his wife go to the temple, and a cloth is spread on four sticks placed in the ground (kunda): four rams are then killed. One at each corner and then the Nār is given as a wali or sacrifice to Shakti. He becomes insensible, is placed in the *kunda*, a rupee put in his mouth, as is done to a corpse, and he is covered with cloths. A sheep is sacrificed on his head so that the bhuts or evil spirits may seize on that instead of the Nār, and then by the power of Shakti the man comes to life again. It is said that in former times the Nār often died, e.g. three died at Mashāra temple near Nagar. The Nār and his wife are given numerous presents by the people present. The idea is that the Mahadeo will save any one bewitched whom the Nār visits in this way, and he is honoured accordingly as a purohit or priest'.

Postel informs that at Basaunā, across Bhuntar, when the Kāhi-kā ceremony is held, a man of Nad (Nauḷ) caste is made to drink ceremonial water with which the masks have been washed. As a result he loses consciousness. Afterwards, *mantras* are chanted and the man comes back to life. Until a few years ago the victim used to be physically beaten or stabbed in order to make him faint which sometimes resulted in his death.

Nauḷ families are found settled in the villages of Bhuttī, Puid, Chuhārā near Bajaurā, Bhraiṇ, Cowkī (Manikaran valley). They also call themselves as Sharma, i.e. Nirved (without Veda)

Pandita. They play important role in the Kāhikā festivals and are associated with the following devatas:

	Name of god	*Name of village where located*
1.	Ajimal (eldest)	Soel
2.	Thirmal	Dhārā
3.	Girmal	Banogi
4.	Siṁhamal (youngest)	Ghot

All the four deities are said to be brothers. It is told that the Nauḷ families came from Curāh (in Chamba), or farther from there, to Uttrākhand (Kullu). Their story is named as *Mahānirsava.* This story has perhaps some connection with the Kāhikā festival also. The Nauḷ have divided their areas in the main valley of Kullu for the purpose of rendering services and obtaining benefits as under:

	Village where the Nauḷ families reside	*Villages assigned for service*
1.	Ghauṭ:	Larāṁkeḷu, Cajogī, Naśāḷā, Jāṇā, Nathāṇ, Soel, Tondlā, Dhārā, Kāīs, Dobhī, Dwāḷā, Puīd, Ghrākaḷ, Seobāg.
2.	Harīpur:	Soel, all the areas above Naggar.
3.	Bhraiṇ:	Half of the Khrāhl, Bandal, Lehnī, Trāmblī.
4.	Chamāhaṇ:	Phāṭi Khrāhl, Kśāvari.
5.	Pīṇī (near Jarī):	Phāṭi Pīṇī.
6.	Caukī:	Some part of Koṭhi Kanāvar.
7.	Mateoḷā:	Some area nearby.

8. Maṇikaraṇ:	Malāṇā, Maṇikaraṇ, Barśaiṇi.
9. Gaḷsā:	The nearby areas.
10. Chohārā:	Kothī Khokhaṇ
11. Bhuṭṭī:	The areas stretching from Lag to Fojjal.
12. Tīhrī (Mandi district):	Kaṭaulā
13. Jogindernagar (Mandi):	Harābāg, Darang, etc.

Role of Nauḷ: In the *melās* of Kāhikā and Bhundā the *Nauḷ* plays an important role and in one way he is made symbolically an object of sacrifice. Both these *melās* are very popular.

i. The Kāhikā Melā: Before the temples of some *devatās* particularly Nārāyaṇa there are seen standing long, about 15-20 meters and thick poles of a whole tree of devadār. These are raised each time the *melā* of Kāhikā of the *devatā* is held. It is told that earlier new poles were planted and the old ones were left undisturbed. But later on when the number of poles became crowded the old poles were uprooted and were replaced by new ones. It is called *dhauj, dhvaj,* flag. The *dhauj* for Bijlī Mahādeva was carried upwards from below through the ridge. At this time a song is sung which is said to be in vulgar language.

Raising of Kāhikā: In the fair of Kāhikā a *vedi*, canopy, is raised. Four poles of branches or trunks of small trees of devadār are raised and a white cloth is spread over it as a roof. This *vedi* itself is called Kāhikā. On the ground in the middle a *kuṇḍ* or *ūkhal*, a small pit, is made in which the *yav,* barley, of the *havan* is thrown. In raising the structure *Nauḷ* plays the central role. He is also the principal actor in the whole Kāhikā. The *Nauḷ* sits nearest to the *kuṇḍ*, and the priests of the devatās and other functionaries sit close to him. The *Nauḷ* starts narrating the story of the god while the other attendants of the god are listening to him. The *devatās* are dancing around him. The lady *Nauḷ*, wife of the *Nauḷ*, or any other *Nauḷ* woman, dances acting indecently behind the *devatās*. The scene continues till the story is finished.

In this play presence of *Nauḷan*, the lady *Nauḷ*, is essential. She may be his wife, otherwise some other *Nauḷ* woman. She is supposed to symbolize Śaktī. They hold wooden symbols of *liñg* and *yoni* and the two play with them and make some vulgar gestures and remarks. They can even tease the *devatā* at this time. In the last the *gur*, priest, of the *devatā* starts playing. It is called *hulkī*. It is presumed that with each *hulkī* a portion of sin is cleansed. Four or seven such *hulkīs* are held. As the last *hulkī* is held the Nauḷ falls and loses his consciousness. Then he is supposed to have died.

At another place it is told that as the story finishes the *gur* of the *devatā* speaks *mantra* in the mouth of the Nauḷ. Arrows are then shot in the four different directions, and the fifth towards the sky. Soon the *Nauḷ* becomes unconscious. He is lifted by some people and alongwith the *devatā* some rounds of the temple are taken. Then the *Nauḷ* is brought at the same place. The *gur* again speaks *mantra* in the mouth of *Nauḷ*, and sprinkles water over him and brings him back into consciousness. And thus ends the principal ritual of the *melā*.

Some people call it as repentance. The *Nauḷ* first dies in the sacrifice and then becomes alive with the aid of power of the *devatā*.

There are different methods of killing the *Nauḷ*. In Hawaī, Diyar and Bashaunā a man carries seven *roṭīs*, cakes, in a *thālī*, plate, smeared with *ghee* and *gur* and as the *Nauḷ* dances he spreads the pieces of the *roṭī* in all the directions. Then the *Nauḷ* is given water from the pot of the god and after the third chance he becomes unconscious. At Śiraḍ, Larāṁ Keḷo, Darpoin, Mathān and Chāṭṭan arrows are thrown in the air.

Kāhikā melā used to be held in Mandi also. The institution of Kāhikā, Nauḷ, Vīr, Phungṇī are common in the states of Kullu and Mandi. Some of the traditions are stated to have come to Kullu from Mandi.

ii. Bhundā of Nirmand: Bhundā is performed in its best form in Nirmand in outer Seraj. On a smaller scale it is performed at Rampur and upper Shimla. It was also held at Balah in Inner Sarāj, where there are temples of Mārkanḍeya Rishi and Bālasundrī, but the custom has now been discontinued.

In Kullu the festival of Bhundā was held at Nirmand in Outer Sarāj, like Kumbh, after twelve years. In the *melā* a man was sent sliding down over a long and thick straw rope in which often accidents occurred and the man died. A death had occurred in 1856 after which a goat was placed instead of a man.

The festival is celebrated in the name of Būḷhā *devatā*. The *devatā* reaches at the place of worship on the first day. On the next day the spirits of the dead Nāgas, the people of the Nāga race of the past, are worshipped on the roof of the temple, as it is believed that they receive peace by it. Thereafter goddess Kālī is worshipped. On the third day the *devatā* alongwith the long rope are taken to Kurpan river for bathing. On return one end of the rope is tied at a height and the other end at a low place so that it gives a slant to the rope. Over the rope at the top end a wooden seat is tied over which a man of the nauḷ caste was kept seated and was let loose to allow him slide down. In this act if the nauḷ or beḷāh dies his funeral is done with great pomp and show. His wife was given land and money for her livelihood from the side of the *devatā*. It is said that no Nāga (serpent) *devatā* can participate in this fair. The fair is considered to represent conflict between the two ancient tribes of Khaś and Nāga. The Khaśas are supposed to have overpowered the Nāgas, thereafter they started celebrating this *melā* of Bhundā in the memory of their victory over the Nāgas.

The straw rope which is about 500 to 1000 meters long is also made in the shape of a Nāga, one end of it is thick, representing the head of the serpent and the other end is thin like its tail. The weaver of the rope is called Meḷāh or Beḷāh and also Jiyālī. Nauḷ who is known here as Beḷāh is considered to be belonging to the Nāga race. The rope is tied by a particular class of Khaśa caste.

Ajnabi writes that, 'This ancient festival commemorates victory of the Khaś race over that of the Nāga. Names of the following villages are mentioned in an ancient song where the yajña were held: Nirmand, Naggar, Nīrath, Kāw-Mamel, Blāh, Nauḷṇā, Badhec, Kulgāoṁ, Dalgāoṁ, Pujārlī, Khaḍāṇ and Nībar. In the celebration of the Bhundā festival a person of the Beḷā caste, considered as the remnant of the Nāga race, is called in the temple of the village. He is given expenses out of the store of the village deity for one whole year. During this period he twists the grass rope which is around a thousand meters long. On the day of the festival one end of the rope is tied to a tree on a hillock and the other end is tied below in the valley. A wheel is fixed on the rope. A person from this family whom the *devatā* has selected is put on the wheel. He is made to stand erect on it. His legs are tied with a stick which works as axel. Two bags filled with earth are tied on either side of the wheel in order to balance it. Then he starts sliding down and the people wait below alongwith the *rathas* of the *devatās*. In the festival the big rope represents the Nāga and the Beḷā as leading his race of Nāgas. As he reaches below he is received with great honour with the pronouncements of *mantras*. This scene ends within two to four minutes. As the Beḷā touches down on the earth he can touch any article lying nearby, however valuable it may be. It is given to him as gift. Ordinarily the Beḷā does not die when on the rope. In case an accident occurs, he is cremated with great honour. His family is given expenses from the bhandār of the *devatā* for life long' (Nem Chand Ajnabi, 1999: 185-187)

BR Sharma writes that, "During the rope sliding ceremony in the Bhundā festival at Nirmand a Nāth was made to occupy the throne of Lord Parshurām and was kept in Parshurām temple for some time. His body was painted in different colours and was worshipped. He was then made to lead a procession through the streets of the village followed by maśāl (wooden torches) and some people carrying baskets full of grains and eatables. At the sunset the Nātha left the village with the objects offered to him and did not come back to stay during the night.

'The villagers believe that by allowing him to stay in the village again would mean that the evil spirits, who might have come to see the fair of Bhundā after hearing the tunes played on musical instruments, would come back with him and would not leave the village. The Nātha in this way represented the deity and was sent out of the village during the odd hours to drive away the spirits haunting the village during the festival period. Nāthas possess magical powers and they are capable of driving away the evil spirits and help people fighting them.'

Bhundā was celebrated in Rampur Bashahar in 1986 after the lapse of 43 years, in which a person of the Beḷā caste was placed on the rope. Measures were taken for his safety. Nets were spread below the rope. These days only goats are made to ride over the rope.

D. Lahul

Lahul is a remote area and it had been extremely difficult to access in the former times. But it is remarkable that Nāthapanth could spread into Lahul even in those days when people had to walk with full load on their back continuously for several days and even weeks. There are number of evidences existing even today revealing its presence in the past. These influences reached Lahul from two directions: one through Chamba and the other through Kullu. It is not much difficult to identify broadly as to which tradition entered Lahul from Chamba and which from Kullu.

Naunāth: One of the outstanding examples of existence of Nātha tradition in Lahul is the presence of the deity Naunāth, also known as Vīrnāth, in the style of Kullu *devata*, in village Rwāling in Pattan, symbolizing the nine early great Teachers of the Panth.

It is a model of Kullu tradition. It has a wooden *rath,* vehicle, as we see in Kullu these days, possessing all the kinds of its paraphernalia like temple, *bhandār* i.e. storehouse, and *mohrās* or metal faces, musical instruments, etc. Presently no deity of this name exists in Kullu, although there are several deities named Vīrnāth. The size of the *rath* is comparatively small.

Although theoretically the deity represents nine entities but practically it is one. However it has exactly nine *mohrās*, and also have no extra *mohrā* in store. It cannot be said that each one of the *mohra* represents one deity. The *mohras* are of different sizes, of different shapes, made of different metals like brass or mixed metal and of silver. As such they appear to have have been manufactured at different times. It may be assumed that the number nine was reached only during the time of Tedhi Singh who donated at least two silver mohras, although comparatively small from those we observe in Kullu, but among those nine these two are the largest in size.

It is told that originally the deity had only one *mohrā*, the three pointed brass *mohrā* at number four. The *mohrā* at number one, a small one weighing about fifty gm, used to be taken to various household in different villages in the area for the performances of the ceremonies of Tādā for removing the harmful spirits. It is named '*tāveez'*, protective amulet. Tādā is a ritual performed by a priest to drive away the bhūt-preta, the evil spirits, that may have overpowered a victim or it may be for the general welfare of the village, etc. In Kullu *devatā* Vīrnāth of Dhalpur performed the ceremony of Tādā in 2009 after fourteen years. On this occasion the *devatā* with its retinue took round of the town moving throughout the night through its fixed traditional route and on the next day a ceremony was performed. The *mohrās* of brass have no moustaches, all the silver *mohrās* have moustaches.

Of these nine *mohras* three have inscriptions in Tankri script. Two *mohras* bear the name of Raja Tedhi Singh (1742-1767) which Khub Ram could read. Another one which is slightly smaller than the two also has inscription. It has date in *sri samvat* but no name of the donor. This appears to be slightly older than the other two.

The *devata* is said to have come from Kāling-Śāling village in Kullu. The *devatā* was installed here in the manner as is done in Kullu although on a very moderate scale. It has a temple of one-room with flat-roof like residential houses of the village, situated above the village. This is both temple as well as *bhandār*. Earlier the *bhandār* was a separate unit situated in the middle of the village. This god came from Kullu after having division from someone there. Vīrnāth of Katrain is said to be his brother. It is told that in the *bhārthā*, pronouncement of the *devatā*, it was narrated that the god came through Gushāl and made friendship with Guru Ghantāl. The *devatā* is said to have first landed in Shansha village.

There live presently two families of the name of *gur*. There was a plot of land in the village called 'land of sādhu' which was owned by the *gur* family. It may be that the *gur* initially came as a *sadhu*. There is another family in the village called Srāngpa, for they have migrated from Srāngme i.e. Shansha.

Naunāth was once very popular deity in the area. The *rath* was decked with *mohras* and was taken in procession once in a year to different villages. Its area extended from Kirting to Tandi.

The people of Shansha made the arrangement for this celebration. The *devatā* was accompanied by musical band. The residents came for paying homage (*ṭhel*) to the god on the occasion of Phagli fair. The custom stopped in around 1960. Nearby the temple of Naunāth there is the one-roomed temple with sloping slate roof of Tilo *devī*. In Kullu the *devī* is known as sister of Vīrnāth. Tilo is said to have come first to Yang Tozing village. There are temples dedicated to the *devi* in some other villages also. The *devi* has no mask. In the temple of Naunāth there is a basket in which shrouds brought by the people are kept and whenever someone needs he takes from here.

Nātha Koṭhiyāḷ: The following is a story told in a song which gives an instance of existence of Nātha family in Lahul who might have immigrated from Kullu. During this time some other families also might have immigrated to Lahul, especially belonging to small professional classes. It preserves an important fact of historical value. The subject of the song is taken from Lahul and it was composed in Lahul.

It states that there existed a Nātha family in a village. They had two sons named Nātha Koṭhiyāḷ and Nātha Bhāguth, born to Zong-Buṭhid. One day they went to Pori festival at Jahlma and came back in the evening. In the night the two brothers had some dispute. Next day the elder one Nātha Koṭhiyāḷ left to Shansha. There the young men of the village were playing bow and arrow. They asked him the purpose for which he had come. Next day he went for hunting across the river. He died there while hunting. He had a matchlock which was manufactured by the local smith named Gorkhu and its trigger was made of silver and the nozzle of gold (Loppa, 1994: 89-90).

In another song it is related that, Nātha Koṭhiyāḷ was resident of village Phura and the family was named *koḷhā*. He was *lambardār* of the village. In another song it is told that Raja Bidhi Singh (1672-1688) of Kullu had sent a *farmān*, an order, imposing *cākri*, free labour, by calling the people of Lahul, to come and join the force for some expedition. Young men of all the villages starting from Nalda to Tandi gathered and went to Kullu. The team of the youngmen of village Phura was led by Nātha Koṭ hiyāḷ.

From the above stories it appears that there existed at least one family of Nātha in Lahul. It was in the employment of the Raja and enjoyed high status in the village. Songs have been composed in their name describing their designation. One of them led the village youngmen. Then it says that he was addressed as Koṭhiyāḷ. Thus he was in charge of the Koṭhi. Koṭhi was the storehouse where the grains collected in levy on behalf of the Raja of Kullu was kept. They were important in the eyes of the Raja of Kullu. Nātha Koṭhiyāḷ is not a personal name. Nātha is a caste, here, family name and Koṭhiyāḷ is his official designation. He must have been looking after all the interests of the Raja in the Kothi.

During the time of visit of Moorcroft in 1820 there was one such kothi at Tandi where there was stationed a kanungo and another official. The impact of Nātha faith however remained confined to Pattan valley. The tradition continued in Lahul for long time. The above traditions have assimilation to the traditions of Kullu and may be assumed to have come from Kullu. The following practices entered from the side of Chamba.

The story of Ban-celā and An-celā: A story current in Pattan valley goes to tell that there lived two beautiful sisters in a forest. Bancelā, the elder, had no son. One day she asked from a *purohit*, 'Is there any son in my luck?' The *purohit* looked in the horoscope. It was found that the luckless woman had no signs of obtaining any son. Yet he did not want to disappoint the woman who had come to him with great expectations. Therefore he pretended to study the book more seriously and minutely. He looked into the horoscope again and more carefully and in it he looked for the movements of the stars. He turned the leaves of the Pothi several times. At last he reached at a conclusion and explained the situation to the lady. 'There is no sign of getting any son according to your past actions. But a coincidence of getting a son is possible according to the dharma i.e. if you do the action of charity.'

The Purohit advised her saying: 'O elder sister Bancelā, you have to ponder over the subjects according to the karma or charity so that your wishes can be fulfilled. You will have to act for twelve years for the accumulation of the merits. You will have to please Guru Gorakhnātha who resides at Gorakh-ṭīlā by means of meditation and true devotion. Then with his blessings you will earn the desired fruit'. Purohit Śrikāntha further explained that, 'this is clearly indicated in your horoscope'.

He further explained, 'O sister! Bancelā, Guru Gorakhnātha will come at your door in the garb of a leper, whom you will have to receive with honour'.

On reaching home, she started doing as was guided and worshipped the guru continuously for twelve years. One day really there appeared a leper, a beggar, at her door. She served him very courteously. Pleased with the services rendered by the woman, the beggar asked, 'O lady ask what gift you wish? She told, 'O great guru, my only wish is to get a son'.

'If this is your desire, you come to Gorakh -ṭīlā on the full moon day. Or on the first Sunday of the Jyesṭh month, you will get the fruit of your penance on that day'. On saying this much the beggar disappeared (K.Angrup, 1993, 33-35.).

There are some other *ghurey,* songs, telling the story of Guggā and others, and other kinds of songs like *sugli,* a kind of song sung on some special occasions.

There were temples dedicated to Nārsiṁha in village Loṭe and Guśāl.

Daḷī Yātrā: People from Pattan valley participate in the annual pilgrimage to Manīmaheśa in Bharmaur which is called Daḷi Yātrā or Jātrā, Pilgrimage to Ḍaḷī, i.e. Ḍal lake in Bharmour. This pilgrimage may be done according to one's convenience during the summer irrespective of the ritual procession held at Bharmaur which begins on a fixed day of the year. Usually they go after the Pori festival of Triloknath which is held in around the middle of August. They go through Kugti Pass and Bharmaur. Presently people also go through Chamba due to availability of vehicular facility. Everybody takes with him as one of the essential items of offerings, a trident of iron called *gajā,* which means yard and is about a yard long. The term comes from Bharmaur where it is found in their important song Aincli concerning the same celebration. The above four customs are most likely to have been introduced into Lahul from the side of Chamba. To this list we may add the instance of the song of 'The Man of Ash' we have already seen.

The prevalence of the practice of the faith in Lahul was recognized outside the area. Following is a *mantra* of Nātha which was popular in the lower areas of Himachal. It has a reference to Lahul.

> संगलदीप का राजा जियापाल, जियापाल का लहूपाल,
> लहूपाल का कुसलपाल, कुसलपाल का नमो नाहरसिंह वीर।
> हाथ में डंडा, पवन का धोड़ा, फिरे नग खेडा, कौण चले।
> नाहरसिंह चले वीर, गद्दी वीर चले,
> पहाडिया वीर चले, वरोधिया वीर चले,
> क्रोधिया वीर चले, वरोधिया वीर चल,
> लाहुला वीर चले, सिंहडु वीर चले,
> दोदिया वीर चले, क्रोधिया वीर चले।
> जटाधरिया वीर चले, केलू वीर चले। (B R Sharma, 1986:141)

This *mantra* enumerates names of several important Vīr deities and one of them is named as Lāhulā Vīr evidently it gives a symbolic representation to Lahul among the class of Vīr deities. This being not a personal name is helpful in recognising the relationship of the Vīr with Lahul. It is of importance that it records the fact that the existence of the faith in Lahul was known outside the area also. This is in conformity with the Lāhulā pītha found named in the Saiva source we have seen.

7 Nātha Leaders in Himachal

A. Bhartharī

Bhartharī and Bhartrhari is a Nātha hero widely known all over the country in the folk tradition. He is also one of the most popular names among the leaders of Nāthpanth known in Himachal. Modern scholars use ordinarily the name Bhartrhari, sometimes interchangeably with Bhartharī perhaps considering Bhartharī a mistake for Bhartrhari. Hence some scholars suggest correction in the use of the name Bhartharī to change to Bhartrhari while reporting from folk traditions. Their information about Bhartrhari is based on their knowledge through literary sources.

Bhartrhari was a great philosopher and grammarian. A reference to Bhartrharī comes in the history in the travelogue of the Chinese scholar pilgrim I-tsing of the seventh century CE. He writes that Bhartrhari was a great scholar and he was famous throughout the five parts of India, and his excellences were known everywhere and in all the directions. He believed in the Three Jewels. The traveller quotes instance of a peculiar behaviour of the philosopher from his life story that he became seven times a priest and seven times returned to the laity. He died in 651-652 CE (I-tsing. 1998: 179-180). I-tsing in his work clearly writes as Bhartrhari and mentions him as Grammarian and Philosopher. He also discusses some of his works.

Murti assigns Bhartrharī slightly earlier date as belonging to fifth-sixth century CE (Murti. 1997: 10). I-tsing and Murti both ignore to discuss some other important and popular works, the three very well known *Śataks*, also attributed to Bhartrharī. They don't refer to these works at all. It may be that by the time of I-tsing the works had not yet been created. In this situation it would be difficult to assign the *Śataks* to the Philosopher-grammarian Bhartrharī.

In the folk tradition, in the oral folk literature from Himachal, Punjab and Chhatisgarh, it is known without ambiguity that they use only the name Bharthari. No reference is found made to Bhartrharī. The Tibetan scholar Taranath in his widely known work History of Buddhism in India, gives description of Bhartharī. He writes that in the country of Mālwā the dynastic line of the kings continued after the death of Viṣṇurāj. After him Bhartharī became king. A sister of the king was married to Vimalacandra, apparently in Bengal. King Govicandra, i.e. Gopicand, was born of the union. During this time Dharmakīrti also passed away. These two kings, Bhartharī and Gopicand, were converted by *siddha* Jalandharipa and Acārya Krsnacārya (Chattopadhyaya, 1990: 249). The story recorded by Taranath about Bharthari agrees with the folk tradition current in India but the period referred by him belongs to a different tradition.

Taranath here writes Bhartharī and not Bhartrharī. He also does not assign him authorship of any literary work. Some scholars write Bhartrharī for Bhartharī correcting Taranath. Taranath was perfectly right in giving his information. The scholar received the story as it was current in his time in the oral folk tradition in northern India through some oral source. His description agrees wholly with the oral tradition about Bhartharī as it exists today in Himachal.

Bhartharī, follower of Gorakhnātha, according to the sagas found about him in Chhatisgarh and Himachal Pradesh all relate that he belonged to Ujjain. Taranath also says he belonged to

Avanti, Ujjain. He is often mentioned as contemporary to some historical personages whose period fall in the medieval period as against the time of Bharṭhari belonging to the first half of seventh century. From these a rough period can be estimated about Bharthari. The folk literature does not assign him any literary work or activity and no work authored by Bhartharī is known to have been found. Bhartharī was related to Gopīcand, another Raja and a leading Nātha teacher. His father's name is given as Vidhi Cand. Man Singh, the king of Delhi was his contemporary. His Guru Gorakhnātha resided at Gorakhpur. There is not wide divergence in the various accounts about Bhartharī found in various regions. Thus we observe that Bhartrharī and Bhartharī have to be taken as two different entities. The two belong to two different periods separated by about seven or eight centuries, the first belongs to the sixth-seventh century CE and the other one to the medieval period. Relationship of Bhartrhari with Nāthpanth is a non issue here.

The propagators of the Nāthpanth relate an incident from the life story of Bharthari how he even possessed of vast amount of wealth, power and pleasure, renounced all of them and became a *yogi*. This is placed as an example before the people in order to impress and stimulate them to join the class of *yogi*. The following piece of song introduces the story of Bharthari at various places and is sung frequently:

> काची बणी काया कोठड़ी काची बणी या संसार।
> दो आ दिने राज़ा ज़िउणा। छाडी देणों संसारा।
> समझा शुणो राज़ा भरथरी।।

This world is temporary and this body is destructible. We have come to live here only for two days, then we will have to leave the world, listen O! king Bhartharī. This is an advice to Raja Bhartharī from his mother stating to abdicate the throne and become a *yogi*. This in the folk song tells the essence of the philosophy of the Nāthas.

The framework of the story of Bhartharī in all the stories sung at different places is the same. Bhartharī goes for hunting and kills a deer, separating the female deer from her beloved mate. Bhartharī is cursed by the surviving male deer. Guru Gorakhnātha advises him to renounce the worldly life. He had to renounce kingship and his beautiful queen. Below are given some stories about him from Chhatisgarh and Himachal.

The story from Chhatisgarh is said to have been related by Allah Udal. Phulwā, queen of Raja Vidhi Chand is childless and is in grief. A *yogi* comes from Vaikunṭh and gives nectar to the queen to drink, saying a child will be born after twelve months. The queen gives birth to a son at the beginning of the tenth month. A *pandita* from Kāshi gives him name Bhartharī. He forecasts that the length of his life is only of twelve years. When still a boy he went to the jungle taking bow and arrows riding a horse for hunting. He kills a black deer. He is cursed by the deer who lost her mate. Then he came home with the dead body of the deer carrying it over his horse.

He goes to Gorakhnātha. The Guru prohibits him from touching his feet for Bhartharī is under the curse of the deer. In order to be free of the curse he should become a *yogi*. The Guru advises him to lead the life of renunciation in the caves and mountains. He then goes to his mother and tells her of his hard decision. Then Bhartharī goes again to Goraknāth who is sitting in meditation.

He requests the Guru to restore the life of the deer. The Guru told that the deer's life can be restored but he himself has to renounce the world. This deer was saint in his earlier birth. He had six score and six female disciples, and he was king of Singhal island. On this Bhartharī promises to embrace the ascetic life.

On return home he tells the story to his mother, who advises him to marry since he has attained the age of 12 years. The barber has been assigned the duty to search a bride. He found Sāmdeī as suitable bride for Bharthārī. The two are wedded. When Bharthārī went to the queen in the bedroom and sat on the golden cot, the cot broke down. He was amazed. The queen laughed. Bharthārī asked for the secret. But she did not tell. She told that her sister Rāmdeī knows the secret.

After ten months of this incident a son is born to Ramdei, the queen of Raja Man Singh, in Delhi. There are Pathan soldiers in his court. Bharthārī is invited to attend the celebration. Here he asks the same question to queen Rāmdeī. But she tells that Rupdei, queen of Garh Narulā, will tell him the secret of breaking the cot. She herself is not able to tell. Then he comes to Rūpdeī. She takes promise from Bharthārī that he will not tell it to anybody else. She tells that Sāmdeī, now his queen, was mother of Bharthārī in his former life. Then he goes to Gorakhnātha. He advises Bharthārī to go and beg alms from his palace. Sāmdeī refuses to give him alms. He comes back to the Guru. The Guru says that he will not accept him as his disciple until Sāmdeī gives him alms saying 'Bharthārī is my son'. Bharthārī then goes again to Ujjain.

He calls 'O mother, give me alms'. Sāmdeī understands that Bharthārī must have known the secret. She tells Campā to send the message to Garh Narulā. There is the queen Mainā, sister of Bharthārī and her son named Gopicand. The two come to Ujjain. Then Sāmdeī gives alms to Bharthārī and he happily goes to the Guru at Gorakhpur and becomes an ascetic permanently. Then he goes to Kāmrūp. He contests with Nainā in magic art but he could defeat her only with the help of Sāmdeī and Rāmdeī. But on reaching back to Gorakhpur he finds all including his Guru under the spell of magic of Nainā. Again he could remove the spell with the help of Sāmdeī and Rāmdeī. Then he became a perfected ascetic (Nandkishore Tivari, 2002).

In the higher reaches of Shimla in the winter when the land outside was covered with snow, people customarily assembled by routine in the house of one family, lit big fire and sat around it working variously on wool. During this time the professional bards or some others sang the Bhartharī sometimes accompanied by music, or stories were related. It took several days to complete the story. Here is given the Shimla version of story of Bharthari from Saleem Gazta (2001: 123-145).

It is told that in the town of Auzab (Ujjain) the king Vidhicand had no issues. After many efforts a son was born who was named Bhartharī. The king died when the prince was eleven years old. Then the prince was placed on the throne. He became devotee of Guru Gorakhnātha and adept in tantric practices.

One day Raja Bhartharī wanted to go for hunting to the Girija jungle. His queen Pinglā tried to desist him from going to the jungle. But he was adamant. In order to console her he gave a cup filled with milk and told her to keep watch over it. When she would see drops of blood in it she should presume that he is no more. There in the jungle he saw a group of deer. He was attracted by their beautiful eyes on which he remarked: 'O God! you have given wealth to miser and beautiful wives to the blind. You have granted beautiful eyes to these deer who remain roaming in the jungles'. Bhartharī threw an arrow but the deer in the hustle were able to save their male companion. But after some more attempts Bhartharī was able to kill the male deer.

The deer cursed Bhartharī, on this, saying, 'You have killed our leader. It could have made no harm if it was someone among the female members of us. Now your own queen will also suffer like us'.

At home the queen saw signs of blood in the cup of milk. She was shocked with the grief and took her life. When the Raja reached home he was dismayed seeing his queen dead. He became like a mad. He took the body of queen Pinglā hanging before his chest and roamed here and there. Meanwhile he met Guru Gorakhnātha. The Guru asked Bhartharī to keep down the corpse and gave him a pitcher and asked him to bring water in it from the waterfall. Meanwhile the Guru lit the corpse in fire. When Bhartharī tried to hold water in the pitcher it broke down and he returned empty handed.

The Guru told Bhartharī, 'This human body too is brittle like the pitcher of raw earth. You therefore should not grieve at the loss of Piñglā. But you are fortunate that Piñglā has taken birth in a place named So-yin Pāl and her name is Birmā.'

Then Bhartharī left the palace of Ujjain and then in the garb of a *sadhu* stayed in the hermitage. His mother asked, 'why have you taken this guitar and stick?' He replied, 'O mother, I have made this guitar for my own entertainment and the stick is for the dogs'. Mother Mauhatī advised him to remain at home and rule this land of nine lakh (population). In the *kuṭir*, hut, the *sadhu* sewed a *gudrī*, cloak, in which he used golden thread.

'Mother, it is not written in my luck to rule this kingdom. In my actions it is written fakiri, asceticism'. 'My son give me this gudrī. It is good that you have reached in time.'

The mother understood that it is not possible to desist Bhartharī from the option he has taken. Then she advised him that he could roam throughout the country but only he should avoid going to the region of Kārañgal. There lives the wife of Kāliyā Nāga who torturing everybody devours them. Then Bhartharī started his journey. On the way he met a group of *sadhus* and he had conversation with them. He asked them, 'Who is the greatest king in the country? Who is the most capable queen?'

The *sadhus* replied, 'We have heard Bhartharī, the king of Ujjain, is the greatest among the kings and the best queen is, we have heard, Birmā. Therefore we are going to Ujjain where we will get meal to our fill.'

They also cautioned Bhartharī, 'You may roam anywhere in the country but don't go to Kārañgal'. Bhartharī went to Kashmir. There before the palace of the king of Kashmir he made a little fire and sat near it. The two queens of the king came to see him. They were both sisters of Bhartharī. He gave them two cakes and told them to open the pack only on reaching in the room. On breaking the cakes they found in it coins and jewels of Ujjain and they recognized the *sadhu* as their younger brother. When they looked for him he had already left the place. Then he went to Kārañgal. There he had competition with the wife of Kāliyā and was able to subdue her.

Then with his power of magic sitting on the wings of an eagle, went to Sandhevara, capital of the country named Sāhi Pāl. He felt assured on seeing foot prints of human beings. A little farther he saw four women filling water. Bhartharī started playing on his guitar. The women were attracted with his music. Then he asked from them to take him to princess Birmā. They told him to follow them. But they warned him that at the gate he should manage himself as there are guards.

He entered the gate and played on the guitar. On hearing the music everybody in the palace came near to him. Princess Birmā also came on the window. Bhartharī threw a few grains of mustard on the ground which were charmed. With the effect of the *mantra* Birmā turned into a dog. All others had become unconscious. Bhartharī took the dog and moved away. When the guards woke up they found princess Birmā missing and also the *sadhu*. They came searching and caught the *sadhu* going with a dog behind him. They asked him about the princess. He told that he does not know. He showed the dog whom he told that this had come with him of its own. They let him go and also the dog. On walking some distance further, the *sadhu* removed the dog of the effect of *mantra* and Birmā turned to her real being. She then started weeping when she saw herself in this situation. She started crying and said, 'My feet are soring. Snow is harming my feet and they have developed cracks. You are cheat. You have brought me here'. Then Bhartharī told Birmā, 'I am Bhartharī' and told her not to worry. 'This situation has arisen only because of you.' Then the two came to Ujjain and spent the rest of the life with pleasure.

This story has been slightly lengthened by adding some more events and making it somewhat different from the others as are found in the folk tales in other areas. The story of Bhartharī here ends with happy notes. The hero leads a domestic life till the end which is altogether unusual. In a story from the same area Bhartharī after this again becomes a *sadhu*. Similarly some stories make him king in the end and others *yogi*.

Padamchand Kashyap (1972: 138 ff.), telling the story of Bharthari, writes that Raja Bhartharī had a beautiful queen named Pinglā. The Raja remained engrossed in her so much that he had ignored the royal tasks of the kingdom. Nor he went even for hunting. He always lived in the *harem*. Once the queen advised him: 'This body is mortal and this world is illusion. Your life is of four days then you will leave the world. O Raja, listen and understand this.' He had no son and daughter. Then he prepared to go to jungle.

In the jungle he killed a male deer. The female deer cursed him. 'O Raja, just as we are widow and mourning here, in the same way in the palace your queen will also become widow. You make singi from the horns and give it to the one who blows nād. Give the eyes to Nainwant, who enjoys sixteen embellishments (solah sṛingār). Give the flesh to a hunter who will cut it into pieces and eat, give the skin to a pandita who will make it a spreadsheet.'

In another story, it is told that when Bhartharī was of twelve years he married seven wives. The first was named Pinglā and the second Kulwantī. He never came to the *harem*, he never went to battle and he never went to hunting. But he was worried that he has no son.

Continuing the story, when Bhartharī is going for hunting, he sees a corpse being carried for cremation. The wife of the dead person is going for *satī*, self-immolation. She is decorated with ornaments. Bhartharī asks Pinglā, 'Are the satī women like those who after the death of their husband wish to get rid of their life?' She says, 'Such women are called Kultā, kusatī, i.e. immoral and unfaithful. She is true satī who after the death of her husband by merely hearing about the incident immediately takes her life.' Bhartharī asked, 'Which kind of satī are you?'

'I am not that kind of satī', told the queen. Bhartharī suspected her being a true satī. He wished to test her. While going to the jungle he gave a cup to Pinglā full with milk and also showed a plant in the park. He told, 'If you see drops of blood in the cup you should presume that I am in trouble but need not take it seriously. If you see this plant drying out then you should think that I am dead'.

In the jungle the Raja tried to kill a male deer and a rhino. Their female partners tried to block his way and prevent him from killing the animals. But anyhow he killed a male deer and a rhino. Then on seeing the condition of the female deers and rhinos he prayed for revival of the lives of the deer and the rhino. He went to guru Gorakhnātha. But the guru told him that he could not do anything. He reminded that Pinglā had already warned him not to kill.

Raja then remembered his desire to test Pinglā. He sent some confident sepoys to tell the Rani that he has died. The messengers informed the Rani accordingly. The Rani went to see the cup of milk. She saw drops of blood in it. Then she went to see the plant. She saw it was healthy. She advised the sepoys to go back immediately to help the Raja. The Raja was determined to test her still more. He sent them back and told to cut the roots of the tree so that it will crumble down by the next day. They did as was told. Next day the sepoys came and told the Rani that the Raja is dead. She saw blood in the cup. Outside the tree also had fallen down. She was now confident that the king is now no more. She took bath, decorated herself with ornaments. Then she took name of Bhartharī three times and on the third she was dead. The sepoys brought the news of her death to the Raja. The king repented. He came back to the palace. He took the corpse of Pinglā in his arms and went out weeping. Burning a fire outside he kept on weeping, saying, 'C Pinglā!' Gorakhnātha came and brought an unbaked pitcher. He filling water in it tried to keep it over the dhunī. It broke out, water fell on the dhunī and put out the fire. Bhartharī kept on watching the scene. Gorakhnātha in the garb of a sadhu cried out, 'Oh dibbī, Oh dibbī (pot)!' Bhartharī had trouble in saying, 'Oh Pinglā, O Pinglā'. He threatened the sadhu and asked, 'What is the need of crying? It is natural that an unbaked pot should break. There is no need to repent'. Gorakhnātha replied, 'If this is foolishness, king is also foolish, who is crying since twelve years for Pinglā. If one can get a second pot one can get second Pinglā also.' The king became angrier. He told, 'I can give you another pot, can you show me my Pinglā?'

The sadhu said, 'Yes.' The Raja went to bring a pot. But he did not find any unbaked pot. The potters had baked all the pots. He returned empty handed. He told the sadhu, 'I did not get any unbaked pot, if you can show me my Pinglā, please be kind to do so.' The sadhu gave his finger ring and asked him to look into it. The Raja could see in it the image of Pinglā. Astonished he recognized the guru. He fell before his feet and entreated him to revive Pinglā. He advised the Raja that, 'It has been twelve years since Pinglā died. She is born in Siṁhala island in the royal family. Her name is Birmā.'

Bhartharī cut his hair, took a jholī, a stick, and set out in search of Birmā. On the way people asked him why he had cut his hair. Why he is carrying the dingī (stick), jholī and phāvlī. He replied that he has done all this for the sake of Birmā. Then he met a person working with hoe and spade. Bhartharī asks him: 'Where does the grain grow in abundance, of which country water is good, of which country the king is good and similarly queen?'

The ploughman answered, 'We hear that the grain grows well in the level fields and water from the hills is sweet. Bhartharī is good among the kings and Birmā among the queens.' Then he meets cowboys. He asks them the same questions. Then he met water carrier girls. Then reaching in the city of Birmā he thinks of taking a cup of wine. He goes at the door of a Kalārin, wine selling woman. He asks for a cup of wine saying, 'I have become mad taking round of the city.'

'If you are able to spend two damadi (= one eighth of a paisā), then you will get madhu, wine, else there is nothing for free', the woman said, 'or keep doda-māl, necklace, as mortgage. Then you will get a cup of wine.' 'You Kalvārī are mad. You don't know my secrets. I can turn gold and silver to stone and wine to water'. Then disappointed he moved away. Playing on ek-tārā, guitar, near the palace he saw there some girls standing. He asked them who they were. They introduced themselves and among them was also Birmā. Then before the palace of Birmā he burnt dhunī and sat down. Then he asks them, 'You are young girls. What is your name? Where do you live?' They replied, 'On the either side there are streams, in the middle is the house of Birmā. Or say on either side are the houses of Brahmins and in the middle is that of Birmā.'

Then Bharthari began playing his kindrī, guitar. Everybody was happy. Birmā, hearing this, also came leaving her meal in the middle. She too started dancing and the two then met like Ganga and Yamuna.

In this version of the story a new element of *satī*, among others, has been added. In this manner merging some current local elements the stories have been given variety and made interesting.

B. Raja Gopīcand

Gopīcand is revered in Himachal together with Bhartharī. RC Temple tells that the legend of Raja Gopīcand is played at Jagadhari in Ambala district. This is one of the most favourite swāngs, dramas, of metrical jokes of the Panjabis, he says. As at other places so in Himachal it usually goes by the combined name of Gopīcand Bhartharī.

According to the story Gopīcand was king of Dhārānagar and he lived in the city of Ujjain. His home was in Gaur Bengal or Bengal and his mother was named Rani Mainawatī, who was sister of Bhartharī, married to the king of Bengal. Gopicand worshipped Gaṇapat.

Gopīcand's mother Mainawatī was weeping. She insisted Gopīcand to become jogī, to embrace the life of saint, saying, 'This world is like a dream, it is a tangle. Name of God is beyond price. They are not born again who approach Harī (Viśṇū). Why not then you take the saintship, and obtain salvation in both the worlds?' She gives example of his father who is no more in this world. Bhartharī had also sought the knowledge of saintship from her. 'Therefore, my son, become yogī, the glorious body will become deathless,' said the Rani. Gorakhnātha was the preceptor of the Rani. She says, 'Carpaṭnāth is my disciple brother.'

Gopīcand replies, he has sixteen hundred queens and his daughter has not yet been married. Lastly he agrees to become jogi. His mother sent him to Jālandharnāth.

The Raja then went to the Garden where Jālandharnāth was sitting and requested him, 'I have come to take saintship. Please accept me as your disciple.' Jālandharnāth, although himself a yogī, forbids him from becoming saint and darting him desists him from renouncing his kingship. 'You are young in the bloom of youth.' Long discussion ensues between the two.

Gorkhnāth took up his abode opposite Kanipa. Kanipa is disciple of Jālandharnāth and therefore he is opponent of Gorakhnātha. The two had discussion. Macchandra Nāth, guru of Gorakhnātha, lives in Siṁhala Isle. Hem Nāth and Khem Nāth, are saintly brothers of Gorakhnātha. Gorakhnātha pierced Gopīcand's ears. Finally Jālandhar becomes his Guru. He is a strict teacher. Jālandharnāth applied ashes to his body and gave him a necklace. He takes the dress of *yogi*. His guru sends him to his own palace for begging alms.

There at his palace none recognised him. He had discussion with one of the Rani named Pāṭan Deī on the subject whether he should become saint or not. Rani Pāṭan Deī forbids him from becoming *yogi*. His daughter also advises him similarly.

Then he goes to his sister Campā Deī who is married to a king in Gaur Bengal and he begs alms from her. He is able to receive alms from his sister. Then Gopīcand comes back and reports to his Guru. Jālandharnāth then tells him to meditate on 'Harī'. Bhartharī was the elder brother of Vikramāditya, in whose favour he had abdicated his kingdom. In the legend Gopīcand's capital was Dhārānagar, which is the seat of Vikramāditya. About the nativity of Gopīcand it is told in the beginning of the story that he is king of Dhārānagar which falls in the western India. At the same time it says that his home is in Bengal. He abdicated the kingdom in favour of his younger brother, Vikrmāditya. Bharthārī's sister Mainawatī was married to a king in Bengal who according to Taranath was named Vimalcandra, and the two had a son named Gopīcand. These two kings were converted by *siddha* Jālandharipa and acārya Krsnācārya, i.e. Kānha. Taranath in another work also writes that Krsnācārya converted king Lalitcandra, a paternal cousin of Gopīcand.

8

The Nātha Deities in Himachal

A. Vīr

There is a class of male deities named Vīr which literally means Hero. Although the pantheon has scriptural origin the practice flourished and developed more in the folk practice.

It appears that the cult of Vīr is as old as Kaul and Yoginī. Magee gives name of a work called *Akulavīrtantram* found in Nepal. It has two manuscripts, one is assigned to Mīnanāth and the other one to Matsyendranāth. Magee assigns date to one of them belonging to about the 13th century CE, (Machael Magee Inroduction:1, in Bagchi, 2007). Although we have no knowledge about the contents of the work, the mention of the term Vīr in the titles of the work give some indication to their relation with Vīr.

According to one explanation, *yogis* entering the *yoga* and *tantric* path are classified into three classes and Vīr is placed in the middle between Paśu and Divya. Briggs explains that there are three classes of practitioners (*sādhakas*): (1) Paśu, those seeking self-control, and desiring what adepts enjoy. They strive to master their passions and impulses. (2) Vīra (controlled), those who have attained complete self-control and do not forget themselves even in the most trying and tempting circumstances. They enjoy freedom. They are not only allowed but are definitely instructed to include such things as the five *makārs,* in their offerings to god. The Paśu is not allowed even to touch or to see these things. Finally the method as prescribed for the Vīra is

Kaula. (3) The Dīvya, free from the trials of the Vīra is allowed to take substitutes for all material things in his process of worship. In the highest stage of attainment, Kaulācāra, the *sādhaka* does away with all rules and injunctions of the *Śāstras*. 'For the Kaula there is neither merit nor demerit, virtue nor vice.' The theory is that as poisons contract poisons, so men must rise by those things through which they so often lose their manhood (Briggs, 1938:282-283).

In Tibetan system there are twenty-four Vīr (*dPa'-bo*). They are deities, protectors of twenty-four *Pīṭhas*, regions, of the *vajrakāyā*. They appear bound with *śakti* in *yab-yum*, father-mother, posture. They are enthroned and propitiated during the rituals (Tucci, 1935, II-2: 42).

In the folk tradition collectively Vīrs are fifty-two and as such is traditionally known as Bāvanjā- Vīr and each individual has name. Most of the names of the Vīrs are generally unfamiliar and uncommon. There are several lists enumerating the names of the 52 Vīrs and the names differ widely from one list to that of the other. There are names outside the lists also. Thus the actual number of Vīrs is much larger.

Vīrs do not appear to be historical persons like the *siddhas*. But there are a few like Bhairava, Hanumān, Nārsīṁha, etc. belonging to the classical pantheon who have been incorporated among the Vīrs. Their role as Vīr is different from that of their original position in the scriptures. Here they are quite active. One of the popular functions of a Vīr appears to be that of a guardian of some deity or deities or some establioshment, etc. For example Nārsīṁha and Kāliyā Nāga are considered as Vīrs, guardian deities, of Guggā. Virs also function as *dwārpals*, door keepers, i.e. guardians of the presiding spirit of the temples. Figures of such deities are seen installed at the doors of some temples.

In Lahul, in the Mirkulā devi temple, there are two ferocious looking life-sized statues made of wood and are placed inside the main door on either side of it. They are called *dwārpāls* and also Vīr. The statues had once under one of their foot a small image like a child trampled under them. Of the two one was missing. On the visit to the temple the next time it was observed that the other one was also missing and the foot was found hanging in the air. On enquiry it was told that the figure was causing nightmares in dreams. Therefore on the advice of the presiding *devī* the figure was thrown into the river. A superstition has also been developed around the *dwārpāls*. It is believed that if a visitor at the moment of his departure says to his companion, 'let us go', the guardian Vīr accompanies them and might cause them a kind of harm.

Atkinson narrates the origin of a class of Vīrs in the area of Jaunsār Bawār in Uttrakhand in the following manner. He writes, in Jaunsār Bawār there are four deities known collectively as the Mahāsu devtas: Bāsak, Pibāsak, Buthiyā or Baithā and Caltā or Haldā. The first three abide in temples dedicated to them at Ranor in Khāt Bawār, Tahnu in Khāt Pacgaon and at Anwar. The fourth or Caltā Mahāsu took up his residence at Behrāt in Khāt. These deities came from Kashmir some four or five hundred years ago in this way. Una Bhat lived in Khāt Mendrat and had a large family of relatives and dependents.

At this time a demon named Kirbīr Dān (dānava) made his appearance at the confluence of Tons and Jumna near Kalsi and day by day ate Una's people until only Una, his three sons and one daughter remained. He fled to jungles of Jumuna. One night the devata Mahāsu appeared to him and told him to seek the help of the four Mahasus who live in Kashmir. Una then built houses for Kelu Bīr, Kadāsiri Bīr, Sakrār Bīr, and sixty-four other Bīrs, who attended the Mahāsus (Atkinson, II-II, 1882:836-838).

Pīr and Vīr: Pīr and Vīr are often used as synonyms. Pīr is a Urdu equivalent of the Hindi term Guru, Teacher. In the following case Pīr and Vīr are treated as two different deities but they are propitiated without distinction. Briggs writes that after the death of a Nātha *yogi* on the third day *roat* (cake) are offered. After a year (*barsī*), or a year and a half, *śrāddha*, or funeral rite is performed. In the watch before dawn fish, or *pakauṛi*, or *khīr*, or *palāu* or flesh is distributed. Six or seven thrones (gaddī) are erected, to the Pīr, to Joginīs, to Sakhya (or witness), to Bīr, to Dhandarī (cook of Guru Gorakhnātha), to Goraknāth and to Neka or Ant. *Mantras* are recited, clothes and coins of gold, silver and copper are distributed, and a cow or some other gift is made to the Pīr. Gifts are made also to *Yogis*. The silver goes to Sakhya, copper to Bīr, the cow to the Pīr, water to Gorakhnātha.

This term Pīr is also found used with the names of Hindu saints. Tibetan guru sTagtshang Raspa who visited Urgyan writes names of such saints as Pīr Balnāth, Jā-pīr and Jinta-pīr. Below are given details about certain Vīrs and Pīr.

Khwājā Pīr: Harikrishan Murari writes that Khawājāpīr in Kangra is a god of the labourers and farming class similar to Khetarpāl, Jakh and Lakhdātā. Those who propitiate the latter three don't propitiate Khwājāpīr. Normally there is no *maḷhī* (small temple), *sthān* (place), or shrine dedicated to Khawājāpīr. At places where there is a *maḷhī* a lamp is lit as an offering.

Prayers are offered to him near the rivers or streams. After the prayer he is offered *roat, halwa,* milk, curd, *ghee*, etc. All these are placed on the leaves of banana with incense sticks and lamps. Offerings are also thrown into the river, for he is believed to live in the rivers. This is known as offering of boat to Khwājāpīr. After the harvesting of crops and when a buffalo is conceived this kind of prayer is also offered. Chinj or wrestling matches are organized near the *maḷhī* by the owners of *maḷhī* of the deity regularly in his honour. If there is no *maḷhī*, it is held near the rivers or streams (Harikrishan Murari, 2008: 13-14).

Vīrnāth: In Kullu Vīrnāth is a *devatā* like many other *devatās*. There are Vīrnath in different villages with the same name or sometimes also known as Gohrī *devatā*, *devatā* of the high region

Candraśekhar Bebas says that in whole of Kullu there is only one Vīr named Vīrnath, who was a *siddha* of the Gorakh sect. He displayed miracles and brought benefits to the people. Thieves killed him. His sister Bhāgāsiddh fled to the village of Prīnī in order to save her life. There she is a *devī* and presently she is one of the powerful *devīs* in whole of Kullu. Vīrnāth's mother took revenge from the villagers of the killer, then Vīrnāth was propitiated as a *devatā*. He says that the temple of Virnāth at Dhalpur in Kullu was founded by Raja Man Singh.

MR Thakur says that in Kullu region the story of Vīrunāth or Vīrnāth is very famous. He travelled in many areas in Himachal, at places in the form of a *yogi*, and at others like an ordinary man. His story is told in the pronouncements of the *devatā* called *deva-bhārthā*. He started his journey from the bank of Ganga. In the hollow of the stick that he carried, he put pebbles from the bank of the Ganga, which made sounds. He reached at Tungal-Pingal in Mandi, from there came to Shamshi in Kullu. He pitched his tent at Khokhan and he discarded the form of *Autar*, i.e. form of *sadhu*. He left his sister there, and went with his dog named *koṇḍu*. At Bharesani in Koṭhi Tārāpur, at the place of the *devatā*, he met Katrusī (Kṛṣṇa) Nārāyaṇa and the two had discussion about their lives. He exhibited the power of *devatā* and reached *thātch* (place where the shepherds stay in the night) of Māshnā. There he played dice with two *gaḷhīs,* attendants of the forts. He lost his life in the game. It is said that the two *gaḷhīs* suspected that the *yogi* had coins in his stick, therefore they contrived to kill him. The faithful dog *koṇḍu* went to *yogi's* sister Tilu at Khokhan and brought her to the place where her brother Vīrnāth was burried. When she dug up the place she found flowers in place of corpse. Spreading flowers in all the directions, Tilu said,

"My brother, if it was your fault, you have been punished. If you are faultless, you will be revered like a god. The residents of Thātch Māshnā were the worshippers of Gohrī *devatā* before this. After this incident they started worshipping Vīrunāth and other Gohrī *devatas* also followed the custom.

The Bhārthā gives further itinerary after his death. It says from there he came to Baḍāgrāṁ where he was established as *devatā*. From there he went to Gadiyārā and played dice with Hurang Nārāyaṇa. At Bhekhlī there erupted a commotion and he had to please the goddess by offering basket of flowers and he was then established at Kaṭāhar. Some people identify Gohrī *devatā* and Vīrnāth as the same *devatā*. MR Thakur differentiates between Gohrī and Vīrnāth.

Following is a part of the composition.

गंगा री गटी छणकाई बेठा। तुंगल पिंगल फिरी बेठा।
सोमसी पोधरा एजरी बेठा। खोखण धूणी जरुंह जगाई बेठा।
औतर रूप छरुोडी बेठा। तिलू बेहणी ब ाई बेठा।
कोंडू कुती साथ ढणाई बेठा। राह जरुंह देई बेठा।।

The shingles collected from the bank of the river Ganga were making sound in the hollow of his bamboo stick. He roamed in Tungal and Pingal, in Mandi and reached at the Somsi plains in Kullu, near Bhuntar. He went to Khokhan where he stayed and lit dhuni. He abandoned the garb of Autar. He left his sister Tilu there and took Konḍu the she-dog with him. He made the way for others.

This poem is an excellent piece of composition in Kullui language and belongs to the medieval period.

There are some Vīr deities who are known in more detail.

Pahārī Vīr: In some villages some people engage Pahārī Vīr in harming their enemies and extracting benefits from them. There are *celās* who know how to recognise him and control him. Amid the large gatherings of the villagers he dances playing musical instruments like *ḍamru*, or bell metal *thālī* chanting *mantra*. He then comes in trance. When he recognises the victim he smears a streak of vermillion on his body. The *celā* beats with fire tongs of iron and directs the spirit possessed in the victim to go away to some other place. In case he refuses to leave, he asks again, "What do you want? The *celā* then promises him that offering of a goat will be made for him soon (Ramlal Pathak 1987: 81-86).

Kālu (or Kahlu, Kailu) Vīr: In Chamba, this spirit is supposed to live in the mountains and his anger causes landslips. It must be appeased with sacrifice. In a different practice Kailu is said to be Kotwāl of Guggā and therefore he is much feared. 'Seizures by him are very violent and hysteria among women is attributed to his attentions. He is very arbitrary and capricious. His qualities are likened to those of Hanumān, his counterpart.'

Lakhdātā Vīr: Lakhdātā is said to be popular both among the Hindu and Muslim devotees. He is supposed to be a form of Lakṣ maṇ and that Muslims have kept him hiding in a Mosque. He thinks that he can get released if he gets sprinkles of water from the Ganges. Annual wrestling fairs are held in his honour. Musicians beat big drums and move around the wrestling ground. He then becomes pleased and fulfills the wishes of his devotees. He is offered milk on the occasion of first conception of a buffalo in a house. In Mandi at places diminutive roofed shrines are seen raised in his honour and his Muslim connection is shown by a grave adjacent to the shrine. He is prayed for the safety of the family members and cattle of the family (Ramlal Pathak 1987: 81-86).

The cult of Lakhdātā or the Bountiful, in Chamba, it is said, is the same as that of Sākhī Sarwar Sultān common in the plains. He belongs to the 12th century. Wrestling matches called *chinj* are held for Lakhdātā yearly in every *parganā* of Curāh, in some *parganās* of the *Sadar wizārat*, as well as in Bhattiyāt. About a dozen of his shrines are counted in Chamba.

Nārsiṁha is considered, in some accounts, as a Vīr and he is the Sardār, chief of the Bāvanjā Vīr, the group of fifty-two Heroes. There exist a few lists of the 52 Vīrs in Himachal Pradesh and elsewhere. Following is a list from Kullu:

1. Kālū Vīr. 2. Ka-i-lū Vīr. 3. Kadarpa Vīr. 4. Sugrīv Vīr. 5. Hanumat Vīr. 6. Narsiṁgha Vīr. 7. Ajiyāpāl Vīr. 8. Cakravarībh Vīr. 9. Karotal Vīr. 10. Nadahad Vīr. 11. Votar Vīr. 12. Kalavīr. 13. Kūkal Vīr. 14. Kalanal Vīr. 15. Supracaṇḍa Vīr. 16. Pracaṇḍa Vīr. 17. Timardanta Vīr. 18. Pradativīr. 19. Rodatī Vīr. 20. Kumati Vīr. 21. Trinetra Vīr. 22. Jhukara Vīr. 23. Hañkā Vīr. 24. Hekar Vīr. 25. Kīlīkal Vīr. 26. Rāmasabuddhavīr. 27. ūrdhakeś Vīr. 28. Maśaṇa Vīr. 29. Baknāth Vīr. 30. Lauñkḍā Vīr. 31. Daitasa Vīr. 32. Sukhpāl Vīr. 33. Gaūmukh Vīr. 34. Jarsandh Vīr. 35. Krītudal Vīr. 36. Tīkal Vīr. 37. Vaman Vīr. 38. Dughat Vīr. 39. Sumasana-sakapa Vīr. 40. Devadūt Vīr. 41. Manabhadra Vīr. 42. Sabhadra Vīr. 43. Madan Kas Vīr. 44. Madamath Vīr 45. Jalaidhara Phuphudra Vīr. 46. Ahukale Vīr. 47. Arajaṇmatala Vīr. 48. Jhapaḍa Vīr. 49. Vījhapaḍa Vīr. 50. Vakale Vīr. 51. Sīkhaḍa Vīr. 52. Jarsathi Vīr. There exist two more similar lists here.

B. Yoginī

The term Yoginī literally is feminine form of *yogi*, a practitioner of *yoga*. But in this aspect it is not found much in use. The best example of ideal *yoginī* may be observed in the tradition of the 84-*siddhas*. Among the 84-*siddhas* the four female *siddhas* are also known as *yoginīs*. These *yoginīs* received teachings from their preceptors, meditated on an object or a thought, attained accomplishment, delivered teachings to others and smoothened their way to the next world. Some scholars translate the term *yoginī* as sorceress or demon. *Yoginī* in practice are spirits, malevolent or benevolent, but ordinarily are indifferent. They are not seen propitiated as an independent deity. They are not principal deities and do not appear to possess the status of a deity who presides over a temple. The practice has flourished and developed more in the folk tradition than in the classical or the greater tradition.

Yoginīs are associated with some superior powers and they accompany them. One of their functions is that they are attendant to a superior deity. Thus there are four or eight yoginīs attendant on Durgā. Atkinson tells that Śañkara Ācārya built a temple for the worship of the goddess Durga, the consort of Śiva and her band of *Joginīs* and placed the service of the temple on the Kedarnath establishment. This example shows the status and nature of *joginī* or *yoginī* who is in benevolent aspect. But this role appears to be minor. Their chief role appears to have been as partners in the tantric performances which might have been their original function and cause of the birth of the cult. Thus the school has origin alongwith the *siddha* tradition.

Regarding the origin of the Yogini cult Magee says that the cult of Yoginī, the *Yoginī -Kaul Mārg*, has origin from Matsyendranāth who founded it as a new sect of the Kaula school. Its chief seat was at Kāmrūpa where he taught his doctrines, (Michael Magee, Introduction, 41; in Bagchi, 1986.). Magee also writes, 'Matsyendranāth seems to be propounding the views of a section of the Kaulas known as Yogini-kaula school. A preference for the 64-yoginis is obvious, and the *cakra* system seems to be based on this classification.' Bagchi and Dvivedi also maintain that Matsyendranāth caused the initiation of the 'Yoginī Kaul Mārg' sect which later on developed into Nāthpanth (Dvivedi, 1996: 2-3).

Magee presumes that the doctrine of Yoginī-Kaul Mārg on the basis of identification of Matsyendra with Lū-hi-pa the first among the 84-siddhas must have had something in common with Buddhist mysticism as expounded in the writings of the Siddhācāryas. He writes, 'The fundamental doctrine as expounded in these writings is the doctrine of Sahaja. The Sahaj is the ideal state of the yogin, a state in which the mind enters into vacuity' (Machael Magee, ibid: 64).

Magee identifies the two as one in the manner saying that among the 84-siddhas, 'It seems that Lui-pāda was identical with Matsyendranātha. In the Tibetan list Lui-pā is the first *Siddha* (ādi *Siddha*), whereas in the Indian list Matsyendra takes that place. Lui-pā had connection with Śavari-pā whereas we have already seen that Matsyendra just precedes Śavarānanda in the Haṭhayoga tradition. Both of them are said to have belonged to the fishing caste and moreover Lui, Lohita, Rohita, 'the king of fishes' is synonymous with Matsyendra. The Tibetan translation of the name of Lui as *na-lto pa* when faithfully restituted gives the form Matsyodara. This, in fact, agrees with the Indian legend, according to which Matsyendra was born from the womb of a fish. We may, therefore, take Lui-pā and Matseydranātha to be the same person' (Michael Magee, ibid: 28). Magee places Matsyendara to c. 900 CE.

We cannot comment on the nature of the doctrine of the Yoginīṣkaula, whether it was Sahaja or somewhat different. But Magee's identification of the two great Siddhācārayas Matsyendra and Lū-hi-pa as one and the same person, the premises upon which his proposition of the form of the doctrine of the Yoginī-kaula cult is based, calls for a little of our attention.

In the account of the 84-siddhas we find two different accounts on the lives of Luī-pa and Mīnapa and there is no reference to Matsyendra in the work. We attempted to identify

Mīnapa with Matsyendra. Between Luīpa and Mīnapa or Matsyendra the only relationship that we have observe is through only the term fish. Mīnapa who belonged to fisherman's profession or caste acquired the perfection in the environment where the fish abound and Lū-hi-pa sustained on the food of fish during the period of his meditation. They differ in all other respects. The descriptions about Matsyendra from other sources have not much in common with Lū-hī-pa. Therefore it is difficult to agree with the above proposition of identification of the two Mahāsiddhas as one.

Causaṭh Yoginī: In the cult of *yoginīs* there is the special group of 64 yoginīs famous as *causaṭh yoginī*. This classical number is followed in the tradition faithfully.

There are temples dedicated to the 64-yoginīs named as 'Chausaṭh Yoginī temple' located at important places in several states, viz. Madhya Pradesh, Orissa, Karnataka, Kerala, Uttar Pradesh, Tamil Nadu, etc. Fergusson describes the temple at Khajuraho dedicated to the 64 yoginī as, 'the temple called the Chausath jogini, or sixty four female demons consists merely of a courtyard, measuring 202 feet by 59 and half feet and surrounded by sixty four small cells with one larger in the back wall, each of which is surmounted by a small spire. This is essentially like a Jaina arrangement.'

It is said that at places they have decorated idols, some riding vehicles, and at others they have been seen in dancing posture. At places the presence of Bhairon is reported in these temples. Bhairon is a god usually of terrific nature. At Rānipur Jhariāl, south of Sāmbhalpur, it is told, there are numerous series of temples, among which one is dedicated to the Causaṭh Yoginīs. It is circular, its outside diameter is about 56 feet having sixty-five cells. Another similar temple is situated at Bherāghāt, 12 miles below Jabalpur, with eighty one recesses for the sixty four joginīs and their cogenes. Both of these are circular enclosures with shrines ranged round, inside of the walls. It probably belongs to the 9th century, or is older. It is built of granite and its plan and the forms of its shikhara in my view are exceptionally old, (Fergusson, 1910- II: 51, 53). These may be taken as examples of classical tradition. We observe that they are propitiated as a group. Looking at the Yoginī temples scholars hold that the cult flourished during the period between 9th and 12th century CE.

There are lists containing names of the 64-yoginīs. This aspect has developed more in the folk tradition where it is found that there are different lists at different places and the names given in one list do not match with those in the other in their entirety. Yoginīs are numerous.

Atkinson describes the nature of the yoginīs saying that Yoginīs wander about the country causing disease to the people and blight to their crops if the oblations at the temple are of little value or the worship of their mistress is neglected. The goddess is represented among the boulders near the temples by the simple mass shining with mica (Atkinson, II-II: 796 note).

Yogini in Himachal

In Himachal the tradition of yoginī is followed both in the established classical form and liberal folk tradition. In the folk tradition a yoginī is usually called joginī or joganī. These are generally considered as spirits living in the high mountains in the clean environment and wandering in the air. Here it is found that although the classical tradition of the 64-yogins is followed without any variation but it is not known if there exists or existed any establishment dedicated to the whole group of sixty-four yoginīs as are found elsewhere. Carvings of yoginīs are said to be found in some temples like in Mandi district, but they don't represent the whole group of 64 yoginīs.

Shami Sharma tells that Yoginīs or Joginīs are 64 in number. All of them have name and in the prayers they are addressed by name. They are constantly moving in the air. Whenever a *mandal* of offering is established they are invited there and then prayer is made. They are prayed, and it is very important, so that there occurs no obstruction in the ceremonies. If they become angry there may take place some inauspicious happening or some unexpected obstruction may arise. Having the nature of rākṣasī, demoness, she is able to kill the enemies imagined in the form of demons (Shami Sharma, 2004: 23-24).

Nilmani Upadhyaya explains that in Mandi the Yoginī carvings have direct relationship with the *Devī* and Śakti. Carvings and stone-slates dedicated to the yoginīs are found at the temples of Śyāmākāli at Tarnā, Bhīmākāli temple of Bhyulī and other Śakti temples. Similar to those of the gaṇas of the Śiva, the yoginīs function as assistants to the Śakti. Propitiation of the Yoginīs is related to the Tāntrik practice which was prevalent in Mandi in the ancient and medieval periods.

Upadhayaya further tells that there are two kinds of figures of the Yoginīs propitiated in Mandi. In one of the practices impressions of footprints are found engraved at sacred places. They are symbols of powers of the spirits. Therefore they are considered as pure and worth propitiating. In some prosperous ancient villages such stones are found at the entrance of the village. In Mandi town such stones are found at Cauhaṭṭā, Khuhā Rānī and other places. Circumambulation ceremony of the stone slab at Cauhaṭṭā is essential in the marriage ceremony. In the second form the figures of the yoginīs are found engraved on stones. They represent the figures and beauty of the woman, and the yoginī empowered with Śakti. Such configuration of the figures of women can be observed on the pathways towards the *garbhagṛah* of the Bhimākālī temple.

Upadhayaya gives names of the 64 Yoginīs as under

1. Divyāyogā, 2. Mahāyogā, 3. Siddhayogā, 4. Maheśvarī, 5. Piśacinī, 6. Dākinī, 7. Kālrātri, 8. Niśācarī, 9. Kañkālī, 10. Raudravaitālī, 11. Huṁkārī, 12. ūrdhvakeśī, 13. Virūpākṣī, 14. Śuṣkāñgī, 15. Narbhojinī, 16. Phatkārī, 17. Vīrabhadrā, 18. Dhūmrākṣī, 19. Kalahapriyā, 20. Raktākṣī, 21. Rākṣasī, 22. Ghora-raktā, 23. Viśvarūpā, 24. Bhayañkarī, 25. Kāmākṣī, 26. ūgracāmundā, 27. Bhīṣṇā, 28. Tripurāntakā, 29. Vīrkaumārikā, 30. Caṇḍī, 31. Vārāhī, 32. Muṇḍa-dhariṇī, 33. Bhairavī, 34. Hastinī, 35. Krodha- durmukhā, 36. Pretavāhinī, 37. Khaṭvānga- dhīrgha lamboṣṭhā, 38. Mālinī, 39. *Mantra*-yoginī, 40. Asthinī, 41. Cakriṇī, 42. Grāhā, 43. Bhuvaneśvarī, 44. Kaṇṭakī, 45. Kārakī, 46. Śubhrā, 47. Kriyā, 48. Dūtī, 49. Krālinī, 50. Śañkhinī, 51. Padminī, 52. Kṣīrā, 53. Asandhā, 54. Prahāriṇī, 55. Lakṣmī, 56. Kāmukī, 57. Lolā, 58. Kāk-dṛṣṭī, 59. Adho-mukhī, 60. Dhūr-jaṭī, 61. Mālinī, 62. Ghorā, 63. Kapālī, 64. Viṣa-bhojinī.

The author says that the names can be classified into the good and bad classes. Some others belong to the class of Nāyikās, heroines, in the Kāmśāstra. Yoginīs are also related to the jyotiṣ-śāstra, astrology and tantrik practices. They are meditated upon and are propitiated for the *siddhi*, riddhi and smriddhi: accomplishment and prosperity' (Nīlmaṇi Upādhayāya, 2004: 25-27).

Candraśekhara Bebas of Kullu says that although there are various kinds of yoginīs in Sanskrit literature and commonly they are counted sixty-four but according to the Jyotiṣ-śāstra there are eight yoginīs. He gives two lists of Joginīs. Of the two, one appears to follow more of literary tradition and the other one carries the folk tradition. Therefore the names in the two lists differ quite a lot. Only a few names are common.

Bebas gives another list from a local manuscript which he says is about more than two hundred years old which was found written in Tāñkri script. Its author was Upādhayāya Sadānanda of village Lāḍ located in the Bhangāl State, now part of district Kangra, whose boundaries touch also with Kullu and Chamba. The Pādhās (Upādhayās) from Lāḍ are famous for ojhāgirī, sorcery. Bebas transcribes the names as follows, leaving blank wherever it was not legible. These are 64 in number. They are divided into eight groups, one group located on each of the eight cardinal points. He writes, this is the manner of worship of the yoginīs or jogaṇī. The rite is performed for the removal of some physical obstructions.

Jayadā - Vijayā, Jayantī Nandā, Bhadrā, Bhīmā, Śridevī and Aṣṭamī, I bow to all these eight jogaṇis. These eight should be worshipped in the eastern direction.

Huṁkārī- Bhāskarī, Dīrghā, Kalah Priyā, Jvalāṅgī and Tripurā, Pātakī I bow to the jogaṇis on part of east-south.

Divya Jāgī - Mahājogī, *Siddha* Jogī, Gaṇeśvarī, Śākinī, Kālrātri, ūrdhva-keśī, Niśākarī, I bow to the jogaṇis in the southern part.

Rākṣasī Ghonāva, Bhayañkarī, Śañkarī, Raudrī, Bītālī, Māṁsa Bhakṣṇī, I bow to the eight jogaṇis in the direction of south-west.

Ghambhīrīṣ Bhīṣṇī and Kalmā-upic, Pānakī, Ulkī, Bhairavī *devī*, Bhadrā, Nandā, all the eight in the part of west, I bow to the jogaṇis.

Vīr bhadrā and Kālī, Kṛpālī, Vikṛtānami, Koṭ Rakṣī, Vīrbhadrā and Vāyu Vegī, Bhyañkarī, I bow to the eight yoginīs in the part of the west-north direction.

Viśālīṣ Phañkanī Jā, Icchā Siddhī, Prajā Tuṣṭī, Sarva Sidhhī, Brāhmaṇī, Kṣetraṇī, I bow the eight yoginīs in the part of the northern direction.

Brāhmaṇī ṣ Vaiṣaṇavī, Raudrī, Mātañgī, Caṇdakeśvarī, Vārāhī, Narsiṁhī, Śivadūtī, I bow to all of you. I bow to the eight joganīs of the part of north-east direction. This is the method of propitiating the sixty-four jogaṇis (Bebas, 2000, Part IV: 76-79). This document was written under the aegis of Rai Pṛthī Pāl, of Bhangāl, in the year 62 equivalent to 1686 CE. Pṛthī Pāl's two sisters were married to Siddh Sen (1684-1727), Raja of Mandi and Man Singh (1688-1719), Raja of Kullu, who were both known to be the most powerful Rajas in the history of their respective States.

Yoginīs in the folk tradition

It is observed that the cult has developed much in the folk tradition and has given birth to many number of *yoginīs*. In the folk tradition there are many yoginīs outside the lists of the 64-*yoginīs*. In some areas in Himachal they are named as *jogaṇīs* or *joginī* instead of *yoginī*. In Kullu they are more popular as *Jogaṇī*. There are some smaller groups as: Sāvanī, Surgaṇī, Phuñgnī, etc. Occurrence of Phuñgnī is confined to Kullu. The former two groups have sixteen numbers each and the last has seven. Individually they have no name. Even those independent single *jogaṇī* have no name. It is believed that the *jogaṇīs* dwell in the pure natural environment on the mountain tops and passes, in the waterfalls and remain roaming in the air. In Jubbal, Rohru, etc. in the Shimla region they are known as *Sāvanī* and are taken in the class of goddesses. Their sphere extends to Kinnaur.

Jogaṇīs are worshipped on different occasions for seeking their favour in the accomplishment of works, fulfillment of wishes, removal of obstructions, including that created by the spirits themselves, therefore it is in order to please them. They are worshipped periodically which should not be missed or they may cause harm.

Shami Sharma explains the faith of Joginī as it exists in Himachal Pradesh, specially in the Kangra region. He says that Joginī is the corrupted form of the word Yoginī. Yoginī or Joginī are spirits roaming in the air. In the Puranic tradition they are sixty-four in number. They are essentially propitiated in the yajñas lest they should create barriers in the task. They are entrusted to live in lonely places. Their residences are trees embedded with tridents, iron nails and other articles of iron. Some women may get possessed of the spirit of joginī then her hairs become loose and dishevelled. They are related to the Śiva and Śakti faiths (Shammi Sharma 2004:23-24).

Harcourt gathered that in the context of Kullu yoginīs are forest fairies. Candraśekhara Bebas writes that in Kullu there exist a number of classes of Joginī such as Joganī, Phuñgnī, Naunī, Brāñgnī, Solā-Surgani, Kūhatī, Kupaḍī, Bhoṭ, Bhoṭalī, etc. They have a collective name as Jagaṇāh or Jagaṇyāh. Solah Sāvnī also comes under this class. He further writes that among the Lok-Joganīs, Folk-Joganīs, there are benevolent and malevolent. In Kullu they are divided into two classes Hāchī (acchi= good) and Bāgaṛī (inferior). First kind of the spirits have white complexion, healthy body, wear colourful clothes and their favourite food is wheat. Tobacco, leather of some kinds of animals, impure articles and touching by untouchables is prohibited for them. Bāgaṛī is removed of all these kinds of restrictions, wears black clothes and likes coarse grains. Their nature is exhibited accordingly (Candraśekhara Bebas, 2000 Part IV:80- 81). Surat Thakur writes that in Kullu the shepherds offer sacrifice of lambs to the Joganīs for the protection of their herds of sheep. People also ask for rain from them in the time of draught.

In Kullu it is believed that some of the joginīs are of the origin of the godly nature and some others have taken form from girls and women. They are pure, untouched of drinks. Women beg from them for getting their desires to be fulfilled. They accompany every *devata*. In the villages there are temples dedicated to them. The structures are generally of medium sized of one room and sometimes nicely designed. These are located slightly away at a distance from the temple of the principal deity of the village. Generally it is also built slightly away from the residential areas. The objective appears to be that the joginīs should not get polluted accidentally. People generally avoid to go near it. The temple is empty, no image or statue represents the deity. She also does not have any particular name. It is simply known by joginī temple.

Phuñgnī: In Kullu there is a class of joginīs known as Phuñgnī. They came from Suket. It is told that once in Sunder Nagar, Suket, there was draught. The king ploughed in the field. There he found an earthen pitcher. Something came out from it. These were the seven sisters of Phuñgnī. They came towards Kullu. From Suket they came to Phuṭā Khaul (Gogḍā Dhār, Mandi). From there to Tyūn and then Samālang (Lag valley, Kullu). From there they scattered to different directions. Presently there is one each in the villages of: Vyāsar, Bhekhalī Dhār, Māthī Shīl, Baḍī Shīl, Jilānī and Jalauharī.

At Banogī in the area of Jindauḷ a mela is held in the month of Bhadoṁ which is dedicated to Phuñgnī. On the day of this melā sickle is first touched to the standing crop of the season and then harvesting of the crop begins. Ears of barley are pasted with cowdung over the frame outside the main door of the house. Earlier one bundle of barley used to be kept separate for offering to the deities. Then grain was ground into flour at home and a *roa*t, a large cake, was offered to the *Joganīs*. In some residential houses the uppermost floor is kept for the *Joganī* where tobacco is prohibited. The whole region of Jindaur is divided in eight sections and one of them belongs to the Nāthas. Phuñgnī is also said to be related to Nāga. Surghanī, another class of *joganī*, are sixteen in number.

C. Nrsiṁha and Nārsiṁha

Nrsiṁha is an incarnation of Visnu according to the classical tradition. In this respect the deity has limited aspects and functions. In the folk tradition, specially in the Nātha cult, the deity has active role, is worshipped in numerous forms and has a variety of functions. In Himachal he has been a very popular deity, presumed to be very powerful. He is named in the folk as Nārsiṁha or Nāharsiṁha.

There are temples dedicated to Nārsiṁha at many places viz.: Bilaspur, Solan, Mandi, Kullu at Naggar, Kangra, Sirmaur and other places. In Bilaspur, it is stated, Raja Dīpcand built a temple for the deity at Dhaulrā in the year 1650 CE. In Suket the Rajas had granted 145 acres of land in *jagir* for the temple of Nārsiṁha. In Kangra the temple of the deity was built at Shahpur about 250 years back and at Rehlu about 200 years back, writes Angiras Angiras (Amardev. 2007: 59-63). He attributes all these temples situated in Himachal, including that of Bharmaur, to Nārsiṁha. At Bharmaur, the ancient capital of Chamba, there is a temple in Śikhara style which enshrines a brass statue of Nrsiṁha or Nārsiṁha. The temple and the statue was got erected by Tribhuvanrekhā as is mentioned in a copper plate inscription of Yugākar the son of Sāhila, and has, therefore, been placed in the period of tenth-twelfth century.

In the folk tradition Nārsiṁha is a young celibate Brahman boy, aged from twelve to twenty years. He wears white dress, vermillion on the forehead, kuṇḍal of pearl in the ears and necklace of pearl in the neck. He walks in the lonely places in the night wearing *khadāūṁ*, wooden sandals. He also sometimes wears the necklace of human skulls. He can live by miracle in the body of some beautiful women and play with them.

Women worship him. He is believed to appear in their dreams in the form of a Brahman and bless them with fertility. It is said when a mother or mother in law worships Nārsiṁha, her daughter or daughter in law must also do so. Barren women consulting a priest or a jogi are usually advised to worship Nārsiṁha for grant of offsprings. A special costume made for this purpose only is worn by the devotees during the worship.

Worship: The old Gazetteer of Kangra records that in Kangra, about two thirds of the women, and some of the men are believers in Nārsiṁha. The following is description of one of the methods of worshipping Nārsiṁha.

'They worship him every Sunday or on the first Sunday of each month. They put the *narjil*, cocoanut, on a brass plate (*thāli*). First washing it with fresh water, they then put a *tilak* of the *chandan,* vermilion, on it in the same way that Brahmans mark their foreheads. Then an *achhat,* washed rice, of as much as will stay on three fingers of the right hand, i.e. on the thumb, first and second or middle finger, is placed on it. When this is done they adorn the *narjil* with flowers, and then burn some *dhup,* a pastilles of a root from the Chamba hills, besprinkled with powdered camphor, sandal wood, almonds and spices. The *narjil* is then worshipped as Nārsiṁha, and sweetmeats offered to it. These being subsequently distributed to the children and other members of the household and the neighbours. Nārsiṁha worshippers also wear a *bahuta* (amulet) containing a picture of him in the form of a man. This *bahuta* is of silver, and is worshipped like the *narjil.* A ring generally made of silver with a projection towards the nail, as worn on the little finger too is worshipped', (Kangra District Gazetteer: 1926, Part A: 207-208).

It tells further that when a woman is sick a *celā* is sent for to charm away the illness. If he says that Nārsiṁha anger has caused it he orders a *baiṭhak*, sitting. If she does not happen to have a *bahutā* or the proper rings or clothes or a *narjil*, the *celā* orders any of them that may be wanting to be procured before performing the *baiṭhak*. Then on a Sunday or any other fixed day the *celā* comes with a *baitry* or singer of sacred songs who plays on a *dopatra* an instrument made of two *tumbas* (ascetic 's bowl) connected by a bamboo rod. A wire runs along this rod fastened to the extremities so as to give out a sound when twanged. The *baitry* sings his song and the *celā* repeats his magic words, and then Nārsiṁha comes and shakes the body of the woman or of the *celā*. The tremors continue for two hours or more, during which time the man or woman into whom the spirit has entered tells the fortunes of those attending the *baiṭhak*. They are usually told to worship some deity who will cure the sick woman. While in patient or the *celā* keeps shivering with the force of the spirit in him the *baitri* sings the following incantation accompanying him on the *dopatra*.

This is a part of a prayer to the deity: Oh my Nārsiṁha, Niranjan Vīr! O, you have captivated me. All the people talk that Niranjan has captivated me. He was born at the fort of Mathura.

In Mandi: The old Gazetteer records that in Mandi as in Kangra, Nārsiṁha is the god of women, whom he is supposed to visit in dreams. He is the ideal type of the divine lover and appears in the form of a handsome Brahman dressed in clothes white as snow, with a red turban, flowered and crested, on his head, a *dhotī* reaching to his knees, wooden shoes on his feet and garlands of jasmine round his neck. He is specially venerated by childless women and priests often refer those desirous of children to his mercy.

Gazetteer notes that in Mandi there are shrines of three different and distinct divinities: Lakhdātā, Nārsiṁha and *Siddha* under a single tree. Nārsiṁha was represented by several *pinḍs*, balls, beneath the shade of the *simbal* tree in which his spirit was supposed to dwell, several threads of cotton had been tied round the trunk of the tree and the god thus was invested with the *janeo*.

Nārsiṁha a historical person: There is a story describing Nārsiṁha as a Raja of some State. Devrāj tells that he came from

Rajsathan and became Vazīr of Guggā. At the worship places of Guggā there are also found the statues of Nārsiṁha, who is known as a Rānā of Rajsathan. There are some varying information on some vital points.

It is also told that Nāharsṁha or Nārsiṁha is a king cotemporary to and minister of Raja Dev of Dhārā (Jagdev Parmār 12th century). Therefore he is called *Vazīr*. He came here from a place named Koṭ Kamol. When any follower offers prayer to Nārsiṁha he also explains his pedigree as the king of Galh Māru.

The following couplet tells the pedigree and the native place of Nārsiṁha.

नाहर सिंह
राजे पाल का पड़पोता
भूमिपाल का पोता
राजे अजमेर का बेटा
माता सोनी का जाया
गढरु मारूए का राजा कहलाया।

Translation: Nārsiṁha is grand-grand-son of Raje Pāl, grandson of Bhūmi Pāl, son of the king of Ajmer, born to mother Sonī, and he was King of Galh (fort) Mārū.

The following description gives a different pedigree of Nārsiṁha and adds some more names related to the deity. Here is he given as a Raja.

शशि पाल का अजयपाल
अजयपाल का गजपाल,
गजपाल का अब, अब का कबः,
कबः का का ाब, का ाब का शूरबीर,
शूरबीर का नार सिंह।

राजा नार सिंह वीर,
माता संदावलिया का बेटा,
अच्छरा बहन का भाई, अखाडरु का सरदार,
परियों का अगवानी, ऊद्धोनाथ का चेला, बांका वीर अलबेला।
(Angiras, 2007: 59).

Translation. Son of Śaśipāl was Ajaypāl, his son was Gajpāl, his son was Aba, his son was Kabah, his son was Kāśab, his son Śūrbīr and his son was Nārsiṁha. The Raja Nārsiṁha is hero. He is son of mother Sandāvaliyā. Name of his sister is Acchrā. He is hero in the wrestling ground. He leads the fairies. He is pupil of ūddhonāth. Such is the description of the handsome and wonderful hero. Angiras also writes that the name of Nārsiṁha's father is Brahmaṛṣi. His Teacher is Kāśi Riṣi and he was born at Multānpurī and that he accompanies the 52-Vīr, 64-Yoginīs and 84-siddhas. In Chamba he is known as Bābā Sinḍu (*Pahāṛiyā*) and is venerated as *Vazīr* of Guggā.

BR Sharma writes that the tāntriks, and priests, believe that Nārsiṁha is one of the fifty-two Vīrs and he is also their chief at whose call all the Vīrs can gather before him. They pronounce *mantra* in order to invoke him. They place one vessel or a pitcher on the ground. Over it is placed a plate of brass which they beat violently. The victim's eyes are closed and incense is burnt. They then start pronouncing the *mantra* loudly. With the kindness of the deity the victim becomes unconscious and starts moaning. Then the one who plays the plate asks the priest. If he can see Nārsiṁha. He will say, 'I can see a person taking a smoking pipe (*hukkā*) in his hands in white clothes like a gaddī shepherd. He is coming towards us'. Such *mantras* are called *bharnī*. Nārsiṁha is considered, in some accounts, as a Vīr. Nārsiṁha can cure a person infected by a bad spirit and grant fulfillment of the wishes of his devotees.

Below is given a couplet describing Nārsiṁha who is like a *gaddī* shepherd who live in Chamba. Here he is shown as belonging to Bhangāl, a remote place.

कुलुए भंगाला ते आया मेरे मितरा ओ
डेरा बसोलिया लाया, मेरे मितरा ओ
हत्था त तेरे नरेलू बराजदा ओ
लक्का बराजदा डोरा मेरे मितरा।
(B.R. Sharma. 1986: 144).

Translation: Nārsiṁha, my friend, has come from Bhañgāl in Kullu. He has pitched his residence at Basohli. In his hand he holds *hukkā* and on the waist there is the long and thick *ḍorā*, waist band.

Another similar couplet describes in this manner: Nārsiṁha has come from Bhañgāl in Kullu. The ridges are covered with snow. On his back he carries a *kiraḍu* (a bamboo basket). My friend, on his waist he holds the thick waist-band. Below are given some more couplets sung in praise of Nārsiṁha Vīr.

संगलदीप का राजा जिया पाल, जियापाल का लहूपाल,
लहुपाल का कुसलपाल, कुसलपाल का नमो नाहर सिंह वीर।
हाथ में डण्डा, पवण का घोड़ा, फिरे नभ खण्डा कौण चले।
नाहर सिंह चले, गद्‌दी वीर चले, पहाडिरुया वीर चले,
वरोधिया वीर चले, तुगनिया वीर चले, तुगल वीर चले।
(B.R.Sharma. 1986: 141).

Translation: Jiyā Pāl is the king of Sañgal dīpa (Sihala dvīpa), his son is Lahu Pāl, his son Kusal Pāl, and his son is Nāharsiṁha or Nārsiṁha. I pray you, O! Nāharsiṁha Vīr. He goes there in the sky riding a horse of air, holding a stick in the hands. Nāharsiṁha is accompanied by Gaddī Vīr, Pahāḍiyā Vīr, Varodhiyā Vīr, Tugniyā Vīr, and Tugal Vīr.

Here is another similar description:

रौणू वीर चले, जिहण्डू वीर चले, मिहण्डू वीर चले।
हाजर तो हाजिर, मुहम्मद अली वीर चले।
वीर वैताल चले, सवाया सेर का तोसा खाए।
लगा लगाए, हाके हंकारिया, भेजया भिजाया।
जल में राधे, स्थल में राधे, मन में राधे।
मन में करे विचार, जादू हांकने वाली रण्डी, पुरूश मरे।
मन का संसा टले, चलेमन्त्र फुरे वाचा।
देखो बाबा नाहरसिंह, तेरे इलम का तमाशा।
(B.R.Sharma. 1986: 142).

Nārsiṁha is Vīr and is followed by other Vīrs.

Translation: Raunū Vīr is coming, Jihaṇḍū Vīr is coming and there comes Mihaṇḍū Vīr. Vīr Muhammad Ali is also present here. There comes Vaitāl Vīr who has taken one and quarter seer of sweets. Those who were to be engaged have been engaged; those who are to be coaxed have been coaxed; and those who were to be sent, have been sent. Rādhā lives in the water, Rādhā lives on the ground and Rādhā lives in everybody's mind. The magician flirts a woman that the man should die. Suspicion of mind may be removed. May the *mantra* and the words be effective. See oh saint Nārsiṁha, how effective is your knowledge!

Nrsiṁha and Nārsiṁha: There is some debate as to whether Nrsiṁha Avatār of the classical form and the Nārsiṁha or Nāharsiṁha Dev of the Nāthpanth or of the folk tradition are the same or the two are different entities of the same deity. The deity at one time was very popular among the folk and he had been attributed with numerous traits and functions which gave him a distinguishing position. Nārsiṁha then attained great heights and gained wide popularity.

As we have noticed above that the temples of Nrsiṁha or Nārsiṁha situated at various places in Himachal, including that of Bharmaur, all have been attributed by Āngriras to Nārsiṁha. Others also have the same view because in tradition they have been recognized as such in the faith of the people. But the metal statue of the deity at Bharmaur is not different from that of Nrsiṁha and today all take him as Nrsiṁha. Iconographically it represents Nrsiṁha. It appears that although popularity of deity flourished during the medieval period and some varying historical colours were also given, but ultimately they all vanished and today the deity is in its original form.

The devotees don't seem to make any distinction between the two.

D. Guggā

Guggā, a very popular folk deity, still enjoys veneration from its devotees in several districts in Himachal **viz.** Mandi, Una, Bilaspur, Kullu, Kangra, Chamba, Shimla, Rampur and Sirmaur. Songs are sung in the praise of Guggā telling the stories of his life and struggles. Annual fairs are held in his memory. A good amount of literature is available about the deity. It is almost wholly in the form of verse and exist all in oral tradition. Recently some scholars have tried to put them down to writing. The propitiation of Guggā was practiced widely in Rajsthan, Punjab, Haryana, Uttrakhand, and Himachal. Its link extended upto Kāmrūp, Assam, to which belonged the Guggā's bride Surhil. The stories current in Himachal mostly indicate that the deity belonged to Rajsthan.

Alexander Cunningham writes that, 'The story of Guggā is known all over Northern India, from the Himalaya mountains to Narbada. Songs are sung in his praise on every return of his birth day, and he is worshipped equally by Hindus and by Muhammadans, by the former as Guggā Cauhān, the invincible champion of their faith, and by the latter as Guggā Pīr and Zahir Pīr, the brave convert to Islamism. He is more especially revered by the people of low class' (Alexander Cunningham, ASI Report, XIV-2000: 81).

Guggā is said to belong to Cauhān Rajput family. Most of the legends relate that Guggā was a hero, a warrior and fought many battles against the invaders.

Guggā in Rajsthan: James Tod relates the story of Guggā as it existed in Rajsthan. He writes, 'It is related by Rajput romances that Goga had no children; that lamenting this his guardian deity gave him two barley corns (*java* or *jao*), one of which he gave to his queen, and another to his favourite mare which produced the steed (*Javādia*) which became as famous as Goga himself. The Rana of Oodipoor gave the author a blood-horse of Kathiawār, whose name was javādia.'

'Goga Chohan was the son of Vacha Raja, a name of some celebrity. He held the whole of Jungul-des, or the forest lands from the Sutlej to Heriana; his capital, called Mehera, or, as pronounced, *Goga ca´ Mairi*, was on the Sutlej. In defending this he fell, with forty-five sons and sixty nephews; and as it occurred on Sunday (*Rubwār*), the ninth (*nomee*) of the month, that day is held sacred to the *manes* of Goga by the "thirty-six classes" throughout Rajpootana, but especially in the desert, a portion of which is yet called *Gogadeo-ca-t'hul*. Even his steed, Javadiā, has been immortalized and has become a favourite name for a war-horse throughout Rajpootana, whose mighty men swear 'by the *saca of Goga'*, for maintaining the Rajpoot fame when Mahmood crossed the Satlej' (James Tod, 1832-II: 362).

James Tod here shows that the country of Guggā lay between Sutlej and Haryana which indicates that quite a substantial part of Guggā's territory fell in the area of the present Himachal. Alexander Cunningham also reiterates the same fact.

As regards the name of the capital of Guggā given by Tod as 'Mehera or, as pronounced, *Goga ca´ Mairi*,' these can be interpreted as Maḷhī or 'Guggā kā Maḷhī' which terms we hear commonly in Himachal even today. Maḷhī means shrine and thus shrine of Guggā. Elliot also gives the same name Mehera for the capital of Guggā's province. Cunningham's proposition that Darderā or Dardarerā was the capital of Guggā appears to be quite reliable. We also hear slightly varying names like Dhundanherā or Dunesh in this context in the stories from Himachal.

Guggā in Hissar: Elliot states that the agriculturists of the Delhi territory and the Upper Doab regard Gugga with reverence and crowd to his shrine with their offerings in the month of *Bhadon*. 'His tomb lies nearly two hundred miles to the south-west of Hissar, and twenty miles beyond a place called Dadrera. Goga Pīr is called by the Mahrattas as Zahir Pīr, and is with them a favourite saint. The local tradition respecting him is that he was the son of a Chauhān Rajput, called Vachā according to some, and according to others Jewar. There is a clan of Chauhāns even now resident in the neighbourhood of his tomb. The Gogāwats of the desert are descended from him and the 'Gogadeo ka thal' is called after his name. His capital was Mehera on the river Gasra (Ghora). He is said to have been contemporary of Prithvi Raj' (Elliot, 1859-I: 255-256).

Elliot also writes that, 'Chāhil or Chāhira, is the name of a tribe of Rajputs who live in Hissar district and on the borders of Bikaner who are connected with Goga Chauhān, whose wife Siriyāl, was the daughter of Sinja, the Chāhil, Raja of Sirsa Patan. The memory of this relationship is still preserved by the Chāhil tribe being the exclusive manager of the Saint's tomb'.

Elliot's identification of some places connected with the life of Gugga are important. He mentions Dadrera from where a twenty miles away is located the tomb of Guggā. Dadrera in another legend is named as Daruhera through which Muhammad Gauri passed and he got erected a Malhī in honour of Guggā.

Alexander Cunningham notes that Sirsava, Sirsa, is birthplace of Bachal Rani, mother of Guggā Chauhan, daughter of Jayml or Jewar, a Tomar Raja and some tell Kara or Kunwar Pal, Raja of Kanaur. During the time of Mahmud she was married to Vacha or Vatsa, the Chauhan Raja of Bagar des, or the wild tract of half desert country from Hansi to the Satluj on the west and to Bikaner or the south-west. Dardera or Dardarera was its capital (ASI Report XIV-2000: 80-81).

Thus it may be concluded that the name of the kingdom of Guggā was Bāgar and his capital was named Daderā, Dadrerā, Dāruheḷā, Dhundanheḷā or Duneś which was situated near Hissar in Haryana.

RC Temple writes that Guggā counts his devotees by thousands in the Panjab and the United Provinces. Some thirty years ago their number was estimated at 35,000 for the Panjab and 123,000 for the United Provinces.

Guggā in Himachal: Guggā in Himachal is known by a variety of names: Guggāmal, Guggā Cauhān, Guggā Rāṇā, Guggā Pīr, Guggā Jāhar Pīr, Guggā Guru, Guggā Vīr, Zahir Pīr and Zahir Diwān, Bāgarvālā (from his reputed homeland) and Mundlīkh (in Chamba). Bāgar is a community in Haryana having its own distinct language.

The story from Bilaspur: The story of Guggā Jāhar Pīr as is told in Bilaspur area is comparatively more detailed. An extract is given here: It is told that Baldev Rāj was king of Gazni. Once he had gone on an expedition and remained there engaged for long time. When he returned home after twelve years he found two girls playing in the courtyard of his palace. He asked them about their identity. They proudly told that they were daughters of king Baldev Rāj of Gazni. The king at once took out his sword. Soon there appeared his Minister. He showed a letter from the queen. As the king read the letter he lifted the two daughters in his lap. The queen had expected the situation and had appointed the Minister as their guardian. The two daughters were born after the king had left Gazni. They were named Bāchlā and Kāchlā. According to the custom in those days daughters in the family of the Rājā were killed immediately on their birth. The daughters were born on Tuesday. Therefore the queen had considered them as auspicious and wanted to protect them.

Raja Baldev Rāj then married the two daughters with Raja Je-oor of Dhundanherā or Dunesh in Marwar, Māru, Rajsthan. Unfortunately both the queens did not have any issue for long period. Then on the advice of the Brahman of the family, Bāchlā, the elder Rani went to Gorakh Tīlā, and meditated there upon Guru Gorakhnātha. As she was about to complete the period of her meditation of twelve years the earth started shaking. The pupils asked for the reason from their Teacher.

The Teacher told that the wish of Rani Bāchlā had been fulfilled. The Guru told her to come again when she would be given a fruit to eat after which a child would be assured to her. She went home and told the story to Kāchlā, her younger sister. Kāchlā was envious and was also very clever. She then requested her elder sister to lend her clothes as she wanted to go to meet her Pir, guru. Bāchlā gave her the key of her box. Kāchlā wore the old clothes of Bāchlā and went to Guru Gorakhnātha in the mid of the night. The Guru asked the reason for her coming in the late night. The Rani replied that she had come for the promised fruit and the Brahman had told that this is auspicious time. The Guru taking out two seeds of grain from his bag gave to the Rani. This helped her to bear two sons named Arjun and Surjan.

In the morning Bāchlā came to the Guru with flowers and sweets in a plate. The Guru asked, 'You had come shortly before and now you have come again'. The queen told that it might have been her younger sister. Then Gorakhnātha searched his bag but did not find anything. Then he asked Vidhi Mātā, the mother of Fate. She also could not help. He also asked the Lords Brahmā, Viṣṇu and Śiva. They also could not help. The guru was very eager to help the queen. Then the Guru went to the nether land and asked from Vāsukī, the Nāga, to give an effective fruit. He told the Guru that he could take any kind of fruit he wanted. Gorakhnātha said, 'Vāsukī, if you want to give me fruit then give me the Nāga that is sitting on your right hand side who spreads light in all the directions'. Vāsukī expressed his helplessness saying that, 'If I give that to you, the whole of the nether world will become dark'. The Guru was adamant. He converted the Nāga into pastilles of guggul and put it in his bag and returned.

Then the Guru gave the pastilles of guggul to Bāchlā and assured her that this boy will be stronger and more promising than the sons of Kāchlā. He will become famed in the world.

On reaching home the Rāni took bath and ate the fruit. She gave a piece of it to the mistress and its peels to the mare. To the mare was born a pony who was named Nīla. The mistress had a girl who was named Gugrī. A son was born to Rani Bāchlā after eleven months who was named Guggā. Gugrī who played with Guggā became his sister and she accompanied him in many battles. The horse Nīla became faithful and favourite horse of Guggā. From this incident it may be assumed that the name Guggā has emerged from the term guggul.

Another story says that a piece of the fruit was received by the Brahman lady of the family from whom was born Nārsiṁha. According to another description, after Bāchlā had conceived Guggā she set out on a bullock cart to her parents' home. On the way she wanted to take rest and left the bullocks loose to graze. At this time Nāga Kalihar bit one of the bullocks called Dhaulā (white, the other one was named Nīla, blue). The Rani then started wailing. The boy started talking from the womb and consoled her. He advised her not to worry. He told her to tie a thread on the wound of the bullock. Bāchlā did as advised and the boy from the womb blew a *mantra*. The bullock immediately recovered and rising up started grazing grass as before. Then she started her journey again towards her parents' home. But the boy in the womb advised her mother to return to her home in Māru (Marwar). She did as told by her son. Here Bāchlā had to face a treachery played by her sister Kāchlā. She had given her a poison in order to kill the child in her womb. But the boy saved himself from the threat. Then the mother gave birth to her son. He was named Guggāmal Cauhān.

Once Guggā, still young, was playing on a swing. The younger mother, by merely seeing him, grew envious. She went to the nether world, aroused Kalihar Nāga from his slumber and invoked him. He made an army of a lakh snakes and moved to the world of mortality, to attack on Guggā. As the snakes attacked on Guggā he caught one by one and sucking like sugarcane, started killing them. In this way the king of the Nāgas, Vāsukī, when he observed his offsprings and community being annihilated went to Guggā, entreated him to save his progeny and community. He also promised that the snakes will remain always under his command and will follow his orders. Wherever the name of Guggā is pronounced, power of the Nāga will become ineffective. After a little thought Guggā pardoned the snakes. This instance shows how Guggā gained power in controlling the snakes and curing their bites for which he is famous.

Marriage of Guggā: In the state of Kohu or Kauru, also called Mālap, there lived a Raja named Sanjhi. He had a daughter named Surhil. As she attained the age of twelve years, the Raja became anxious for the marriage of his daughter. He invited a Brahman who guided him to send a messenger to the country of Māru where he told, 'there is a prince named Guggā Rāṇā of Chauhān lineage. He is the most suitable groom'. The messengers sent there saw the boy and finding everything suitable gave the *tilak* (symbol) and contracted the marriage.

As the messengers had left to Māru there arrived a similar party from the country of Kachhu, a country like Mālap, but bigger and more powerful than Māru, to seek the hands of Surhil. It was decided to give the daughter to the prince of Kachhu, since Māru is small and deserted country. The Raja sent a message to Māru stating that he will not give his daughter to Guggā of Māru. At this time Guggā was playing pāsā (cowrie) with his cousin brothers Arjun and Surjan. At this Arjun and Surjan made joke of Guggā who became enraged and got engrossed in deep worry. His mother asked for the reason. He told that he will marry only with Surhil or will die.

He enquired from his mother about Guru Gorakhnātha as he wanted to take his help. His mother tried to evade and told that Gorakhnātha lived far away in distant land. Guggā took his horse Nīla and set off in search of Guru Gorakhnātha. He went through the jungles and rivers and ultimately reached Gorakhnātha. He related his story to the Guru and also told that if this marriage fails he will die.

Firstly Gorakh also tried to dissuade Guggā. Then the Guru called his pupil Kahan or 'Kahnī'. He asked him to go to the Pātālpurī, the nether world, to call from there 'Kalihar Nāga'. Kahan was afraid. But the Guru assured him not to worry of the Nāga. The Guru gave him three unbaked pitchers to take with him. Kahnī reached the residence of Kalihar Nāga and knocked at the door. His queen Padmanār sent alms with her servant which Kahnī refused to accept. He sent message that he will take alms only from the hands of Padmanār. She became enraged and she told this fact to her husband Kalihar. He came out at the door hissing with a lot of poison in his fang. As Kalihar came out he spit at Kahnī but Kahnī showed forward a pitcher on which the serpent spit and the pitcher became fully backed. Likewise the second pitcher also became baked. But when the third pitcher was placed before the serpent, there was no sign of change visible in it, since the serpent had exhausted his stock of poison.

Kalihar was surprised with this mystery. He begged pardon and bowed before the guest and also asked his purpose of coming. He told that he is pupil of Gorakh and he had come to invite him. Kalihar came with his son Taksak to Gorakh.

Seeing Guggā there he stopped at once. He told that he could not move forward because his enemy was sitting there.

Gorakhnātha confided him. The Guru ordered the serpent to go to Mālap state and arrange the marriage of the princess Surhil with Guggā. Kalihar sent his son Taksak assigning the job and he himself went away to his palace.

Taksak went in the form of a crow and reached the garden of the king of Mālap. Surhil was playing there in the garden with her companions. They threatened away the crow. Then he went in the form of a Brahman and asked for water. He told that he will take water only from the hands of Surhil. When Surhil came out he bit her. Then her parents sent for doctor. Taksak again appeared in the form of a Brahman and told that he could cure the princess but only on the condition that if her marriage was fixed with Guggā. The king agreed and then Taksak cured Surhil. Marriage of Surhil was fixed on the ninth day from the day.

Taksak went with the news and told to Gorakhnātha. The Guru conveyed the message to Guggā. Guggā on hearing the news came to the Guru and started weeping instead of being pleased. The Guru asked reason for it. Guggā told that it is impossible that this marriage can be ceremonised because the time of the marriage has been fixed too short. He told that it takes six months journey from Māru to reach Mālap. Therefore this marriage is not possible.

The Guru consoled him not to worry. He flew towards the Kailash mountain. At that time Śivajī was sleeping but with his inner vision he could visualise Gorakhnātha coming towards the Kailash. Śivajī suggested Parvatī that, 'Today Gorakhnātha is coming to meet me. We have not met since long. But we will not give him the things for which he is coming to demand'. Śivajī told Parvatī that he will hide himself among the buffaloes in the cave. She should not tell him anything about it.

When Gorakhnātha reached Kailash he enquired Parvatī about Śivajī. Initially she refused to tell but on the insistence of the Guru she had to tell the truth.

Gorakhnath took Bhairava with him for company and went towards the cave where Śivajī was hiding. The Guru stayed over the gate spreading his legs apart and asked Bhairava to drive out the buffaloes so that they would pass under him. Five of them came without any hesitation, but the sixth one would not move out even after Bhairava tried by striking with the stick. Then at last Śivajī came in his real form. Gorakhnātha begged pardon for his this indecent action. Then he told about the marriage of Guggā. For this he requested the articles: ash, armlet, flying shuttle, *nād* and *amrit,* life-water. Śivajī gave him all these things. Gorakhnātha went back and told to Guggā to go to Māru and make preparations for marriage.

Guggā asked from the Guru as to how he could make all these arrangements. The Guru told that he had gone to Kailash mountain to meet Śivajī. He brought from him Flying shuttle by which the whole journey would be covered within the required time. Moreover if there is any trouble at any moment, I have brought ash and armlet. If somebody dies during the fight I have brought for it the life giving water. For inviting the gods in the marriage party I have brought *nād*. Guggā was very much pleased and he went to Māru for making preparations for the marriage.

Then Gorakhnātha, Kahni celā, and Nīla the horse rode the flying shuttle and reached Kurudesh. Gorakhnātha chose to stay at the cemetery. The rest went to the garden of the king. There the gardener did not allow them to enter. They told that they had come in the marriage with the bridal party. Even then he did not allow them. Then they had to enter forcefully. The gardener complained to the king. There was then a contest of strength of magical powers and attempt to overpower the opponent. The inhabitants of the area were famous for possessing magical powers. At last the party of Gorakhnātha subdued all the opponents easily and the marriage was ceremonised happily. Guggā went to his home with his bride.

While Guggā was away from home his cousins Arjun and Surjan had taken over the reign of the kingdom. On his return Guggā had first to contest with them whom he was able to defeat convincingly. A Brahman advised the two brothers to go to Delhi to seek the help from Prithvi Raj Chauhān, the Raja of Delhi. The Raja sent a man for compromising and dividing the kingdom into two parts. But this was not acceptable and the envoy returned. Then the King went himself. There was a fierce fighting. With the aid of Guru Gorakhnātha, Guggā's army won the battle. His two cousins were beheaded. Then Guggā went home and met his mother. He gave the news of his victory and showed the heads of his two brothers. Mother became angry and told to Guggā to leave the place immediately and never to come before her again.

Then he received teachings from Guru Gorakhnātha on Yoga. Surhil saw her husband in the dream who was holding a spear in his hand was riding a horse. She told the story to her mother in law. She advised her to spend her time in prayers and meditation. She prayed the almighty who accepted her prayer and then Guggā came everyday in the night to meet her. Guggā told her that this fact should not be known to his mother at all.

On one auspicious day the women of the area came adorned in sixteen kinds of embellishments and they invited Surhil also to come with them for the prayer. Bāchlā told them that her daughter-in-law is like a widow she cannot come. They went away. But Surhil on this started crying. Bāchlā compelled her to tell the truth. Then in the night when Guggā came, his mother tried to catch the reign of his horse. Guggā broke his necklace and the beads got scattered on the floor. He told his mother to pick up the beads. By the time he managed to escape saying, 'O mother remember your words once you told me, never to show my face to you.' To Surhil he said, 'You have broken the promise and told the secret to my mother'. Then he left the palace forever.

When Muhammad Ghuri reached Dāruhedā, while going to Delhi, the drums of his army suddenly stopped sounding. On enquiry he heard the story of Guggā and he promised that if he won the battle he will build a temple here for the deity. Thus he constructed a Malhī at Dāruhedā. Thus ends the story.

RC Temple writes that when Guggā separated himself permanently from his family, he prayed Mother Earth, to take him into her lap or else he will die himself. Mother Earth advised him to go to Rattan Hājī who in turn advised him to go to Ajmer and worship Khwājā Muhinuddin Ciṣtī. Ultimately Gard Darora, Mother Earth, received him.

Vogel writes that according to a version current in Kulu, the bride of Guggā, named Suryār Nāgnī, was the daughter of 'Bāski Nāg'. In the shrine of Guggā at Sultanpur, the capital of Kulu, he saw Vāsukī Nāg in the form of a snake issuing from the ground in front of the hero's statue.

In this story it is related that the home of Surhil, Gugga's bride, was situated at a distant land, to which it took about six month's journey. This apparently indicates to Kāmrūp which is known from another story given below.

Guggā rides the blue horse, carrying spear, sword, and battle shield, on the back and a cap like that of Tāntya Tope on his head. Sometimes he is shown like Rānā Pratāp Singh carrying arrow and bow. He is accompanied by his retinue.

A Variant Version of the story: In another variant story it is narrated that Raja Dev Raj belonged to Dakhan (south) who had two queens: Bāchlā and Kāchlā. Both of them received a fruit each from guru Gorakhnātha. Bāchlā ate half of it and the other half she gave to the mare that she was riding. To Kāchlā was born a daughter named Gugrī, and to Bāchlā a son, named Guggā, and the mare in turn had a foal. Guggā and the foal were brought up together. When Guggā attained adult-hood he heard the fame of a beautiful maiden. Riding the horse (his foster brother) he went to woo her. For years he lived with her being changed by day by the sorcery of the country to a sheep, and by night resuming the form of a man. During his presence no one could enter the maiden's room. The door-keeper used to grow blind when Guggā went out of the room and became normal on his return.

After long absence from home his cousin Gugrī sent a letter by the hand of a brahman to Guggā in Bangāhal. Guggā, realizing the state of affairs, abandoned his life of pleasure and with the help of the Brahman escaped from the web of the sorcery that had bound him. By the same aid the horse that had grown old and thin was restored to youth. Thus Guggā once more mounted his steed and reached his home town. On his return home Guggā and Gugrī both performed miracles. They fought the enemies and once Guggā even fought for some time after he had lost his head. After death he was venerated as god, and has thereafter been always represented on horseback. Any person suffering from a snake-bite is usually taken to a Guggā shrine, where in some cases he gets cured. The others who die are supposed to have committed some deadly sin from which the only redemption was death.

RC Temple gives another version. He writes, Jewar, a Cauhān Rajput, was the Raja of Bāgar, in Bikaner. Some call it a tract in Gujarat and Malwa. He was always a lawful man. He had no offspring, therefore, no guardian of his kingdom. Queen Bāchlā was the favourite wife of the Raja.

Guru Gorakhnātha visits the Raja. He comes with a splendid retinue with carriages, horses and palanquins. The Raja took the shawls and hangings, and filled a golden platter with pearls and coral for the *yogi*. Queen Bāchlā requested the *yogi*, 'I have no child. Kindly fulfill my desire.'

Queen Kāchlā, sister of Bāchlā, was the second wife of the Raja. She too begged for a son from Gorakhnātha. Deceptively the two fruits were given to Kāchlā instead of one each to Bāchlā and Kāchlā. But the Guru blessed Bāchlā too with a son. Bāchlā, on the complaint by a person, was blamed by the Raja for going to the Guru in the garden. She then went to Ghazni Fort, her parental home.

Then a miracle happened. Guggā was in womb for twelve months. He advised his mother from within her womb not to grieve but call at Gorakhnātha. Then on the request of Guggā from womb Raja Jewar asked the minister to call the queen back. At home the handsome Guggā was born. He was a brave and miraculous prince.

Guggā was then engaged to a beautiful princess Chhariyāl, Sariyāl, or Sioriyāl, daughter of Raja Sanja, king of Kāmrup. When Guggā's father had died, his betrothal was broken. Some unfriendly relative speaking evil of Guggā had done this.

His mother was wailing. Guggā was enraged. He went to forest, took a bamboo stick and made a flute. He sang Rāg Bhairav and called Gorakhnātha. He played all the six rāgs and thirty-six rāgnīs on his flute. When Vāsukī, king of the serpents, heard the tune, he was displeased in his heart. This awakened all the snakes.

Tātig Nāga, the servant and priest of Vāsukī Nāga, was sent to bring the details. Guggā replies: "I am Jewar's son, Guggā, a name given by Gorakhnātha. My bride named Sariyāl lives seven rivers across. My betrothal has been broken off. Sānjā is her father's name. She lives at Dhupnagar seven rivers across, in the country of Kāru. Their goddess is Kāmākhya. The people there are great sorcerers. I have come in the forest to complain. Then Vāsukī Nāga ordered Tātig to do as requested by Tātig requests Gorakhnātha to grant him power. He went to Kāru and bit the girl and was successful in getting the betrothal revived.

Mundlīkh: In Chamba, the old Gazetteer notes, that the deity is worshipped in the name of Mundlikh who represents the valiant Rajput champion, Guggā Cauhān, of the time of Prithvi Raj, the last Hindu King of Delhi of 1170-93 CE. Guggā is said to have fought many battles with the invaders and in the last his head was severed from his body, hence the name Mundlīkh, from *munda,* head, and *līk* a line. He is said to have continued fighting without the head and by some to have disappeared in the ground, only the point of his spear remaining visible. The legend is sung to the accompaniments of music by the hill bards, and with such pathos that their audiences are often moved to tears. Mundlīkh's death is supposed to have taken place on the ninth day of the dark half of the moon in Bhādon, and from that date for eight days his shrādha, called *Guggṇaih*, is observed yearly at his shrines. Mundlīkh has about four shrines in Chamba.

Guggā and Muhammadism: Guggā enjoyed a very wide popularity among the various religions and social classes. There are stories telling how Guggā was converted to Muhammadism. In the legends the deity is shown partly Hindu and partly Muslim.

Vogel writes that, 'Strange to say, that this 'Cid Campador' of the Hindu faith is not only worshipped by all castes of Hindus, but also by Muslims on the strength of a tradition that Guggā before his death became a convert to Islam, and even made a pilgrimage to Mecca. He is known under a great variety of names – Guggā Bīr and Guggā Pīr, Zahir Pīr and Zahir Diwan, Bagarvala (from his reputed homeland), Ram Deva (in Hisar), and Mundlikh in Chamba (Vogel, 1926:265). RC Temple writes, 'He is now a days one of the Chief Muhammadan saints or objects of worship of the lower classes of all sorts, and is also known as Zahir Pīr.'

In Kullu it is believed that Guggā was eaten up by a fiendess. Then he appeared in a herd among the sheep. They became afraid. When the shepherd saw him coming out of the earth he hit over his head with a hammer of about 20 maunds. Guggā was able to come out only half. The part of the body of Guggā which is seen above the earth is called Jāhar. Therefore he is called Jāhar Pīr and he is propitiated by the Muslims. The part which is under the earth is called Alakhdātā and it is propitiated by the Hindus. There is a Malhī of Guggā at Sultanpur. Guggā, his vazīr and Gugrī are riding horses. Nārsiṁha, Kāliyāvīr and Guru Gorakhnātha accompany him. In another description the part of the body of Guggā which is buried is described as Mohammedan and the part above that as of Hindu.

In district Sirmaur in a song it is narrated that Guggā had meeting with an unknown Mughal Emperor of Delhi. The Emperor prays Guggā, 'O Goga Miyan, I will construct a Malhī for you on the top of a ridge. It will be constructed from marble which will be polished and minute carvings will be done on it. You please relieve us from your vision which has affected us badly, you please remain in your kingdom of Bāgar' (Saleem, 2001: 151).

Historicity of Guggā: Whether Guggā was a historical person cannot be said. But there are some references in the legends and traditions which appear to possess some historical nature. Based on these facts Guggā could belong to any time during the period of around six hundred years. According to one tradition he fell in battle with his forty five sons and sixty nephews, while opposing

Mahmud of Ghazni, c. 1000 CE. Guggā, in some legends, is shown that he was ruler of Bāgar, the great prairies of Rajputana and Haryana. He is said to have been a valiant Rajput of the Chauhān clan and was a contemporary of Prithi Raj Chauhān, the last Hindu king of Delhi, the last quarter of the twelfth century. A third account places him in the time of Aurangzeb, the last quarter of the seventeenth century.

RC Temple writes, in life he appears to have been a Hindu and a leader of the Chauhān Rajputs and fought against Mahmud of Ghazni about A.D. 1000. One of the tales would connect him with the Rajputs reigning in Kabul before the Muslim rule came there, but Tod disputes the identity of the Rajput of Gazni with Ghazni. RC Temple from another source deduces the date for the deity at A.D 1309 or 1312 (Temple, 1884-III: 261).

Temples of Guggā: Shrines of Guggā are small of one room called malhī. In some villages statues are kept in an open place or under a tree, which are called *sthān* or *sthāpanā* or *Gugā-rā-sthān*, place of Guggā. Vogel writes that shrines of Guggā, called *Guggā malhī*, or *khāngāh*, may be seen in almost every village throughout the sub-montane tract and in the Kangra Hills. Snakes are part of the rude ornamentation of his shrine which usually contains a group of clumsily fashioned figures of stone or earth.

It is told that in Bilaspur there is a little shrine dedicated to Guggā Pīr in almost every village, containing the image of Guggā mounted on a horse and supposed to be specially efficacious for snake bites. There is a story as to how a new temple was founded. A person in the village of Guggā Baṭeḷ had a son who was bitten by snake and he was almost dead. The boy's father meditated upon Guggā and wished if his son regained life he will go to Māru country and offer *roat*, cake, there at the *maḷhi* of Guggā. He will bring soil from there and will construct a *malhī* here. As soon as his son regained life and his wishes were fulfilled he did as he had wished and got constructed a *malhī* in his village. This is also the story of another village named Gehdavīṁ.

At village Thor, in Pachāḷ, Sirmour, there is an ancient temple with a gilt dome but it has no image. Worship is held every evening with music, incense, and the sound of conch. The temple was originally founded by Mahant Tāwarnāth and was reconstructed by Mahant Māyāgīr, eleventh in descent from Tāwarnāth. The Mahant Viṣṇugīr is the 17th in descent. The temple has legends associated with Raja Māhī Prakāsh (1659-1678 CE) of Sirmaur. The temple originally belonged to the Yogīs (Nātha). At the temple of Garīb Nāth near Paontā it is believed that if a woman, who is barren or whose children die in infancy, takes bath in the water of the wells of the temple she is cured of sterility.

The Śiva temple at Pairīwālā, near Nahan, is said to have been built by Śaṅkara Acārya. Near it, it is said, there are ruins of a palace and wells ascribed to the famous Raja Rasālu, son of Sālivāhan.

Iconographically Guggā is always seen dressed as a warrior, carrying a sword or a spear and shield and riding his horse named Nīla. Others in his retinue are Gugrī, his sister; Kailu Vīr, his Vazīr (guardian); Gorakhnātha and Nārsiṁha Vīr. The first three may be riding horses and the others following on foot. Guggā himself on horseback occupies the place at the centre. This is exceptional that in some temples of Guggā the statues of the following deities are also said to be found: Ghog: A Brahman woman, nurse of Guggā; a Nāga with raised hood; Pithu Bhadiār, Guggā's sister's husband.

Guggā Naumī: The great popularity of Guggā in Himachal is attributed to the belief that, when duly propitiated, he can save from snake-bite, and bestow sons and good fortunes. An annual fair called Guggā Naumī is held in honour of Guggā in many villages where many feats and miracles are exhibited to the visitors.

Date of Fair: The fair starts from the first day of Bhādon, the day of Rakshābandhan, of the bright half of the month and lasts for nine days. From the first day to eighth, Guggā Aṣṭamī, mandalīs, groups of traditional singers, go on round and the fair is held on the ninth day. At places it it told the car of Guggā Jāhar Pīr is taken out on round on the day of Rakshābandhan festival. This date is said by some to be the date of birth of Guggā and by others to be that of his wedding or of his martyrdom. At places in the Punjab such fairs were held on a day called Anant Chaudās.

The Procession: For eight days the mandalī, constituting group of about eight to sixteen members, goes from village to village and house to house within the respective traditionally known area, singing songs narrating stories from the life of Guggā. At some places they call themselves *sevak*, servants of Guggā.

The head of the Mandalī is called *celā*, head priest. The *celā* carries an iron rod in his hand. Its head is made in the shape of head of serpent. Sometimes it is three faced. On it are tied articles like bag, ribbon, colourful cloth pieces, etc. Pastilles of dhoop, incense, are also placed on it. One of them plays the instrument like *thālī*, a plate of brass and others *damru*, small drum. They are called *bajantarī,* players of musical instruments.

On reaching before a house the *celā* strikes the stick on the ground before the door and fixes it there. Firstly a prayer is made then a context from the story of Guggā is sung. At other places it is said on this occasion his *chaḷī* or stick, consisting of a long bamboo surmounted by peacock feathers, a cocoanut, some fans, and a blue flag, is taken round by Jogīs who ask for alms.

A person from the house comes out with grain or flour in a plate and flowers in a piece of cloth. People also give something like cocoanut or cash. One of the persons in the group carries a *jholī,* long bag made of thick cotton cloth, in which the alms of flour etc. given by the villagers are collected. In the nights they stay with a household with an invitation from them. They sing and tell the stories of Guggā in the night. During these days they sleep on the ground. These are some samples from the prayers:

जय गुग्गा जाहर पीर, मां बाछल का बेटा, नीले घोडे का स्वार।

Hail! Guggā Jāhar Pīr, son of Bāchal, and riding the Nīla horse.

जय गुग्गा जाहर पीर, नीले घोडे का स्वार, कीडे कंडुओं का पहरा देना।।

Hail! Guggā Jāhar Pīr, riding the Nīla horse, protect us from serpents and poisonous wormss.

Similarly many other songs are sung and the people are explained their meanings.

The epic poem sung by these singers is called '*Guggā kī Vār*' which contains the full life story of Guggā. The service of visiting the villages and houses is known as 'Guggā kī Kār', service of Guggā. Kār is normally translated as alms.

Naumi, the Ninth day: On the ninth day they come to the *Guggā sthān* and the festival is held on this day. The people gather and celebrations are held. The *sevaks* sing Bhārath, pronouncements of the deity, and *khel*, spirit possession, is also arranged. An example of a *mantra* in translation recited at this moment is given as: 'The deity Nārsiṁha tying a rope of wool like the gaddīs in the waist is my friend. He has in his hand a small *hukkā*. He is coming towards me.'

Mandi: The old Gazetteer notes that in this part of the State, Guggā, the serpent demi-god, is a popular object of worship, especially in cases of snake bite. He is not venerated much by the Kanets of the upper villages, but in the lower hills he is generally recognised and certain Rajput clans regard him as their ancestral god. His special followers are the Nāthas, and in Mandi itself some of them pretend to special skill due to his power, in catching snakes and curing their bites. On the day of *Guggā Naumi* the Nāthas carry the images of himself and his attendants, with their canopies of cobra hoods, from house to house, singing songs in his honour and begging for alms.

Guggā Naumī in Una: From the first day of the month the followers of Guggā go in groups on the round called *kār*, for begging alms, in the neighbouring villages.

The leader of the group of the *kār,* called *celā*, moves with an umbrella in his hands and an iron chain on his shoulder. The other members of the group, called *Bainṭi,* who belong to *Bhanjdā* community, narrate the story of Guggā playing on a *ḍamru*. They sing and relate the story of Guggā while moving in the day. They halt in the night on the way. This part of the routine is called '*dehāḷi*'. They had been following the tradition from generation to generation, since long past. The *celā* and the *bainti* walk barefooted for eight days. During these days they don't sleep on the cot and don't kill any worm, snake, etc. On the ninth day they add their own contribution to the material collected during the Round from the villagers and prepare *Roat* and offer to Pīr Guggā and the public.

Worship of Guggā in Kangra: Guggā in Kangra is considered as a deity possessing the power of curing from the effects of snake-bite, magic and evil spirits. It is believed by the people that if a person bitten by a snake is taken to the place of Guggā, he can be cured. The victim is given water of Guggā's place and he is made to vomit.

From the day of *rakshābandhan* to the ninth, for nine days the followers of Guggā wander from house to house singing the praises of Guggā and collect the articles donated by the people like rice, flour, gur, *dori* (coloured thread), cash, etc. They play musical instruments like *dhol* (drum), *thāli* (plate), *cimtā* (pincer) etc. One person carries the *Chatra* (umbrella) made of leaves, called the 'Umbrella of Guggā' with a stick in its centre. In the inner side of the umbrella are tied to it cloth pieces and threads given by the people.

On the *Guggā Naumī*, the ninth day, the *maḷhi*, or *Sthāpanā* (place) of Guggā, is prepared and cleaned for the celebration. In the malhī there is a statue riding a horse, at places there may be three such other statues. At many places the statue is raised in the open spaces or under the trees. *Guggā kī bār*', songs telling the stories of Guggā, are sung the whole of night. *Roat* is prepared by adding own share in the collections made from the villagers and are presented to every house. It is said that now a days many groups collect alms without singing the '*Guggā kī bār*'. On the tenth day *yajña* is held.

Guggā and the Nāgas: People believe that the serpents fear from Guggā and Guggā has power to cure from the snake bites.

Here an attempt has been made to find out as to how Guggā came to acquire this skill, power and knowledge by studying some of the related events from his life. We observe some instances in the legend of Guggā when he exhibits his superiority over the serpents. Vogel says that the legend of Guggā shows infinite variation. He quotes an example of his close affinity with Nāga. In one important instance the Nāga assisted Guggā in getting his broken betrothal revived and marriage ceremonised. Denzil Ibbetson writes that, 'Guggā is supposed to be the greatest of the snake-gods.' In fact life of Guggā is very closely associated with Nāgas. There are number of incidents related in the life story of Guggā when he has fierce confrontations with the snake gods; he overpowers them who bow down to serve him and follow his orders for life long.

1. Association of Nāgas with the life of Guggā begins before his conception. Bāchal was devotee of Gorakhnath and

Kāchal that of Kāliyā Nāga. When Bāchhal, Guggā's mother, went to Guru Gorakhnath for seeking child, the Guru found that he had already given away the charmed article to Kāchal. He after searching all the sources went to Vāsukī, the king of the Nāgas, seeking for a fruit. The guru asked for the Nāga who was making light and was lighting the whole Nāga world. Vāsukī refused to give saying that whole of his world will become dark. The guru killed the Nāga, turned it into a guggul pastilles, together with the female Nāga who resisted from killing her husband, and returned carrying them. He gave the pastilles to Bāchal who mixed it with water and drank which caused conception of the son. Thus Guggā inherited the seeds of power of the Nāgas in him from his birth.

2. According to another story Gorakhnātha had granted Vāsukī Nāga itself in the form of fruit to Bāchlā. Therefore he was blessed by the Guru to be able to subdue the serpents.

3. Another story tells that once when Guggā was still young he was playing on a swing. Kāchhal, his younger mother, seeing him thus, grew envious. She went to the nether world, aroused Kalihar Nāga from his slumber and invoked him and requested for his assistance. He made an army of a lakh of snakes and moved to the world of mortality, in order to kill Guggā. As the snakes attacked on Guggā, he caught one by one and killed sucking them like sugarcane. In this way the king of the Nāgas, Vāsukī Nāg, when observed his offsprings and community being annihilated, entreated Guggā to save his progeny and community. Vāsukī gave assurance that the snakes will remain always under Guggā and follow his orders. Wherever the name of Guggā is pronounced, power of the enemy Nāga will become ineffective. After a little thought Guggā pardoned them and did as was requested to him. This incident shows

that the whole Nāga world was filled with fear from Guggā and they became bound to him permanently.

Curing Snake-bite: Guggā is propitiated for three reasons: He cures a patient who is bitten by snakes. Secondly he frees the persons influenced by the evil spirits and malicious spells. Lastly he is supposed to fulfill the desires of the devotees by granting son, etc.

People believe that from the day of *Rakṣābandhan* festival when the *Kār* of Guggā Jāhar Pīr is taken out to the end of Guggā Naumī the poisonous snakes and other harmful insects go to hide. Otherwise also during these days they don't bite. Even if a snake bites during these days it has no effect. It is believed that during this period all poisonous snakes come under the *Kār* of Guggā, circle of influence of Guggā, so their bites become ineffective.

On the day of *Guggā Naumī* the people affected with snake bites come to the *Guggā sthān* for cure. They sing the context of Vasukī Nāga and raise the slogan 'Jay Guga Jāhar Pīr'. The method of treatment differ slightly from place to place.

Patients come with offerings like wheat flour, etc. which is used for preparation of *roat*. Sometimes the person who is cured offers silver snake at the place of Guggā. Then the process of extracting the poison starts. Dhoop, incense, is burnt and the slogans like '*Jai Guggā Jāhar Pīr*' are raised several times. The *celā* ties a thread to the patient. As the patient circumambulates the statue of Guggā he starts vomiting which is a sign of his having been cured. At places the patients affected with snake-bite and spells are given the earth of the place of Guggā to eat and water to drink.

Some priests give the patient leaves of the trees growing in the premises of the shrine to eat and rubbing some of it on the wound. Others sprinkle holy water on the affected part. Pilgrims who came from long distances took away some of this earth as a protection. While curing a patient affected by a spirit possession the *celā* plays beating with iron chain.

In Bilaspur it is told that Guggā can cure a patient where all attempts of treatment on him have failed. On the ninth day of *Naumi* the Mandali sings *bhārath* (songs of Guggā) throughout the night. *Khel*, the play of spirit possession, is also held. The patient is produced before the Mandali. *Bhārnī*, prayers, are made to different deities. Then a spirit enters the patient. He is asked many questions and is asked the cause of the disease. The patient beats with an iron chain over his own shoulders and on his back. Under hallucination he gives description of Nārsiṁha coming towards him in the garb of a gaddī. Thus a great cause is fulfilled.

Bibliography

Abul Fazal Allami, *The Ain-i-Akbari*, translated. 1891. by H.S. Jarret, Vol. II, Asiatic Society of Bengal, Calcutta.

Agrawala, V.S. 1966. The Devanagari Script, in *Indian System of Writing* (pp. 12-16), Publications Division, Ministry of information and Broadcasting, Delhi.

Atkinson, E.T. 1973. *The Himalayan Gazetteer,* Vol. II, Part II, reprinted, Cosmo Publications, Delhi.

Bagchi, P.C. 1986. *Kaulajnananirnaya of the School of Matsyendranatha*, Prachya Prakashan, Varanasi.

Beal, Samuel: 1884. Si-Yu-Ki, *Buddhist records of the Western World*, London, reprinted 1969, Oriental Books, Delhi.

Bhattacharya, Beoyntosh. 1968. *The Indian Buddhist Iconography*, Firma K.L. Mukhopadhyay, Calcutta.

Briggs, G.W. 1938. *Gorakhnātha and the Kānphata Yogīs,* YMCA, Calcutta.

Census of India. 1961. Vol. V. *Himachal Pradesh,* Part VII ṣ B, *Fairs and Festivals.*

Chatterji, Suniti Kumar. 1966. *Brahmi – The Mother of Indian Scripts*, in Indian System of Writing, Publications Division, Delhi.

Chattopadhyaya, Debiprasad (Ed.). 1970. *Taranath's History of Buddhism in India,* translated by Lama Chimpa and Alaka Chattopadhyaya, Motilala Banarsidass, reprint, 1990, Delhi.

Cunningham, Alexander. 1924. *The Ancient Geography of India*, reprinted 2002, Munshiram Manoharlal, New Delhi.

Cunningham, Alexander.2000. ASI Report Vol. XIV, reprint, Archaeological Survey of Indian, New Delhi.

Dey, N.L. 1927. *The Geographical Dictionary of Ancient and Mediaeval India,* reprinted 1979, Cosmo Publications, New Delhi.

Dowson, John. 1993. *A Classical Dictionary of Hindu Mythology and Religion,* Reprinted Rupa & Co., New Delhi.

Dutt, Nalinaksha. 1977. *Buddhist Sects in India*, Indological Book, Varanasi.

Edward C. Sachau. 1888. *Alberuni's India*, Ludgate Hill, reprinted Rupa & Co., New Delhi, 2002.

Elliot, Henry M. 1859. *North Western Provinces of India*, Vol. I, reprinted 2004, Low Price Publications, Delhi.

Fergusson, James. 1910. *History of Indian and Eastern Architecture*, reprinted 1998, Munshiram Manoharlal, New Delhi.

Gazetteer of India, Himachal Pradesh, *Bilaspur,* 1975.

Gazetteer, *Gazetteer of the Chamba State,* 1904. 1904. Reprinted Indus, New Delhi, 1996.

Gazetteer, Punjab District Gazetteers, 1926. *Kangra District*,Volume VII, Part A, 1924-25, reprinted Kangra Cultural Society, Dharamsa, H.P., 1995.

Gazetteer of the *Kangra District*, Parts II to IV, *Kullu, Lahul and Spiti,* 1897, first published 1899, reprinted, Indus, New Delhi, 1994.

Gazetteer of the *Sirmur State* 1934 Part A. 1934. Reprinted Indus, 1996, New Delhi.

Gazetteer of the Simla Hill States, 1910 (Punjab States Gazetteer Vol. VIII). 1911. Lahcre. Reprinted 1995, Indus, New Delhi.

Gazetteer , Punjab. 1920. *Mandi State*, Volume XII-A.

Goetz, Hermann. 1955. *The Early Wooden Temples of Chamba,* Brill, Leiden.

Grierson, G.A. 1878. The Song of Manik Chandra, *in Journal of the Asiatic Society*, No. 3, Calcutta.

Gupta, Shashibhushan Das. 1995. *Obscure Religious Cults*, Firma K.L.M., Calcutta, reprinted.

Hutchison and Vogel. 1933. *History of the Panjab Hill States*, Vol. I, Lahore, reprinted, Himachal Pradesh, Department of Language and Culture, Shimla.

I-Tsing. 1896. *A Record of the Buddhist Religion as Practised in India and the Malay Archipelago*, translated into English by J. Takakusu, reprinted 1998, Munshiram Manoharlal, New Delhi.

Joshi, Lalmani. 1967. *Studies in the Buddhistic Culture of India, during the seventh and eighth centuries A.D.*, Motilal Banarsidass, Delhi, reprinted 1987.

Joshi, Tika Ram. 1911. *A Dictionary of the Pahari Dialects*, Journal Asiatic Society of Bengal. Reprinted by Himachal Academy of Arts, Culture and Languages, 1989, Shimla.

Levi, Sylvain. 1882. The Local Divinities, in *Ancient Nepal*, Nos.53-56, August 1979-March 1980.

Magee, Michael. 1986. *Introduction* (pp. 1-94) in Bagchi, P.C.1986. *Kaulajnana-nirnaya, of the School of Matsyendranatha,* Text edited & translated into English by Michael Magee, Prachya Prakashan, Varanasi.

Majumdar, R.C. 1971. *History of Ancient Bengal*, G. Bhardwaj, Calcutta, reprinted, 1974.

Murti, M. Srimannarayan. 1997. *Bhartrhari, the Grammarian*, Sahitya Academy, New Delhi.

Nautiyal, K.P. 1969. *The Archaeology of Kumaon*, Varanasi.

Newell, William H. 1965. *Report on Scheduled Castes and Scheduled Tribes* (A Study of Gaddi Scheduled Tribe and affiliated castes, Census of India, 1961, volume XX, Part V-B, Himachal Pradesh.

Poastel, M.; A. Neven; K. Mankodi. 1985. *Antiquities of Himachal, Project for Indian Cultural Studies,* Volume I, Bombay.

Publications Division. 1966. *Indian System of Writing*. Publications Division, Government of India, Delhi.

Rose, H.A. 1883. *A Glossary of the Tribes and Castes of the Punjab and North West Frontier Provinces,* Vols. I to III, Government of Punjab, Lahore, reprinted, Patiala, 1970.

Sen, Kshitimohan. 1935. *Medieval Mysticism of India*, Luzac, London.

Sharma, Kamal Prashad. 2001. *Manimahesh Chamba Kailāsh,* Indus, New Delhi.

Singh, K.S. (Gen. Ed.). 1996. *People of India, Himachal Pradesh*, Vol. XXIV, Anthropological Survey of India, Manohar, New Delhi

Singh, Mohan. 1934. *Kabir and the Bhagti Movement*, Atramram, Lahore.

Sircar, D.C. 1973. *The Śākta Pīthas,* Motilal Banarsidass, New Delhi, reprinted, 2004.

Temple, R.C. 1884. *The Legends of the Punjab*, Vols. I ṣIII, reprinted 1988, Language Department , Punjab, Patiala.

Templeman, David. 1989. *Taranatha's Life of Krsnācārya/Kanha*, Library of Tibetan Works and Archives, Dharamsala.

Tiwari, Nankishore. 2002. *Bharthari, A Chhatisgarh Folk Epic,* Sahitya Akademi, New Delhi.

Tod, James. 1829: *Annals and Antiquities of Rajasthan*, Vols. I & II, reprinted Rupa & Co 1997, Calcutta.

Tucci, Giuseppe. 1935. *The Temples of Western Tibet and their Artistic Symbolism, Tsaparang, Indo-Tibetica* III.2, Ed. By Lokesh Chandra, 1989, Aditya Prakashan, New Delhi.

Tucci, Giuseppe. 1940. *Travels of Tibetan Pilgrims in the Swat Valley,* Calcutta.

Vogel, J.Ph. 1911. *Antiquities of Chamba State*, Vol. I, reprinted 1994, Archaeological Survey of India, New Delhi.

Vogel, J.Ph. 1926. *Indian Serpent Lore or The Nagas in Hindu Legend and Art*, Arthur Probsthain, London.

Wilson, H.H.1846. *Religious Sects of the Hindus*, reprinted 1972, Indological Book House, Varanasi.

Journals

Pandey, Ram Niwas. 1970. *Ancient Nepal,* No. 12, July, 1970.

Sax, William. 2013. *Divine Kingdoms in the Central Himalayas,* (internet 20 Feb., 2013).

Sax, William. 2009. *Roopkund,* National Geographic Channel, 25 September, 2009.

Tucci, Guiseppe. 1931. *The Sea and Land Travels of a Buddhist Sadhu in the Sixteenth Century*, The Indian Historical Quarterly, Vol. VII, No. 4, December, 1931, pp. 683-702.

Hindi Books

Abhinavgupta. 1986. *Tantrasār,* Hindi translation by Hemendranath Chakravarti, Varanaseya Sanskrit Sansthan, Varanasi.

Aatreya, Kanshiram. 1994. *Mandīyālī Lokgīt aur Lokgāthāyeñ,* Himachal Kala Sanskriti Bhasha Akadami, Shimla.

Acharya, Sriram Sharma and Chamanlal Gautam. 1978. *Tantra Mahāvidyā,* Sanskriti Sansthan, Bareili.

Ajnabi, Nemchand. 1999. *Himachal Pradesh, Itihās Sanskritī va Praśāsana*, H.G. Publications, New Delhi.

Anuragi, Keshav. 1997. *Gorakhpānth ke Paripekṣya Me Dholasāgar*, in *Garhwal aur Garhwal*, (pp. 195-197), edited by Chandrapal Singh Rawat, Winsor, Delhi. .

Upadhayaya, Nagendranath. 1958. *Tāntrik Bauddh Sādhnā aur Sāhitya*, Nagripracharini Sabha, Kashi.

Kashyapa, Padamchandra. 1972. *Kulluī Lok Sāhitya,* National Publishing House, Delhi.

Kashyap, Padamchandra. 1986. *Himachali Sanskritī kā Itihās,* Arya Prakashan Mandal, Delhi.

Gautam, Khushiram.1992. *Sirmaurī Lok Sāhitya,* Himachal Kala, Sanskriti evam Bhasha Akadami, Shimla.

Gautam, Dayanand (Ed.). 2000. *Bebas Sāhitya Sādhnā,* Dayanand Gautam, Kullu.

Jaswal, B.R. 2010. *Himachal Pradesh me Guggā Paramparā,* Himachal Kala Sanskriti Bhasha Akademi, Shimla.

Jaswal, B.R. 2010. Hamirpur janpad me Guggā Paramparā in *Himachal Pradesh me Guggā Paramparā,* (49-139), (Ed. B.R. Jaswal), Himachal Kala Sanskriti Bhasha Akademi, Shimla.

Jasrotia, Ramesh. 1998. Sānchā Vidyā me *Mantra*-Tantra-Yantra in *Himachal Pradesh kā Prāchīn Tantra Granth, Sānchā,* (90-101), Ed. By Sudarshan Vashishtha, Himachal Kala, Sanskriti, Sahitya Akadami, Shimla.

Thakur, M.R. (Ed.) 1986. *Himachal Pradesh ke Ghaṭnā aur śram pradhān gīt*, Himachal Kala Sanskriti aur Bhasha Akadami, Shimla.

Thakur, M.R. 2008. *Himachal ki Lok Kalāyenñ aur Asthāyeñ.* National Book Trust, New Delhi.

Thakur, Surat. 2004. *Himachal kī Dev Sanskṛtī*. H.G. Publications, New Delhi.

Thakur, Surat. 2013. *Himachal ki Devgathayen* (manuscript).

Tiwari, Nandkishore (documented by), H.U. Khan and Arvind Macwan (Translators). 2002. *Bhartharī, A Chhattīsgarhī Oral Epic*, Sahitya Akademi, New Delhi.

Dorje, Sempa (Tr.). 1998. *Caurāsī siddhon kā vṛtānt,* Central Institute of Higher Tibetan Studies, Varanasi.

Dvivedi, Hazariprasad. 1996. *Nātha Sampradāya,* Lok Bharti, Allahabad.

Narendradev, Acharya. 2000. *Bauddh Dharma Darshan,* Bihar Rastrabhasha Parishad, 2nd Edition, Patna.

Pathak, Ramlal. 1987. Kucch Devi-davata in *Himachal Pradesh, Lok Jeevan aur Paramparāyeñ,* Eds. Banshiram Sharma, Moluram Thakur and Saroj Sankhyan, Himachal Kala, Sanskriti aur Bhasha Academi, Shimla.

Pandey, Badridatt.1990. *Kumaon ka Itihās*, Shyam Prakashan, Almora (U.P.).

Bahuguna, Abodh Bandhu. 1997. Garhwal ke Gorakh Panthi Granth, in *Garhwal aur Garhwal,* Ed. By Chanderpal Ssingh Ravat, Winsor, Delhi.

Bebas, Chandrashekhar. 2000. *Bebas Sāhitya Sādhnā,* Dayanand Gautam (Ed.) Dayanand Gautam, Kullu.

Manjul, Rasik Bihari. 1991. *Caurāsi Bauddh Siddha*, Radha Publications, New Delhi.

Murari, Harikrishan. 2008. *Śivālak Janpad ke Śramik-kriśak varg me Mānya lok Devi-devata,* Author, Rait, Shahpur, Kangra, H.P.

Loppā, Satish Kumār. 1994. *Gīt-Atīt, Lāhulī Lok Gāthāoñ kā Sañkalan*, Rinchen Zāñpo Sānskritik evam Sāhitik Sabhā, Kyelang.

Varma, Syama and Sunrita Gautam (Eds.). 2004. *Himachal Pradesh ka Prachin Tantra Granth, Sancha,* Part II, Himachal Kala Sanskriti Bhasha Akadami, Shimla.

Varmā, Shyāmā and Sūnṛtā Gautam (Ed.). 2004. *Himachal Pradesh kā Prācīn Tantra Granth, Sāncā,* with Hindi translation of Pābucī, Part II, Himachal Kala, Sanskrit, Bhasha Academy.

Vashishtha, Sudarshan. 1998. *Himachal Pradesh kā Prachīn Tantra Grantha, Sancha*, Himachal Kala, Sanskriti Bhasha Akadami, Shimla.

Sharma, Jagdish. 2000. *Himachal kī Lokgāthāyeñ,* Himachal Kala Sanskriti Bhasha Academy, Shimla.

Sharma, Dev Raj. 2004. *Guggā Gāthā athva Guggā Jāhar Pīr,* H.G. Publications, New Delhi.

Sharma, Banshi Ram, 1986. *Himachal Lok Sanskṛitī ke Srota,* Arya Prakashan Mandal, Delhi.

Sankrityayan, Rahul. 1953. *Himalaya Paricaya (1), Garhwal,* Allahabad Law Journal Press, Allahabad.

Salīm, Lacchiram Gazta, 2001. *Hamārā Sānskritik Itihās, Mahāsuvi Lokgāthāeñ,* Author, Shimla.

Singh, Virbhadra. (Ed.). 1984. *Bharthrī Lokgāthā,* Himachal Kala Sanskriti Bhasha Akademi, Shimla.

Journals

Angiras, Amardev. 2007. Naarsingh Vazeer, Bavan Veeron ka Sardar, *Somsi,* Jan. ș June 2007, (59-63), Himachal Kala, Sanskriti Bhasha Akadami, Shimla.

Upādhyāya, Nīlmaṇi. 2004. Causaṭh Yoginiyāñ: Arcanā tathā Sādhnā, in *Somasi*, April-June, 2004, (25-27), Himachal Kala Sanskriti Bhasha Akadami, Shimla.

K.Angrup. 1993. Bancelā Ancelā, in *Chandertāl,* Ed. By Banshi Ram Sharma, Himachal Kala Sanskriti Bhasha Akadamy, Shimla.

Jasata, Hari Ram. 1999. Himachal me Nāth Sampradāya, in *Vipāsha*, Jan.- Feb. 1999, pp. 77-84, Department of Languages and Culture, Himachal Pradesh, Shimla.

Sharma, Jagdish (Ed). 2000. *Himachal Pradesh kī Lokgāthāyeñ,* Somsi, December 2000, Special Edition, Himachal Kala Sanskriti Bhasha Akadami, Shimla.

Sharma, Jaya Krishna. 2004. Guggā Jāhar-Pīr, (pp.84-90) in *Samaj-Dharam*, October 2004, Mahatpur (Una).

Sharma, Yog Raj. 2004. Nātha Pherī, in *Himbhārti,* Shimla, January-June, (pp.10-12), Himachal Kala Sanskriti Bhasha Akadamy.

Sharma, Yog Raj. 2007. Bharthari Gopicand, in *Somsi*, Jan-June 2007, 17-25, Himachal Kala Sanskriti Akadeami, Shimla.

Sharma, Shami. 2004. Jo-Joganiyan aur Himachal Pradesh, in *Somsi*, April-June, 2004, (pp, 23-24), Himachal Kala, Sanskriti, Bhasha Aakadami, Shimla.

Sharma, Svaran Kanta, 2000. Gugga Chhatri, in *Himachal Pradesh ki Lokgāthāyeñ*, Himachal Kala Sanskriti Bhasha Akadamy, Shimla, Special Issue, *Somsi* (104-110), December 2000, Ed. Jagdish Sharma.

Bhoti/Tibetan

au-rgyan mkha'-'gro'i gling-gi lam-yig thar-lam bgrod-pa'i them-skas. sTag-Tshang Ras-pa (Travelogue of sTag tsang Ras-pa to Orgyan, the land of Ḍakinīs).

Taranath. *bKa' babs bdun gyi rnam-thar* (Biographies of five lineages).

Gu-ge mkhan-chhen ngag-dbang grags-pas mdsad-pai mn'a-ris rgyal-rabs, Dharmsala.

'phags-yul grub-chhen brgyad-chu rtsa-bzhi'i byin-rlabs skor las lo-rgyus rnam-par-thar-pa rnams bzhugs-so, (Account of lives of 84-Mahasiddhas of Aryadesh), reprinted 1972, by E. Kalsang, Buddhist Temple, Sigra, Varanasi.

rgyal-ba rgod-tshang-pa mgon-po rdo-rje'i rnam-par thar-pa mthong don-ldan nor-bu'i phreng-ba bzhugs-so. (Biography of rGod-tshangpa).

Index

K

L

M

N

T

❐ ❐ ❐

Plate-1. Devata Virnath, Kullu.

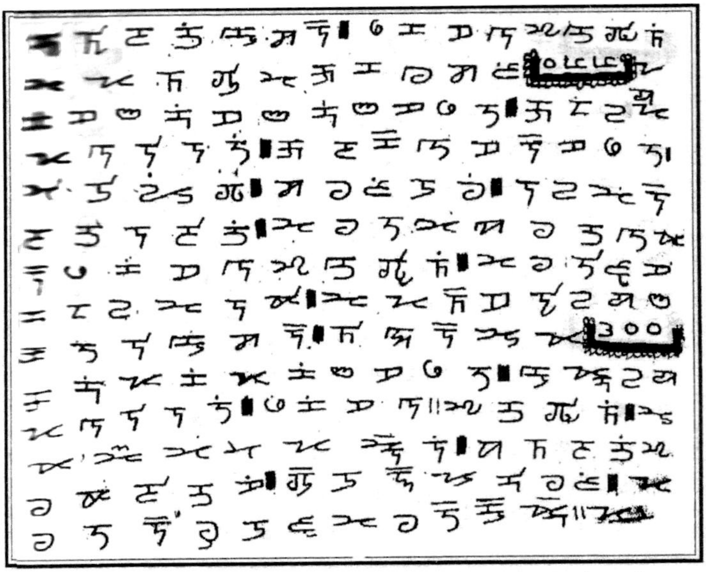

Plate-2. Sancha script used by the tantrics in the interior of Shimla (Courtesy Shyama Varma, Academy, 2004).

Plate-3. Jogini temple, in the unpolluted environment, away from the residential area, Kullu.

Plate-4. Jogini dehri, miniature temple,
in the unpolluted wild, Kullu.

Plate-5. Chamba Tibetan Mane' inscription
(Courtesy, Kamal Prashad Sharma, 2001).

Plate-6. Images of Vasuki Naga and his Vazeer, Chamba. The simple figures with club is a typical iconographical style of the sect and those allied to it. (Courtesy, J.Ph. Vogel, 1926.)

Plate-7. Silver mohra (mask) of one of the Naunath deity, Lahul, gifted by Raja Tedhi Singh of Kullu, c. CE 1750.

Plate-8. Brass mohra (mask) of one of the Naunath deities, Lahul, among the oldest.

Plate-9. sTag Tshang Repa (sGrub-dbang ngabang-rgya mtsho), drawing in biographical book, with typical cap and the Natha earrings (Shamonath).

Plate-10. sTag Tshang Repa, wall painting, as Shamonath, (Courtesy, Snellgrove and Skorupski, 1977).

Plate-11. sTag Tshang Repa, a drawing on stone, Ladakh, in the garb of Nath adept (Shamonath), in teaching posture, with two disciple monks, on either side, (photo. anonymous.)

Plate-12. A Natha householder, chins resting on the wooden spade, Kullu.

Plate-13. A Natha householder, holding gorkhdhandha, Kullu.

Plate-14. A Natha householder with symbolic earrings, Kullu.